Brigham Young University
2012–2013 Speeches

Frequently Used Abbreviations

CR—*Conference Reports of The Church of Jesus Christ of Latter-day Saints.*

DBY—Young, Brigham. *Discourses of Brigham Young.* Selected by John A. Widtsoe. Salt Lake City: Deseret Book Company, 1941.

GD—Smith, Joseph F. *Gospel Doctrine.* 5th ed. Salt Lake City: Deseret Book Company, 1939.

GI—McKay, David O. *Gospel Ideals.* 2nd printing. Salt Lake City: Improvement Era, 1954.

GS—Grant, Heber J. *Gospel Standards.* Compiled by G. Homer Durham. Salt Lake City: Improvement Era, 1941.

HC—Smith, Joseph. *History of The Church of Jesus Christ of Latter-day Saints.* 7 vols. 2nd ed. revised. Edited by B. H. Roberts. Salt Lake City: The Church of Jesus Christ of Latter-day Saints, 1932–51.

Hymns—*Hymns.* Revised and enlarged. Salt Lake City: The Church of Jesus Christ of Latter-day Saints, 1948 and 1985.

JD—*Journal of Discourses.* 26 vols. London: Latter-day Saints' Book Depot, 1854–86.

Lectures on Faith. Compiled by N. B. Lundwall. Salt Lake City: N. B. Lundwall, n.d.

MD—McConkie, Bruce R. *Mormon Doctrine.* 2nd ed. Salt Lake City: Bookcraft, 1966.

PMG—*Preach My Gospel: A Guide to Missionary Service.* Salt Lake City: The Church of Jesus Christ of Latter-day Saints, 2004.

PPP—Pratt, Parley P. *Autobiography of Parley P. Pratt.* Edited by his son Parley P. Pratt. Salt Lake City: Deseret Book Company, 1973, 1985, 1994.

Sing—*Sing with Me: Songs for Children.* Salt Lake City: The Church of Jesus Christ of Latter-day Saints, 1970.

Songbook—*Children's Songbook.* Salt Lake City: The Church of Jesus Christ of Latter-day Saints, 1989, 1995.

Teachings—Smith, Joseph. *Teachings of the Prophet Joseph Smith.* Selected by Joseph Fielding Smith. Salt Lake City: Deseret Book Company, 1938.

TETB—Benson, Ezra T. *The Teachings of Ezra Taft Benson.* Salt Lake City: Bookcraft, 1988.

TGBH—Hinckley, Gordon B. *Teachings of Gordon B. Hinckley.* Salt Lake City: Deseret Book Company, 1997.

TSWK—Kimball, Spencer W. *The Teachings of Spencer W. Kimball.* Edited by Edward L. Kimball. Salt Lake City: Bookcraft, 1982.

PRINTED IN THE UNITED STATES OF AMERICA

ISBN: 978-1-8425-2846-7

speeches.byu.edu

13-803/P004664   750M

CONTENTS

Time: A Precious Commodity; a Finite Resource

Thomas H. Morris

It is an honor to be with you. I pray the Spirit may dwell with all of us.

Today I would like to share some thoughts about time. To illustrate some aspects of time, I wish to tell you about a few of my heroes—one from the Book of Mormon, one from the field of science, and one who is very personal. I, like you, have many heroes: the great coaches and teachers I have had, my PhD advisor, my colleagues, my brother and sister, my great parents, my sons, my sweetheart, and many, many others. These people have believed in me and have given me a chance. I will be forever in their debt, for they shared their time with me—and time is one of the most precious commodities of this life.

As a petroleum geologist, I am awed by the power of fossil fuels. Think of it: we can dump a little bit of gasoline in a tank, start up an engine, pile ten people (or undergraduates, as the case may be) into an 8,000-pound van, and drive up a mountainside at seventy miles per hour—simply by depressing a pedal a couple of inches.

Thomas H. Morris was a professor in the BYU Department of Geological Sciences when this devotional was given on 1 May 2012. © Brigham Young University.

This alone would make fossil fuels a precious commodity, but in our modern hydrocarbon society, many of us also use them to heat our homes, cook our pancakes, and warm our morning showers. To all of us, fossil fuels are a precious commodity. Yet fossil fuels are also a finite resource. It has taken Mother Nature millions of years to deposit, generate, migrate, and trap this precious commodity in the rocks buried deeply beneath Earth's surface. Yet it is estimated that, starting from the Industrial Revolution, it will take humankind only 300 years to deplete this finite resource—a blip on even the human-history timescale.[1] This then begs the following questions: What is my stewardship of this resource? and How will I use it?

Today for a few moments I would like us to consider these same questions relative to *our time* on Earth—this short mortal existence. Carl Sagan, the author and great spokesman for the television series *Cosmos*, used to browbeat us by telling us that we as humankind are arrogant to assume that there is not life beyond our planet, given the immensity of space and the universe. This concept was easy enough for LDS people to grasp; yet after a lifetime of study, Sagan found no solid evidence for extraterrestrial life. In fact, in viewing our tiny blue planet from space, he said, "It underscores our responsibility to deal more kindly with one another and to preserve and cherish the only home we've ever known: the pale blue dot."[2]

Before his premature death due to myelodysplasia,[3] Carl Sagan suggested that life on Earth is pretty precious and that we should take care of our planet. May I suggest that *time* on Earth is pretty precious. Maybe we should take better care of *it*. Indeed, just like fossil fuels, it is a precious commodity and a finite resource. The questions resurface: What is my stewardship over my time on Earth? and How will I use it?

As a geoscientist I have thought a lot about time. We geologists commonly throw around big numbers relative to time and the age of Earth. For example, with solid evidence geoscientists contend that Earth is approximately 4.7 billion years old—assuming time as we know it. Can we even comprehend what one billion years is? That is a very difficult task, so let's pare it down.

For several years my students and I have been engaged in studying a Jurassic-age formation in Utah's Colorado Plateau. The Entrada Sandstone has created the splendor of Arches National Park, Goblin Valley and Kodachrome Basin state parks, and other spectacular scenery in Utah. We have now determined that the Entrada Sandstone was deposited from approximately 162 to 165 million years ago,[4] so the Entrada Sandstone has been around for at least 162 million years. This is only 3.4 percent of Earth history, but it is still a big number, so let's pare it down some more.

Milutin Milankovitch, one of my scientific heroes whom I will discuss later, determined that the elliptical path that Earth carves around the sun varies. At times it is more circular, and at other times it is more elliptical. This variation in the shape of the elliptical orbit has a distinct periodicity of approximately 100,000 years.[5] This and other orbital variations affect the amount of incoming solar radiation and force Earth in and out of ice ages. When Earth goes into a cold glacial condition, it stores ocean water on the continents as huge ice sheets. This process of building continental-scale ice sheets effectively lowers sea level by hundreds of feet. Therefore, Earth's oceans rise and fall at a precise periodicity of 100,000 years—a mere 0.0021 percent of Earth history. One hundred thousand—still too big of number to comprehend? Let's get closer to home.

Have you ever wondered why our campus is so flat when it is located literally a mile from the Wasatch Front, which quickly rises to 11,000 feet above sea level?[6] It turns out that our campus was created when the Provo River deposited its sediment as a delta into a great freshwater lake called Lake Bonneville. Yes, just a mere 15,000 years ago,[7] if you were sitting exactly where you are now, you would be under sixty feet of water watching fish and an occasional iceberg float over your head. As the climate changed during the past 15,000 years, due primarily to Milankovitch orbital variations, Lake Bonneville began to dry up and shrink, effectively concentrating her salt into what is now the Great Salt Lake. So our campus was created just 15,000 years ago. Its existence represents only 0.00032 percent of Earth history.

Let's go one more time with the analogy. The life expectancy of the average person in the United States is 78.49 years.[8] So if you are average—and I know all of you are exceptional—you will be part of only 1.7×10^{-6} percent of Earth history. That's 0.0000017 percent. No, I am not trying to make you feel like a zero—but, in a relative perspective, life is short!

The scriptures teach us that our time (here on Earth) is not the same as God's time. To help me comprehend time, I think in terms of being sent to this earth life and being placed within an envelope of time. When this life is over, we are plucked out of that envelope and returned to Heavenly Father's realm—a place in which time as we know it does not exist. In this way I can barely get my head around the eternal nature of God and man.

One of my heroes in the Book of Mormon is King Benjamin. In my mind he was a man's man, because he taught by example. He walked the walk. He was focused on a clear eternal perspective. He knew what he was about. And what was he about? He described himself in Mosiah 2:14: "And even I, myself, have labored with mine own hands that I might serve you." He taught that service to our fellow men is inseparable from service to God. He taught this principle by example. He used his time to serve others by teaching and leading through word and action. He also taught that this time in life is given to us from day to day and moment to moment:

> I say unto you that if ye should serve him who has created you from the beginning, and is preserving you from day to day, by lending you breath, that ye may live and move and do according to your own will, and even supporting you from one moment to another—I say, if ye should serve him with all your whole souls yet ye would be unprofitable servants. [Mosiah 2:21]

The question returns: If my time is given to me from one moment to another, even from breath to breath, what will I do with it? King Benjamin chose to serve others.

A little more than a year ago a former graduate student, Shane Long, returned to campus to recruit geoscientists for his company. In a presentation that I had requested he give to our students, he shared an experience that had changed him. This story also had a profound impact on me.

Shane was on assignment for his company in Lagos, Nigeria, the eighth-most-populous country in the world and one in which there is much poverty. As he was driven in a bulletproof vehicle from the airport to the meeting facility, people and children were abundant in the streets. Shane spent three and a half hours in that vehicle, as progress was slow. During those hours he had time to observe and ponder what was around him just outside of the vehicle. At one point he observed two little girls in the dusty street. They were playing hand games. Shane's attention to them intensified because he recalled a similar experience he had had just a couple of weeks earlier. It was his own daughter who, while waiting to be picked up from her swimming lessons, was playing similar hand games with a friend. The circumstances of these two experiences, however, were vastly different, and, in Shane's words, "the contrast could not have been more striking." In those precious, quiet moments, clarity came to him. He received a vision, or personal revelation, that told him directly that, from that moment on, he was to be a steward over his salary. He fully internalized how he was a product of hard work, good people, and the blessings of circumstance. He was to be wiser and more caring with the gifts that were given him. In that poignant moment he resolved to change.

I have thought a lot about the experience of this great young man. I have thought about his willingness to share that experience with our present students. I have thought about the degree to which I serve others by sharing my gifts—my time being the most precious of them all. Am I doing my part? Am I serving my God by serving others to the extent that I should? Or do I waste a lot of the most precious gifts that are given me? When was the last poignant moment that I had wherein I resolved to change? Maybe it's about time.

President Marion G. Romney said:

Service is not something we endure on this earth so we can earn the right to live in the celestial kingdom. Service is the very fiber of which an exalted life in the celestial kingdom is made.[9]

Service, then, is the ultimate way of spending our time.

Let's examine a way in which another one of my heroes spent his time. Milutin Milankovitch was a Serbian mathematician. As a young man in the early 1900s he got caught up in the fervor of the possibility that Earth had experienced more than one ice age.[10] Encouraged by the work of several predecessors, including Scotsman James Croll, Milankovitch realized that several variations in Earth's orbit around the sun affected the amount of incoming solar radiation that hit Earth. This variation in solar radiation, he reasoned, could throw Earth in and out of ice ages. The mathematical proofs, however, were difficult to develop. Indeed, it took thirty years of his life to finally produce and conclude these proofs and associated graphical curves.[11]

Milankovitch died in 1958 at the age of seventy-nine at a time when most geologists had rejected his theory of the ice ages. Almost three decades after his death, with technological advances that were unheard of during his time, geoscientists finally proved that Milankovitch was right all along. Unfortunately, Milankovitch was long gone. Time had deprived him of the experience of knowing that his geological colleagues fully acknowledged the validity of his theory.

Milankovitch's theory has now been widely accepted and evidenced from a variety of disciplines. His calculations have been shown to be the driving mechanisms of the great ice ages of the geological past. They are now considered fundamental in understanding Earth's past climates. Furthermore, they have been extremely useful in petroleum exploration because as Earth stores vast quantities of ocean water on the continents in the form of massive continental ice sheets, global sea level drops. When Earth enters a warm interglacial period, the ice melts. That meltwater runs back to the ocean, and sea level rises again. This fluctuation in sea level is around 400 vertical feet. Therefore, the shorelines and great deltas of the world shift their locations over 200 miles across the continental shelves from sea level's lowstand position during cold glacial maximums to its highstand position during warm interglacials. The great deltas of the world are prolific in producing accumulations of oil and natural gas. A knowledge of the driving mechanisms of these movements through time has greatly aided in the discovery of fossil fuels on the world's continental shelves. So, in a very broad sense, Milutin Milankovitch has affected each of our lives. Certainly the time he spent on his calculations has served mankind well.

On a more personal note, Milankovitch directly affected my life because as a graduate student at the University of Wisconsin, I studied Milankovitch cycles in the Arctic Ocean. Upon graduation I was fortunate enough to be given several offers of employment by oil companies while my colleagues, many of whom were brighter than I, struggled to get even one offer. I quickly realized that the multiple job offers were not a result of my sterling personality but were indeed a direct reflection of my knowledge of Milankovitch theory. Milankovitch helped me to secure my first real job, which has trickled down to other opportunities, including my present position here at BYU.

There is one more story about Milutin Milankovitch that gives him hero status in my life and directly addresses the topic of time. I stated that it took Milankovitch thirty years of his life to produce his mathematical proofs. Early in this process he was confident that his theory was correct. All he needed was time to make the necessary calculations. Then, to his dismay, World War I broke out. The invading army captured him and took him to a fortress. He spent the next six months in confinement as a prisoner of war.

Of the day he was put into prison, he later recalled:

The heavy iron door was closed behind me. The massive rusty lock gave a rumbling moan when the key was turned. . . . I adjusted to my new situation by switching off my brain and staring apathetically into the air. After a while I happened to glance at my suitcase. . . . My brain began to function again. I jumped up, and opened the suitcase. . . . In it I had stored the papers on my cosmic problem. . . . I leafed through the writings, . . . pulled my faithful fountain pen out of my pocket, and began to write and count. . . . As I looked around my room after midnight, I needed some time before I realized where I was. The little room seemed like the nightquarters on my trip through the universe.[12]

Milankovitch was focused on his goals and his life purpose. He knew what he was about. He despaired only momentarily before awakening himself. He chose not to waste his time, so to speak. He turned his circumstance around and seemingly relished the six months he spent in confinement as a prisoner of war.

Brothers and sisters, do we relish our time on Earth? Do we have enough purpose in our lives to shake off despair and apathy? President Uchtdorf recently challenged us to prioritize all of the "good" things we do in order to do the best things we can.[13] I have found that on occasion it is healthy for me to step back and contemplate what I really want to gain from this life and the precious time that I have. It often invigorates me and gives me more focus.

When I was recently discussing time as a precious commodity and a finite resource with one of my bright undergraduate students, the student blatantly stated, "Doc, we don't have time to make mistakes in this life. It's too short, and we lose the opportunity to accomplish something good." How profound.

Please permit me to tell you about one last hero of mine—one who is very personal. This story also started with a moment of despair. In 1990 my wife and I were blessed with the birth of our third son, Connor. Within moments of his birth he was whisked away by the nurses for cleaning up and ordinary checkups. Soon thereafter, however, a solemn doctor returned to my wife's recovery room to inform us that our son had Down's syndrome. As the words came out of his mouth, I vividly remember the deep despair that sank through my body. I felt ill and turned away from the doctor and prayed silently to Heavenly Father, asking Him to turn back time and to not let the doctor say those words. It didn't happen; time went on.

Over the course of the next two days I was in deep despair, thinking of all the challenges that the future would hold. On the morning of that third day, I said a prayer asking Heavenly Father to deliver me from despair. I felt like I couldn't go on, and I needed His help. That afternoon a good neighbor and friend came to visit. He took me aside and told me that our little boy needed a name and a blessing and then prodded me to go with him to the hospital and give him one. I agreed, and as we finished the blessing, I watched our little Connor in the incubator struggling for life. In that instant these words came to my mind: "One day at a time, Tom. One day at a time."

The despair seemingly melted away. I had my answer. My little boy was fighting for life. I was surely going to give him my best— one day at a time. Since that moment I have never worried too much about the future with Connor. We've taken it one day at a time— moment by moment. Connor taught me to not be overwhelmed and fall into despair but instead to break life down into bite-size pieces, chew hard, and savor the moment.

For nearly twenty-two years our life's ride with Connor has been awesome. I have often thought that all I have to do is provide him with a good life and then hang on to his coattails, for he will surely whisk me back to the celestial kingdom. He is a perfect example of unconditional love. He has been the glue to our family. He has made each of us a better person—especially his Papa Bear. And may I add that he is a great field assistant and a superb fishing partner! Connor seems to know what he is about. He wastes no time in sharing his talents: smiles, hugs, and unconditional love to all he meets.

In Doctrine and Covenants 60:13 the Lord instructs his early missionaries to "not idle away thy time, neither shalt thou bury thy talent that it may not be known." This instruction seems fitting as we soldier on through life, one day at a time.

My three heroes have provided great insight into the use of time. King Benjamin used his time to serve others and thereby his God by word and action. His many acts of service led to the strength of his words. He knew what he was about.

Milutin Milankovitch was also focused on his life's work. He found little time to despair. He plowed forward, sometimes with delight, even under seemingly dire circumstances.

And, finally, Connor has taught me that life comes at us one day at a time. He taught me to not become overwhelmed with problems that might happen in the future but to instead use our gifts and talents from moment to moment and savor our precious time together.

Brothers and sisters, our life on Earth may be our best chance to prove our mettle. It comes at us one day at a time. What will we do in this life? this year? this day? this moment?

Heavenly Father and Jesus Christ have given us this time. They believe in us. They have given us all a chance. They are the real heroes. May we have the wisdom, purpose, and drive to know what we are about and to take advantage of our time here on Earth. May we reflect often and prioritize our time, for time is a precious commodity—a finite resource. In the name of Jesus Christ, the Prince of Peace, amen.

NOTES

1. See Stephen Marshak, *Essentials of Geology*, 3rd ed. (New York: W. W. Norton and Company, 2009), 338–39.

2. Carl Sagan, "We Are Here: The Pale Blue Dot"; www.youtube.com/watch?v=2pfwY2TNehw; see also Carl Sagan, *The Pale Blue Dot: A Vision of the Human Future in Space* (New York: Ballantine, 1994), 7.

3. See Carl Sagan, Wikipedia; en.wikipedia.org/wiki/Carl_Sagan.

4. See Tyson L. Perkes and Thomas H. Morris, "Integrating Facies Analysis, Nonmarine Sequence Stratigraphy, and the First

Detrital Zircon (U-PB) Ages of the Twist Gulch Formation, Utah, USA: Constraining Paleogeography and Chronostratigraphy," *UGA Publication 40—Sevier Thrust Belt: Northern and Central Utah and Adjacent Areas* (2011), 176–77.

5. See John Imbrie and Katherine Palmer Imbrie, *Ice Ages: Solving the Mystery* (Short Hills, New Jersey: Enslow Publishers, 1979), 81, 83, 100.

6. See Provo Quadrangle, Utah—Utah County, 7.5 Minute Series (Topographic), United States Department of the Interior Geological Survey, 1975; photorevised from 1948 and 1969.

7. See Donald R. Currey, Genevieve Atwood, and Don R. Mabey, "Figure 4. Changing Size of Lake Bonneville and Great Salt Lake Through Time," Map 73: Major Levels of Great Salt Lake and Lake Bonneville, Utah Geological and Mineral Survey, May 1983.

8. See "Life Expectancy at Birth," People and Society, United States, The World Factbook; https://www.cia.gov/library/publications/the-world-factbook/geos/us.html.

9. Marion G. Romney, "The Celestial Nature of Self-Reliance," *Ensign*, November 1982, 93; quoted in M. Russell Ballard, "The Greater Priesthood: Giving a Lifetime of Service in the Kingdom," *Ensign*, September 1992, 73.

10. See Imbrie and Imbrie, *Ice Ages*, 97–100.

11. See Imbrie and Imbrie, *Ice Ages*, 100, 111.

12. Imbrie and Imbrie, *Ice Ages*, 102.

13. See Dieter F. Uchtdorf, "The *Why* of Priesthood Service," *Ensign*, May 2012, 59–60.

Prophet, Priest, and King

John P. Hoffmann

It's a pleasure to be here this morning to share some time with you discussing a topic that is important to all of us: our Savior, the Lord Jesus Christ.

I was baptized into The Church of Jesus Christ of Latter-day Saints almost fourteen years ago. But my journey to the Church, which culminated with my baptism, began many years earlier.

On a fall day almost twenty-five years ago I was sitting in a hospital waiting area in San Diego. My fiancée, Lynn, who soon thereafter became my wife, was scheduled to have surgery to remove a blockage in her trachea. The doctor was going to attempt a new procedure using a laser to burn away the excess tissue. Needless to say, I was worried, especially after the doctor who was scheduled to perform the surgery said he had never used a laser before.

In any event, I happened to be sitting next to my future mother-in-law, whom I had just met. The only thing I recall from our brief time together is that she asked me what I believed about Jesus Christ

John P. Hoffmann was a professor in the BYU Department of Sociology when this devotional was given on 8 May 2012. © Brigham Young University.

and Heavenly Father. I don't recall my reply, but I doubt it was very satisfactory. You see, I had never really thought seriously about Jesus Christ or His Father.

A few years after Lynn and I married, I still had not made much progress in my understanding of the Savior. Although I devoted part of my professional life to studying social and cultural aspects of Christian religions, I had not pursued doctrinal studies, nor had I personalized any of the teachings of the Church. Then I had a dream that shook my soul. I was in the entryway of a white building waiting for Lynn. I looked a few feet to my left and saw her talking to a bearded man. Somehow I knew she was very close to this man—I immediately thought he was her best friend—and it confused me for a moment. But then he looked at me in a rueful way and walked away. An intense feeling of sadness overcame me, for I realized that he was my wife's friend but could not be mine.

I joined the Church a few years later and began a new journey—but I still had a lot to learn. In 2005 my best friend passed away from cancer. Sun was not a member of our church, but he was a fine and honorable Christian man with a wonderful family. A couple of nights before the funeral I had a dream about him. If you'll indulge me, I'd like to read a description of this dream, which I delivered as part of his eulogy:

During a fitful night's sleep, having just found out that Sun had passed on to rejoin the Lord, I had a deep desire to see him once more—to make sure he was all right, or perhaps simply to test my faith. I dreamed I was walking along a corridor in a building where I work. I came across a turnoff into another corridor. It was dark, but I could just make out the shadow of a person facing away from me. I could see just enough to realize that it was Sun. He appeared to be waiting for someone. My first thought was one of fear: I did not want him to be in the dark, all alone. So I began to approach him. As I got nearer a light began to glow around him and get brighter. It was then that I realized it was not Sun who was in darkness; it was me. He was bathed in a vivid light that swept me into it. Without saying a word, he turned around and grabbed me in a hug as I began to weep.

I then knew that he was there for me—that he was in an eternal light that would never go out.

We know the source of this light. According to the Gospel of John, Jesus said, "I am the light of the world: he that followeth me shall not walk in darkness, but shall have the light of life."[1] In the Book of Mormon Alma taught his son Shiblon that the Lord Jesus Christ "is the life and the light of the world."[2] Although I have no idea if my dream had a literal quality, I like to believe that my friend has entered into this light.

These episodes from my life, as well as many others, have led me to want to know more about our Savior. This desire involves both an intellectual and a spiritual pursuit that requires study and faith. I wish to get to know Him better and to know about His mortal life, His role in bringing forth the Atonement, and His many teachings that we need to understand and follow so that we can achieve true happiness. Therefore, please let me share a small part of this pursuit, because I think it has improved my life in ways that I probably don't appreciate enough.

We all know that there are many metaphorical and literal names for the Savior. In addition to His mortal moniker of Jesus and His self-ascription as the Light of the World, we also know Him as the Lord, the Son of God, the Bread of Life, the Good Shepherd, the Living Water, the Lamb of God, the Redeemer, Immanuel, Jehovah, and by many other titles.

Although we regularly use several titles in the Church, I would like to highlight three that are often used together. Perhaps we know these words best from the hymn written by eighteenth-century Baptist pastor Samuel Medley: "I Know That My Redeemer Lives." The third verse includes these lines: "He lives, and while he lives, I'll sing. He lives, my Prophet, Priest, and King."[3]

For some reason not entirely apparent to me, I have always been intrigued by this triumvirate. Considering the most common uses of these terms, it seems that prophets, priests, and kings are supposed to be subordinate to the Savior. I therefore wish to dig a little deeper and consider how the Lord takes on these roles.

But first, what is the source of this triple combination? Although the terms are common titles for the Savior, they are not used in this particular arrangement anywhere in the standard works. Thus we must search a little more broadly to find the origin of this phrase.

The historical record suggests that the terms *prophet, priest,* and *king,* as applied to Jesus, originated with Eusebius, the Bishop of Caesarea in Palestine during the early fourth century. In his *Church History,* Eusebius wrote:

> *That his anointing was divine is proved by the fact that he alone, of all who have ever lived, is known throughout the world as Christ and . . . is honored by his worshipers throughout the world as King, held in greater awe than a prophet, and glorified as the true and only High Priest of God.*[4]

More than one thousand years later, John Calvin used the term "threefold office" to designate these roles taken on by the Lord.[5] Calvin was particularly interested in linking the Jesus of the New Testament with these three offices from the Old Testament that represented God's appointed servants. Yet he also saw that these three sacred offices were exemplified and perfected in Jesus Christ.[6] Others, such as Moses and Melchizedek, may have fulfilled these roles during certain dispensations, but Jesus is the only perfect prophet, high priest, and king anointed to rule on earth and in heaven. One scholar wrote that when we understand the Savior in these roles, they "[come] into perfect bloom."[7]

Many others have emphasized another name for Jesus that encompasses the threefold office—that of Messiah. As you know, *Messiah* is a Hebrew word meaning "the anointed." The Greek parallel is Christ, thus Jesus Christ means "Jesus the Anointed." In the Old Testament it was through sacred anointing that prophets, priests, and kings were set apart to perform their duties. They were anointed as a symbol of purification and consecration, being made holy and thus fit to serve God.[8]

For instance, we learn that Moses "poured . . . the anointing oil upon Aaron's head, and anointed him, to sanctify him"[9] so that Aaron could perform his priestly duties. The Lord commanded Elijah to anoint Elisha as a prophet.[10] Samuel anointed David to be king even before he took over the throne from Saul.[11] And we learn in the Book of Mormon that kings were anointed among the Nephites and Jaredites.[12]

The Savior was also anointed to conduct His sacred duties, perhaps—as with His baptism at the hands of John—to serve as an example to others. Some have pointed out that He was anointed three times: once during the premortal existence and twice during His ministry on the earth.[13] Joseph Smith lends support for the premortal anointing: "He, the Lord being a priest forever, after the order of Melchizedek, and the anointed Son of God, from before the foundation of the world."[14] The two mortal anointings occurred when the Savior was baptized and when Mary poured oil on Him at Bethany prior to His entry into Jerusalem.[15]

I'll now examine the three offices that Jesus Christ fulfills: prophet, priest, and king. I have two reasons for taking this step. First, I hope it will help us honor Him better, perhaps by understanding a little more about what it means to say, "He is the Messiah." Second, just as with other sacred roles, it is helpful to see how Jesus perfected them, thus providing an example for others.

JESUS' ROLE AS PROPHET

In simple terms, a prophet is one who represents God to mankind. We learn from numerous passages in the Old Testament and the Book of Mormon that prophets serve as messengers who reveal God's word, call people to repent, teach them to obey God's laws, and prepare them for the coming of the Savior. Thus we recall that Lehi, following his first recorded vision,

went forth among the people, and began to prophesy and to declare unto them concerning the things which he had both seen and heard.

And it came to pass that the Jews did mock him because of the things which he testified of them; for he truly testified of their wickedness and their abominations. . . .

And when the Jews heard these things they were angry with him; yea, even as with the prophets of old, whom they had cast out, and stoned, and slain; and they also sought his life, that they might take it away.[16]

Samuel the Lamanite likewise preached repentance in the land of Zarahemla and was run off by disbelievers;[17] Abinadi was executed for teaching God's will for the people and for teaching about the coming of the Anointed One.[18] Thus we see that the fate of many of God's messengers included persecution, mockery, and even death.[19] Just as many prophets before Him suffered such tribulations, the Savior experienced widespread rejection of His holy mantle.

Two prophets of the Old Testament whose lives most directly anticipated the Savior's were Moses and Elijah. It is no coincidence that these two prophets of old appeared during Christ's Transfiguration on the mount.

Jesus was likened unto Moses by a number of parallel life experiences, including being tempted by Satan,[20] being transfigured on the mount,[21] being saved as an infant from certain death,[22] and confronting powerful political and religious leaders.[23]

Like Elijah, Jesus taught using parables, healed the sick, raised the dead, and suffered rejection and persecution at the hands of His own people.[24] He also preached to people outside of Israel.[25] Unlike most of the prophets before His time, the Savior expressed concern for all individuals, both Jew and Gentile, to conduct themselves according to the laws that He had prepared for them.[26]

Yet the Savior transcended the sacred mantles of all previous prophets. While on the Mount of Transfiguration, Moses and Elijah spoke to Him about His "departure" or "exodus." This referred to His impending death and resurrection,[27] but it also represented the journey that would bring people to God through the Atonement.[28] By offering an atoning sacrifice and overcoming death, the Lord surpassed the prophetic roles of both Moses and Elijah.

The theologian Robert J. Sherman wrote:

> *The New Testament . . . clearly portrays Jesus as more than a prophet: . . . he speaks and acts with his own authority and power. He proclaims the kingdom of God; more than that, he is himself the revelation of God's truth and purposes. Indeed, he not only enlightens, but empowers persons to recognize and claim God's truth as their own true meaning and end, and as such in him prophecy itself is fulfilled.*[29]

Nephi taught that God would raise up a prophet from among the Jews six hundred years from then. Yet this man would be more than a prophet: He would be the Messiah, the "Savior of the world."[30]

JESUS' ROLE AS HIGH PRIEST

Whereas prophets represent God to the people, priests represent the people to God; priests function as mediators between God and mankind.[31] Understanding the Savior's role as a priest can be difficult in a biblical sense because priests were of the Levitical line and the Savior was a descendent from the tribe of Judah. Yet we learn in Psalm 110 that the Lord would be "a priest for ever after the order of Melchizedek."[32] In other words, the Lord was a priest of an order that predated the Levites. We understand through modern revelation that this involves the distinction between the Aaronic Priesthood and the Melchizedek Priesthood.

We are fortunate to have this information since it is difficult to fully understand the Savior's priestly role without our non-biblical sources. For example, who was this Melchizedek in whom we find a higher priesthood? The Old Testament briefly mentions that he was the king of Salem (Jerusalem) and a high priest who blessed Abraham and received his tithing.[33] But if we read inspired scripture, we learn that he also bestowed the priesthood on Abraham[34] and was a man of mighty faith who convinced the people of his kingdom to repent.[35] Because of his great works, Melchizedek was known as "the Prince of peace" and "the king of heaven."[36] These titles suggest that he was the Old Testament figure who resembled the Savior most closely.[37] He was a prophet, priest, and king.

Much of our understanding of the Savior's role as a high priest of the order of Melchizedek comes from the Epistle of Paul to the Hebrews. Paul was writing to a group of Jewish Christians who would have been familiar with the Levitical priesthood and its responsibility for the sacrificial rites held in the temple. He told his readers that Jesus was "the Apostle and High Priest of our profession."[38] Paul's intent was to show that the Savior, in His role as high priest, fulfilled and transcended the law of Moses, because He offered a perfect sacrifice through His Atonement.

At the time of Jesus' mortal ministry, the temple high priest was designated in Jewish tradition to represent the Lord. He wore the name of the Lord on his forehead and was the only priesthood member allowed to enter the Holy of Holies and make the blood sacrifice on the annual Day of Atonement.[39] Paul maintained that Jesus was able to save all because He was sinless, unlike the high priests who presided in the temple. Consequently, there was no longer a need for daily sacrifices—first for the priests' sins and then for the people's. The blameless Lord, "the spotless Lamb of God"[40] whose blood was far superior to any animal's, offered a sacrifice beyond that which any other person could offer.[41] It is only through the shedding of His blood and through His atoning sacrifice that we can be reconciled fully with Heavenly Father.

As Paul wrote in the ninth chapter of Hebrews:

But Christ being come an high priest of good things to come, by a greater and more perfect tabernacle, not made with hands, that is to say, not of this building;

Neither by the blood of goats and calves, but by his own blood he entered in once into the holy place, having obtained eternal redemption for us. . . .

And for this cause he is the mediator of the new testament, that by means of death, for the redemption of the transgressions that were under the first testament, they which are called might receive the promise of eternal inheritance.[42]

The Savior understands our weaknesses and infirmities. He knows the temptations we face.[43] He has suffered for us. He is thus the perfect High Priest and the perfect Mediator for representing mankind to the Father. Yet He is much more than this: unlike other high priests, He was both priest *and* sacrifice.[44] In fact, His one sacrifice is of greater eternal worth than all of those sacrifices that had come before.

JESUS' ROLE AS KING

The third part of the threefold office of Christ is king. Of the three, this is probably the Savior's best-known title. We find it in films, such as the 1961 epic *King of Kings*, and in some of the songs in our LDS hymnbook, such as "I Believe in Christ" and "Jesus of Nazareth, Savior and King."

Christ's kingly duties are also easier to understand than His prophet or priestly duties. We know that the Jesus who lived a mortal life is the Lord of the Old Testament, the one known as Jehovah. He created the earth and continues to lead His Church.[45] Thus He is our Holy Leader, our Lord who reigneth, our "King of kings."[46]

His mortal claims to kingship are due to both His earthly parents being descendants of King David, for it was prophesied by Samuel that one of David's descendants would rule over God's everlasting kingdom.[47] Like David, this Messiah would be a shepherd king who would save Israel. Even before Jesus' conception, the angel Gabriel told Mary:

> *He shall be great, and shall be called the Son of the Highest: and the Lord God shall give unto him the throne of his father David:*
> *And he shall reign over the house of Jacob for ever; and of his kingdom there shall be no end.*[48]

Following His birth, Jesus was recognized by the "wise men from the east"[49] and by Anna the prophetess[50] as the fulfillment of Samuel's prophecy.

However, Jesus was unlike any king who had come before. The Old Testament kings were leaders of nations—often warrior-kings who led their people in battle[51] and administrator-kings who oversaw the running of the state.[52] Most kings eventually ran afoul of God in some way, usually because of their sinful acts.[53] For example, we read that "when Solomon was old, . . . his wives turned away his heart after other gods: and his heart was not perfect with the Lord his God."[54] Others were simply wicked, like King Noah, who encouraged priestcraft and put Abinadi to death.[55] In fact, many of us have been conditioned to dislike and mistrust the idea of a king.

Yet as we search for exemplary kings who were in the image of the Savior, we need look no further than King Benjamin. Not only was he a just ruler who seemed to care little for his own aggrandizement, he was also a genuine servant-king who cared for his people, worked alongside them, and taught them to serve each other.

He exclaimed during his famous address:

Behold, I say unto you that because I said unto you that I had spent my days in your service, I do not desire to boast, for I have only been in the service of God.

And behold, I tell you these things that ye may learn wisdom; that ye may learn that when ye are in the service of your fellow beings ye are only in the service of your God.

Behold, ye have called me your king; and if I, whom ye call your king, do labor to serve you, then ought not ye to labor to serve one another?[56]

This notion of a servant-king was perfected in the Lord. Indeed, He often resisted the title of king during his mortal ministry. The Gospel of John reports that after miraculously feeding the multitude, "Jesus . . . perceived that [the people who had witnessed his miracles] would come and take him by force, to make him a king, [so] he departed."[57]

He also would not give Pilate or Herod the satisfaction of indicting Him for the seditious act of designating himself King of the Jews. He told Pilate, "My kingdom is not of this world."

Then, when Pilate asked Him, "Art thou a king then? Jesus answered, Thou sayest that I am a king. To this end was I born, and for this cause came I into the world, that I should bear witness unto the truth."[58]

The Savior understood His role. He was tasked with teaching the people a new covenant and bringing mankind back from a fallen state into the presence of the Father through the Atonement—the ultimate sacrifice.[59] He was already a king, so there was no need to be given the title. Even those who knew of His divine kingship must have been confused, because His mortal life represented the humble nature of His sovereignty.[60]

Recall that the Old Testament was understood by many as prophesying a messiah who would be king, and this king was to deliver the people from conquest and the physical suffering they endured at the hands of their rulers.[61] Instead, Jesus, who had authority over the entire world, turned the notion of a messianic king on its head.[62] He was born in a stable. He traveled not with soldiers but with fishermen and tax collectors. He dined with Samaritans and sat with the poor and downtrodden. Not only did He refuse all earthly treasures that kings tended to receive, but He also showed the people a humble king, entering Jerusalem on a donkey. He did not come to Jerusalem for a rich, royal feast but to preside over a humble meal with His friends, even washing the feet of those in attendance.[63]

The mistake made by many was assuming He would come as a warrior-king when the Savior actually came as a shepherd-king and as a servant-king. His sovereignty was not demonstrated by temporal wealth or political conquest but by His victory over death and the freedom for mankind that this entailed.[64]

We await His triumphant return that will usher in the Millennium. His kingdom shall be fulfilled, and He will reign as king over the millennial earth. As we are taught in the Doctrine and Covenants, "The Lord shall be in their midst, and his glory shall be upon them, and he will be their king and their lawgiver."[65]

In closing, allow me to quote President Thomas S. Monson:

Who is the King of glory, this Lord of hosts? He is our Master. He is our Savior. He is the Son of God. He is the Author of our Salvation. He beckons, "Follow me." He instructs, "Go, and do thou likewise." He pleads, "Keep my commandments."[66]

It is my desire that all of us may get to know the Savior better, including his roles as the perfect Prophet, Priest, and King. But recall some of the other names we use for the Savior: Son of God, the Anointed One, the Bread of Life, the Good Shepherd, the Living Water, the Lamb of God, the Truth, the Redeemer, Immanuel—which means "God is with us"—the Master, and Jehovah.

Now let me emphasize yet another name for Him: *Friend.* I was mistaken in the conclusion I drew from the dream I discussed earlier. He is my Friend, but as with all close and precious friendships, it requires effort to get to know the Savior better and to appreciate all that He does for me, for my family, and for the world.

I offer testimony that it is to Him that we owe our lives and the promise of full potential as noble children of a Heavenly Father. May we love and honor Him always. I leave these words with you in His sacred name, amen.

NOTES

1. John 8:12.

2. Alma 38:9.

3. "I Know That My Redeemer Lives," *Hymns,* 2002, no. 136.

4. *Eusebius: The Church History,* trans. Paul L. Maier (Grand Rapids, Michigan: Kregel Publications, 2007), 30; see also Michael F. Bird, *Are You the One Who Is to Come?: The Historical Jesus and the Messianic Question* (Grand Rapids, Michigan: Baker Academic, 2009), 164–66.

5. John Calvin, *A Compend of the Institutes of the Christian Religion,* ed. Hugh T. Kerr (Philadelphia: The Westminster Press, 1964), 78; see also Rose M. Beal, "Priest, Prophet and King: Jesus Christ, the Church and the Christian Person," in Gerard Mannion

and Eduardus Van der Borght, eds., *John Calvin's Ecclesiology: Ecumenical Perspectives* (London: T & T Clark International, 2011), 90–106.

6. See Kim Riddlebarger, "The Triple Cure: Jesus Christ—Our Prophet, Priest, and King," *Modern Reformation* 4, no. 6 (November/December 1995): 16–20; see also Bird, *Are You the One?* 165.

7. John E. Johnson, "The Old Testament Offices as Paradigm for Pastoral Identity," *Bibliotheca Sacra* 152 (April–June 1995): 189.

8. See David Rolph Seely and Jo Ann H. Seely, "Jesus the Messiah: Prophet, Priest, and King," in Paul H. Peterson, Gary L. Hatch, and Laura D. Card, eds., *Jesus Christ: Son of God, Savior* (Provo: Religious Studies Center, Brigham Young University, 2002), 249–51.

9. Leviticus 8:12; see also Exodus 29:7.

10. See 1 Kings 19:16; see also Seely and Seely, "Jesus the Messiah," 251–52.

11. See 1 Samuel 16:13.

12. See Jacob 1:9; Ether 9:14.

13. See Seely and Seely, "Jesus the Messiah," 253–54.

14. *Teachings*, 265.

15. See John 12:3; Matthew 26:7, 12.

16. 1 Nephi 1:18–20.

17. See Helaman 13–16.

18. See Mosiah 11–17.

19. See D&C 136:36.

20. See Matthew 4:1–11; Moses 1:12–22.

21. See Luke 9:28–30; Moses 1:1–2, 11.

22. See Exodus 1:22; 2:2–10; Matthew 2:7–8, 11–16.

23. See Seely and Seely, "Jesus the Messiah," 256–57. See also Exodus 7:10–13; Luke 11:45–50.

24. See Luke 11:47–50; see also Daniel J. Harrington, "The Rejected Prophet," *America* (15–22 January 2007): 46; and see Seely and Seely, "Jesus the Messiah," 257–58.

25. See Harrington, "The Rejected Prophet," 46.

26. See Paul E. Davies, "Jesus and the Role of the Prophet," *Journal of Biblical Literature* 64, no. 2 (June 1945): 241–54.

27. See Luke 9:30–31; JST, Luke 9:31. See also J. Severino Croatto, "Jesus, Prophet Like Elijah, and Prophet-Teacher Like Moses in Luke–Acts," *Journal of Biblical Literature* 124, no. 3 (fall 2005): 461.

28. See Daniel J. Harrington, "The Transfiguration of God's Prophet," *America* (26 February 2007): 31.

29. Robert J. Sherman, *King, Priest, and Prophet: A Trinitarian Theology of Atonement* (New York: T & T Clark International, 2004), 220. See also 3 Nephi 9:17; 3 Nephi 12:46; Hebrews 8:13.

30. 1 Nephi 10:4.

31. See Bird, *Are You the One?* 166.

32. Psalms 110:4.

33. See Genesis 14:18–20.

34. See D&C 84:14.

35. See Alma 13:14–19.

36. JST, Genesis 14:33, 36.

37. See Andrew C. Skinner, *Prophets, Priests, and Kings: Old Testament Figures Who Symbolize Christ* (Salt Lake City: Deseret Book, 2005), 25.

38. Hebrews 3:1.

39. See Margaret Barker, "The Great High Priest," *BYU Studies* 42, nos. 3–4 (2003): 68–70.

40. Noel Due, "Christ Ascended for Us—'Jesus Our Ascended High Priest,'" *Evangel* 25, no. 2 (summer 2007): 56.

41. See Hebrews 7:24–28; 1 Peter 1:19; 3 Nephi 9:19.

42. Hebrews 9:11–12, 15.

43. See Hebrews 4:15.

44. See Gerald O'Collins and Michael Keenan Jones, *Jesus Our Priest: A Christian Approach to the Priesthood of Christ* (Oxford; New York: Oxford University Press, 2010), 46.

45. See 3 Nephi 9:15; 3 Nephi 27:7.

46. 1 Timothy 6:15; see 2 Nephi 10:14; Revelation 3:21.

47. See 2 Samuel 7:12–16.

48. Luke 1:32–33.

49. Matthew 2:1–2.

50. See Luke 2:36–38.

51. See Genesis 14:8; Joshua 10:3–5.

52. See 1 Kings 4:21; 1 Chronicles 18:14.

53. See 1 Samuel 13:13–14; 2 Samuel 11.

54. 1 Kings 11:4.

55. See Mosiah 17:20.

56. Mosiah 2:16–18.

57. John 6:15.

58. John 18:36–37.

59. See 2 Nephi 9:6–7.

60. See Jey J. Kanagaraj, "Jesus the King, Merkabah Mysticism and the Gospel of John," *Tyndale Bulletin* 47, no. 2 (November 1996): 349–66.

61. See Jeremiah 23:5.

62. See Sherman, *King, Priest, and Prophet*, 114–15.

63. See John Witte Jr., "No Ordinary King," *Christianity Today* 55, no. 7 (July 2011): 55. See also Matthew 21:7–10; John 13:5–12.

64. See Sherman, *King, Priest, and Prophet*, 119.

65. D&C 45:59.

66. Thomas S. Monson, "Finding Joy in the Journey," *Ensign*, November 2008, 88.

Small Things

J. Michael Hunter

A s I was pondering what to say here today, the phrase "make a difference in the world" kept coming to mind. We often hear this phrase in this season of graduation proceedings and commencement addresses; it's commonly used at a university. When I searched this phrase on the BYU website, I got over five thousand results. It's a phrase that is often expressed in the context of future opportunities and actions, frequently suggesting something extraordinary. In this context, when students hear that they are preparing now to make a difference in the world, they might assume that the difference they are to make somehow lies dormant until after graduation, so that when they do go out into the world, they are prepared to make a big impact.

Today I would like to look at this phrase in a different way. I would like to discuss making a difference in the world in the context of the here and now and the small and simple.

J. Michael Hunter was chair of the BYU Department of Religion and Family History at the Harold B. Lee Library when this devotional was given on 22 May 2012.
© *Brigham Young University.*

Wanting to make a difference in the world, Mother Teresa founded the Congregation of the Missionaries of Charity in 1950. The mission of her small organization was to help "the poorest of the poor" in the slums of Calcutta, India, by educating and meeting the needs of the destitute and starving. She wanted to bring comfort to the sick and dying who often felt unloved, uncared for, and unwanted.[1]

Some twenty years later the BBC sent an award-winning journalist to interview Mother Teresa about her work. The journalist reported that Calcutta was a scene of suffering and despair, the streets crowded with naked, hungry, homeless people whose needs stretched far beyond what the Missionaries of Charity could provide. The journalist suggested that a government agency would be better equipped than Mother Teresa to handle the destitute in the slums of Calcutta.[2] He stated, "Statistically speaking, what she achieves is little, or even negligible."[3] He thought—as he later revealed—that the difference she was making was so insignificant that it was hardly worth the bother.

Responding to the criticism directed at the "insignificant scale" of her work "by comparison with the need," Mother Teresa noted that "welfare is for a purpose—an admirable and a necessary one—whereas Christian love is for a person."[4] She told the journalist that the one was about numbers, the other about Christ.[5] She explained that what the poor need as much as food and clothing is to be wanted and loved.[6] Her simple purpose was to provide that love. She served the one within her reach, doing the best she could with what she had.

At another time Mother Teresa said: "What we do is nothing but a drop in the ocean. But if we didn't do it, the ocean would be one drop less."[7] Through her humble service, Mother Teresa made a difference in the world, drop by drop.

After the interview the journalist concluded: "Christianity is not a statistical view of life. That there should be more joy in heaven over one sinner who repents than over all the hosts of the just, is an anti-statistical proposition."[8]

Jesus Christ taught us to love and serve the one within our reach. Sitting by a well in Samaria, Jesus spoke with a woman from the local village (see John 4:4–28). He spent time with her. He listened. He answered questions. He showed respect. The teachings and miracles of Jesus attracted crowds. People in need—like the woman who reached out and touched His clothes to be healed—pressed about Him, seeking His individual attention. Some tried to bring little children to Him, wanting Him to put His hands on them and bless them. When some of His disciples tried to send the children away, Jesus stopped them and asked that the children be brought to Him. He took time out of His busy schedule to be with them. "He took them up in his arms, put his hands upon them, and blessed them" (Mark 10:16; see also Matthew 19:14).

Jesus spent time in the home of His friends Mary, Martha, and Lazarus. On one such occasion He listened patiently to the complaints of an anxious and perhaps weary Martha, who felt she was carrying more than her fair share of the burden of hosting guests. Jesus responded with kindness, understanding, and love (see Luke 10:41). Later, when Lazarus became sick, Mary and Martha sent for Jesus (see John 11:1–35). When Mary heard that Jesus was near, she ran to meet Him, fell down at His feet, and said, "If thou hadst been here, my brother had not died" (v. 32). When Jesus saw her weeping, the scriptures tell us that "he groaned in the spirit, and was troubled" (v. 33) and that He "wept" (v. 35). He showed great compassion in mourning with and comforting those around Him. Near the end of his mortal ministry Jesus said, "A new commandment I give unto you, That ye love one another; as I have loved you" (John 13:34).

While Jesus sat at the well or visited with friends in their homes, the streets of Jerusalem were filled with the homeless, the hungry, the crippled, the blind, and those with leprosy, but there was nothing negligible about His services. There's nothing negligible about the simple acts of kindness and assistance that you and I offer to those around us on a daily basis. At BYU the one within our reach might be the roommate who has had a difficult day and needs someone to listen, the professor who is having an off day teaching and needs a little patience and understanding, or the guy in the lane next to us who needs us to give him a break by slowing down to let him over so that he doesn't miss his turn ahead. Every day in our homes, in our communities, and in our classrooms right here on campus we can find the one within our reach who needs our assistance. It may only be a drop, but it does make a difference in the lives of those around us.

President David O. McKay was fond of the nineteenth-century quote "Life is made up not of great sacrifices or duties, but of little things in which smiles and kindness and small obligations given habitually are what win and preserve the heart and secure comfort."[9]

Mother Teresa said:

It is never too small. We are so small we look at things in a small way. But God, being Almighty, sees everything great. Therefore, even if you write a letter for a blind man or you just go and sit and listen, or you take the mail for him, or you visit somebody or bring a flower to somebody–small things–or wash clothes for somebody or clean the house. Very humble work that is where you and I must be. For there are many people who can do big things. But there are very few people who will do the small things.[10]

We read in the Book of Mormon "that by small and simple things are great things brought to pass" (Alma 37:6). This is illustrated beautifully in the birth of Christ. The Savior of the world was born in a simple stable in an obscure village to a woman of no great standing in the world. Out of these simple, small circumstances proceeded the Lord's great work of salvation. One of the most recognizable symbols of the Christmas season is the Nativity, with a small babe lying in straw and surrounded by animals. It is a reminder to us all that "out of small things proceedeth that which is great" (D&C 64:33).

When celebrating the birth of Christ, we surround ourselves with symbols to remind us of what life is really all about, why we're here, and what we're supposed to be doing with our lives. There are two very similar fictional stories that have become a part of the Christmas tradition in the United States. One is Frank Capra's film *It's a Wonderful Life*; the other is Charles Dickens' novella *A Christmas Carol*, which has been adapted for film and theater. I believe the broad appeal of these simple stories lies in their ability to remind us of things that we so easily forget but really want to remember. They help us rediscover the small things that get misplaced in the clutter around us. I know it's a little off-season, but I hope you'll indulge me in referring to these stories to remind us today of some things.

The main characters in these two stories—George Bailey and Ebenezer Scrooge—live their lives in relative obscurity, interacting on a daily basis with the people in their neighborhoods and communities and going about the mundane tasks of life. Both are businessmen in the profession of lending money—a trade that brings them into daily contact with individuals who need assistance. Like his father did before him, George Bailey runs his business with his heart rather than his head. He puts people before profits. His purpose in running a building and loan company is to help people get out of the slums. Kindness and respect characterize his daily interactions with those around him. On the other hand, Ebenezer Scrooge is described by Dickens as "a squeezing, wrenching, grasping, scraping, clutching, covetous, old sinner!" He conducts business with his head rather than his heart—a head that Dickens says is as "hard and sharp as flint."[11] Profits come before people. Despising the poor, Scrooge is perfectly content to keep them in the slums.

Despite their differences, these two characters are very much alike. Both have forgotten the significance of their simple, daily interactions with others: the powerful, cumulative effect of daily living is lost on them. They don't get it—not until there is Christmas Eve intervention to remind them of things they probably already know in their hearts but have forgotten in their heads.

George feels like a failure because he did not pursue his dreams of becoming an architect and world traveler. He has lived out his life in the same small town where he was born, doing the same small things day in and day out. He feels like he has made no difference in the world. Looking back on his life, he can find no meaning or purpose to it, and he contemplates ending it.

George's life, however, is saved by an angel named Clarence who has come as an answer to the prayers of George's family—and to earn his wings. Clarence's job is to show George the impact of those small things he did day in and day out. Clarence sets out to prove to George that he really has had a wonderful life by giving him a vision of what life would have been like for others had George never been born.

Visiting that same small town as a stranger who has never lived among them, George finds people without hope living in the slums. He finds unhappiness and despair. He hasn't been there to offer a hand up, and no one else has bothered. George realizes that his little deeds of goodness, his habits of selfless service—his small drops— have brought a better life to those around him and beyond. He's astonished at the reach of his small gestures. George had made a difference in the world without having ever left his hometown.

Ebenezer Scrooge also has Christmas Eve visitors. The first is the ghost of Jacob Marley, Ebenezer's former business partner. He appears "captive, bound, and double-ironed"[12] with a long chain wound about him made of "cashboxes, keys, padlocks, ledgers, deeds, and heavy purses wrought in steel."[13] The ghost explains to Ebenezer that he wears the chain he "forged in life," having made it "link by link, and yard by yard"[14] through the choices he made, being eternally linked to that which he valued most in life. He explains that he is now required to walk the earth and witness what he could not now share "but might have shared on earth, and turned to happiness."[15] Shocked, Ebenezer exclaims, "But you were always a good man of business, Jacob."[16]

The remorseful ghost says, "Business! . . . Mankind was my business. The common welfare was my business; charity, mercy, forbearance, and benevolence were, all, my business. The dealings of my trade were but a drop of water in the . . . ocean of my business!"[17]

And Ebenezer doesn't get it. He doesn't comprehend how the big things count so little nor how the small things matter so much.

He cannot get that flint head of his around it. In the course of that long night he is visited by the spirits of Christmas past, present, and future. They come to show Scrooge that his cold-hearted, tight-fisted ways—his drops—have brought misery and unhappiness to those around him. His single-minded focus on his business has gradually resulted in his turning his back on his family and friends and in rejecting the needs of those in his community.

Both George and Ebenezer have Christmas epiphanies that bring them back to that simple stable in an obscure village. They come to realize that "by very small means the Lord doth confound the wise and bringeth about the salvation of many souls" (Alma 37:7). They remember, as we do through their stories, that the essence of life is in the small and seemingly insignificant daily interactions we have with others.

We are busy people here at BYU. There are appointments to be kept, projects to be finished, papers to be written, assignments to be graded, and any number of things to be organized on any given day. In the rush of our daily lives, we—like Marley and Scrooge—can easily get our priorities mixed up and forget the small things that are the most important. The one we need to assist could be sitting right next to us, but we do not see that person. Perhaps the person needing our individual attention has worked in the same office with us for years, and yet that person is invisible to us. If we become too preoccupied with the distractions that crowd around us, we may not feel the prompting when our Heavenly Father has an assignment for us.

One of my responsibilities at the library is to meet one-on-one with students to assist them with their research. I consider it the best part of my job. I also sometimes have to write reports and attend to mundane office duties. On one occasion I was feeling the pressure of an upcoming deadline. It had been a busy week, and I wasn't sure how I was going to get everything done. On my calendar I designated a couple of hours to get a certain task done. I told the student employees at our desk not to send any students needing research assistance to me that morning. I then went into my office and closed my door.

A short while later there was a knock at the door. I was irritated at the interruption. I went to the door and opened it. The student standing there explained that he really needed to meet with me as soon as possible, and he wondered if now would be a good time. Looking at my face, his smile dropped. Whatever I was radiating that morning, it wasn't friendly.

Before I could answer him, he said, "I see you're busy. I'll come back at another time." As he started to walk away, I received a prompting—a chastisement, really. I had made a bad choice. I had gotten my priorities mixed up. Like Marley and Scrooge, I had forgotten for a moment that mankind was my business. I told the student to stay and that I would really like to meet with him now.

As we talked in my office, the student explained that he had transferred to BYU from a small college. The course work here was more difficult than he had anticipated. He was feeling discouraged and doubting his abilities. He had two papers due, and he hadn't had much experience writing research papers. He found the library to be a large, complicated, and—I'm sure, thanks to me—unfriendly place. I had nothing better to do at that moment than to orient a new student to library research and offer a little encouragement. He returned to me several times for help after that. If I had let him walk away because I was too busy for him, I'm sure he would not have returned—the prompting told me that.

I believe that our Heavenly Father has small daily tasks that He would like us to do right here at BYU to make a difference. He would like to make us instruments in His hands in helping to fulfill His work. President Spencer W. Kimball said:

> *God does notice us, and he watches over us. But it is usually through another person that he meets our needs. Therefore, it is vital that we serve each other in the kingdom. . . . So often, our acts of service consist of simple encouragement or of giving mundane help with mundane tasks, but what glorious consequences can flow from mundane acts and from small but deliberate deeds!*[18]

Knowing that there are angels among us attending to our needs and that no sparrow falls without the Father's notice gives us courage and faith to let go of our own troubles long enough to reach out and help others with theirs. It's a system of give and take that works best when all focus more on the giving and less on the taking. Along the way, our Heavenly Father sends us gentle reminders of the small things that are of the greatest worth.

I first arrived on this campus as a freshman nearly thirty years ago. I had only been a member of the Church for four months, and I was the only member in my family. I was over two thousand miles from my home in Virginia and knew no one here in Utah. It was a lot to get used to all at once. At times I felt like I had landed in a foreign country. I was overwhelmed with all there was to learn and do.

I didn't know who my roommate would be in the dorms that first year, but I assumed he would be a lifelong member of the Church who could explain to me how things worked around here. The Lord, as He often does, had something else in mind. That first roommate of mine wasn't a member of the Church. In fact, he wasn't from a Christian tradition. He was from Saudi Arabia, and he didn't speak English. He had come to participate in BYU's English as a Second Language program. I may have felt like I was in a foreign land, but he actually was. My challenges seemed trivial; his appeared to be overwhelming. He looked to me to tell him how things worked around here, and I hope he has forgiven me for not always getting it right.

President Gordon B. Hinckley told of his experience of feeling homesick and discouraged while serving a mission in England and how he wrote home about it. His father's simple reply was "Forget yourself and go to work."[19] I think that's the message my Heavenly Father was trying to send me that first year. Years ago President Hinckley visited this campus and gave that very message to the students. He said:

If the pressures of school are too heavy, if you complain about your housing and the food you eat, I can suggest a cure for your problems. Lay your books aside for a few hours, leave your room, and go visit someone who is old and lonely. There are many such right here in this valley. Or visit those who are sick and discouraged; there are hundreds of that kind here, including not a few on this campus, who need the kind of encouragement you could give.[20]

I was not left without assistance and encouragement that first year. In fact, I don't have time today to tell you of all the helpers sent my way, but I do want to mention one. Before I left home, my grandmother sat me down to determine if I was really serious about going to BYU. When—to her disappointment—she found out that I was, she said, "You might as well know, then, that your grandfather has a cousin who joined the Latter-day Saints some thirty years ago." She explained the complicated family connection, but it went over my head. She explained that in the course of those thirty years they had only seen this cousin and his wife at a few reunions and that it was her understanding that he now lived in New Mexico. She said that at one of the reunions she had heard that this cousin had a son who worked at BYU. She didn't know the son's name, but she provided me with the cousin's name. I tucked this information away in my mind, thinking that perhaps I would look this person up when I came to BYU.

That first semester I had registered for my general electives, including Biology 100. In my registration materials, the instructor of that biology class was simply listed as "staff." On the first day of class, the instructor introduced himself as Larry St. Clair. I immediately recognized St. Clair as the last name of that cousin. The thought, of course, occurred to me that I should ask him if he was the son of that cousin. However, as the class progressed that day, I started to talk myself out of the idea, thinking that there could be any number of people on campus with that last name and wondering how I would approach the subject since I wasn't exactly sure how we were related. The feeling that I should introduce myself persisted to the point that I felt pushed forward. At the end of class I hung back, waiting for a portion of the class that had surrounded the professor wanting to add his class. If you've ever been in a Biology 100 class, you know that this was a hundred or so people.

My turn finally came, and I introduced myself, asking him if he was the son of Jack St. Clair. When he confirmed that he was, I introduced myself as his cousin. He asked me a few questions. At this point he could have said, "Nice to meet you. Tell the folks hello," and left it at that. Instead he invited me to dinner that week so I could meet his wife, Rieta, and their children. So I went to dinner and met the St. Clair family. At that point Larry had certainly fulfilled any family obligation he might have had, and, again, he could have left it at that with a clear conscience. However, he was in tune enough to recognize the one within his reach who needed his help. He somehow realized that I was a little homesick, a lot overwhelmed, and with no family support in the Church.

The St. Clairs invited me to dinner again and again and again. They invited me over for holidays. They invited me to go to activities with them. A few months after that initial meeting Larry St. Clair bestowed upon me the Melchizedek Priesthood and ordained me to the office of an elder. A year later, Larry and Rieta accompanied me to the Salt Lake Temple for my first visit to the temple. A couple of months after that, Larry drove me to the Missionary Training Center to see me off on my mission.

Jump forward twenty years. I was two thousand miles from home—this time in the opposite direction—on the East Coast at a conference away from my family and home in Utah. I received a phone call from my wife, who was distressed. I could hear our children crying in the background. Our family had suffered a heartbreaking loss. I felt helpless, and I couldn't get home immediately. After we ended our phone call, my wife loaded the children into our van and drove to Larry and Rieta St. Clair's house. The St. Clairs found themselves with a living room full of heart-broken people. Larry took each person, one by one, and placed his hands on them and gave them blessings of comfort.

When we are willing to accept assignments from the Lord, they may only take a moment, but they might also take a month or a year or a lifetime. The important thing is that we are in tune enough to see the one within our reach who needs our help and that we have enough faith to accept the assignment. It won't be convenient. I hope nothing I have said here today has given the impression that I believe "small and simple" means easy, because it doesn't. But I believe these small and simple things will become our most valued university experiences.

When Mawi Asgedom, an Ethiopian native who had once lived in a Sudanese refugee camp, left for Harvard University, his mother said to him, "Always remember where you came from."[21]

Once he arrived at Harvard he got caught up in the rush of everyday university life, which for him involved clubs, sports, a lot of classes, and a part-time job. He said, "Remembering where I had come from seemed far less important than knowing where I was supposed to be every half hour."[22]

During his sophomore year he worked as a delivery man for the Harvard Student Agency. While waiting for a package in the office, he watched as an elderly and feeble woman walked in. She asked if there was someone there who could type a short letter for her— "such a simple, easy thing to do," Mawi later recalled.[23]

The receptionist explained that they offered no typing services and sent her away. Looking a little confused, the woman started to turn away, but another worker in the office called her over, "gently sat her down," and then typed the letter for her.[24]

Mawi said, "Never has a Harvard student seemed so great to me as in that moment."[25] Mawi began to reflect on what his mother might have meant when she advised him to always remember where he came from. He had been the recipient of many such kindnesses in his long journey from a refugee camp to Harvard University. Many angels had helped him along the way, and he had noticed that "most angels don't look like angels,"[26] so it shouldn't have surprised him as much as perhaps it did to find one looking like an ordinary college student at Harvard. Thinking back on those angels and their kind-nesses, he realized that each had taught him something important about life and inspired him to reach out to help those around him. In their small ways they had made a difference in his life.

Mawi graduated with top honors and gave the commencement address at his graduation in 1999. Reflecting on his time at Harvard, he said in his address he had learned "many facts and formulas, many new ways of thinking, a fresh understanding of the world."[27] But he highlighted that seemingly insignificant act of kindness he had witnessed that day in the Harvard Student Agency as a turning point in his education, when he began to reflect on what is most important in life. He said, "While Harvard University taught me well, my true education has come from less-likely sources."[28]

I pray we will always remember where we came from and that we will follow Christ in reaching out to those around us. Christlike love transforms our simple, everyday living into something extraordinary. It's the love of Christ that makes the difference. We don't need to leave BYU to make a difference in the world. There are people within our reach here who need us. There are assignments waiting for us here—we just need to accept them.

In the words of David O. McKay:

There is no one great thing which we can do to obtain eternal life, and it seems to me that the great lesson to be learned in the world today is to apply in the little acts and duties of life the glorious principles of the gospel. Let us not think that because some . . . things . . . seem small and trivial that they are unimportant. Life, after all, is made up of little things.[29]

In the name of Jesus Christ, amen.

NOTES

1. Edward Le Joly, *Mother Teresa of Calcutta: A Biography* (San Francisco: Harper and Row, 1983), 28–29.

2. See Malcolm Muggeridge, *Something Beautiful for God: Mother Teresa of Calcutta* (London: Collins, 1971), 25.

3. Muggeridge, *Something Beautiful*, 28.

4. Muggeridge, *Something Beautiful*, 28.

5. See Muggeridge, *Something Beautiful*, 28.

6. See Muggeridge, *Something Beautiful*, 22–23.

7. Mother Teresa, *My Life for the Poor: Mother Teresa of Calcutta*, ed. José Luis González-Balado and Janet N. Playfoot (San Francisco: Harper and Row, 1985), 20.

8. Muggeridge, *Something Beautiful*, 28.

9. *GI*, 388; quoting Humphry Davy, in John Davy, *Memoirs of the Life of Sir Humphry Davy* (London: Longman, Rees, Orme, Brown, Green, and Longman, 1836), 391.

10. Mother Teresa of Calcutta, *Life in the Spirit: Reflections, Meditations, Prayers*, ed. Kathryn Spink (San Francisco: Harper and Row, 1983), 49; quoted in *Love: A Fruit Always in Season: Daily Meditations from the Words of Mother Teresa of Calcutta*, ed. Dorothy S. Hunt (San Francisco: Ignatius Press, 1987), 26.

11. Charles Dickens, *A Christmas Carol* (Philadelphia: David McKay, 1914), 3.

12. Dickens, *Christmas Carol*, 26.

13. Dickens, *Christmas Carol*, 20.

14. Dickens, *Christmas Carol*, 24.

15. Dickens, *Christmas Carol*, 24.

16. Dickens, *Christmas Carol*, 26.

17. Dickens, *Christmas Carol*, 26.

18. Spencer W. Kimball, "Small Acts of Service," *Ensign*, December 1974, 5.

19. In Sheri L. Dew, *Go Forward with Faith: The Biography of Gordon B. Hinckley* (Salt Lake City: Deseret Book, 1996), 64.

20. Gordon B. Hinckley, "Forget Yourself," BYU devotional address, 6 March 1977.

21. Mawi Asgedom, *Of Beetles and Angels: A Boy's Remarkable Journey from a Refugee Camp to Harvard*, ed. Dave Berger (Boston: Little, Brown and Company, 2002), 135.

22. Asgedom, *Of Beetles*, 136.

23. Asgedom, *Of Beetles*, 136.

24. Asgedom, *Of Beetles*, 136.

25. Asgedom, *Of Beetles*, 136.

26. Asgedom, *Of Beetles*, 30.
27. Asgedom, *Of Beetles*, 137.
28. Asgedom, *Of Beetles*, 134.
29. *GI*, 151–52.

Becoming More Teachable

Melissa Heath

Over the past month our ward has welcomed several newborn babies. Each baby comes to this earth curious and eager to learn. They want to taste everything, chew everything, and pull on everything. I imagine that from a baby's point of view, everything in this world is new and amazing.

As we anticipated our exodus from the spirit world, we placed great trust in the plan of salvation. We trusted Heavenly Father and our Savior. In Their wisdom, They knew that our spirits would initially flourish best in the physical form of a baby. When our spirits were united with our physical bodies, we became helpless and totally dependent on our caregivers. We forgot our previous knowledge and relationships. It must have been a huge shock to have our spirit and physical body unite. But we were confident in the plan of salvation—we were confident that this earthly life, including the merging of our spirit and physical body, was a necessary step in our eternal progression. Confident in our Savior's Atonement, we came

Melissa Heath was a BYU associate professor of counseling psychology and special education when this devotional was given on 29 May 2012. © *Brigham Young University.*

to earth knowing that we could return to our heavenly home. Each of us started our life fresh and innocent, and we began to learn the many things we needed to know in order to function on this earth and continue our eternal progression.

We are children of our Heavenly Father; each individual who comes to this earth is given an extraordinary capacity for learning and growth. We have opportunities in this life to learn information that would have been difficult—if not impossible—to learn in the spirit world. For instance, learning to ride a bicycle would be difficult to accomplish if we only observed others riding their bicycles. Even more difficult would be learning to ride a bicycle if our sole preparation was merely reading books about bicycle riding. Learning by doing is an amazing process. Most of us scraped our knees and elbows as we repeatedly tried to master cycling—without the training wheels. Most of us were successful. We now ride a bicycle without much thought regarding our initial difficulties, fears, and injuries. Fortunately, as young children we were not faced with simultaneous challenges that overwhelmed our capacity to learn and progress. For example, on the same day—or week—that we learned to ride a bicycle, we were not faced with learning to drive a car, pilot an airplane, and fly a rocket to the moon. Typically, as Nephi described in 2 Nephi 28:30, our learning progresses "line upon line, precept upon precept."

At Brigham Young University, before we "go forth to serve," we "enter to learn." We read books, listen to lectures, discuss topics, write papers, and take tests. Many of you will complete a practicum or internship in which you will apply your academic learning to real-life situations. "The glory of God is intelligence, or, in other words, light and truth" (D&C 93:36).

Whatever principle of intelligence we attain unto in this life, it will rise with us in the resurrection.

And if a person gains more knowledge and intelligence in this life through his diligence and obedience than another, he will have so much the advantage in the world to come. [D&C 130:18–19]

Because attaining knowledge is such an important task—and a lifelong endeavor—it is important to understand the meaning and implications of being teachable. When we are teachable, the Holy Ghost bears witness of truth and we increase in knowledge and wisdom. In 2 Nephi 28, the prophet Nephi saw our day and warned us about the challenges of living and learning in these latter days. Even though Nephi offered these words approximately 2,572 years ago, his vision was inspired and crystal clear regarding these perilous times. The chapter synopsis in the Book of Mormon reads:

Many false churches shall be built up in the last days—They shall teach false and vain and foolish doctrines—Apostasy shall abound because of false teachers—The devil shall rage in the hearts of men—He [the devil] *shall teach all manner of false doctrines.*

Likening the scriptures to my personal life, I took this synopsis and placed responsibility on myself, the learner: In 2012 men and women shall join many false organizations—They shall learn false and foolish doctrines—Apostasy shall abound, and I will be pulled into personal apostasy if I listen to and learn from false teachers—Many will allow the devil to rage in their hearts—I will not allow the devil to rage in my heart. I will avoid learning all manner of false doctrines from the devil's teachings.

Although the very existence of false teachings is troublesome, our eternal progression is blocked when we accommodate and assimilate these false teachings into our beliefs and way of life. The end product is misery. As Alma warned his son Corianton, "Wickedness never was happiness" (Alma 41:10). In direct opposition to Satan's false teachings, the gospel of Jesus Christ and our obedience to God's commandments help us move forward in our eternal progression (see Mosiah 2:41). In regard to moving forward, 2 Nephi 28:30 emphasizes the importance of being teachable:

For behold, thus saith the Lord God: I will give unto the children of men line upon line, precept upon precept, here a little and there a little; and blessed are those who hearken unto my precepts, and lend an ear unto my counsel, for they shall learn wisdom; for unto him that receiveth I will give more.

Today I am recommending four strategies to help us become more teachable and to help facilitate our eternal progression: (1) stick to the gospel's fundamental principles; (2) have a grateful heart; (3) conquer pride by choosing to be humble; and (4) recalibrate and get back on track.

STICK TO THE GOSPEL'S FUNDAMENTAL PRINCIPLES

Have you ever studied for an exam without knowing the exact information that you would be required to know? The exam may have covered several textbooks, and the exam's grade may have factored heavily into your course grade. This uncertainty of not knowing what to memorize or what to study can cause great anxiety because you do not know which pieces of information are the most important—or which pieces of information the professor thinks are the most important.

Sometimes we are overwhelmed by the sheer amount of information available through the Internet and library resources. There are literally thousands of books available on every imaginable topic. One important lifelong skill is the ability to prioritize information, focus on the most important pieces, and know how these pieces fit into the bigger picture. During His ministry the Savior boiled down critical information and summarized key points to help us focus on fundamental principles. His words and actions provide a perfect model for us to follow. He emphasized the importance of obedience, and, in response to a lawyer's question, He identified the first and greatest commandment:

Thou shalt love the Lord thy God with all thy heart, and with all thy soul, and with all thy mind.

This is the first and great commandment.

And the second is like unto it, Thou shalt love thy neighbour as thyself.

On these two commandments hang all the law and the prophets.

[Matthew 22:37–40]

His teachings identified the gospel's fundamental principles—the very most important things we need to know and do.

In a revelation given to the Prophet Joseph Smith and recorded in section 42 of the Doctrine and Covenants, the Lord said, "If thou lovest me thou shalt serve me and keep all my commandments" (D&C 42:29). Obedience is important, and—interestingly—love and obedience are paired together. This will not change: we are expected to keep the commandments—to show our love for God we must keep His commandments. This principle is important and is reiterated by every prophet. Contrary to Satan's teachings, being obedient is not restrictive; in fact, obedience keeps us free from spiritual bondage. Obedience allows us to have the constant companionship of the Holy Ghost and keeps our minds open to learning and feeling the love of our Savior and our Heavenly Father. We must stick to the fundamental principle of being obedient because obedience helps us become more teachable and facilitates our eternal progression.

The gospel's fundamental principles—such as faith in the Lord Jesus Christ, repentance and turning from sin, obedience to the Ten Commandments, and avoidance of pride—are repeated throughout the Book of Mormon by the prophet Abinadi, King Benjamin, Alma, and Moroni. In the scriptures several prophets and righteous men closed their earthly lives with a "parting message"—final words of wisdom that clarified the fundamental principles of the gospel. In the movies, dying individuals also give their parting messages as a nice way to emotionally emphasize critical information and manipulate the audience's emotions, often with dramatic music to draw some tears. However, the scriptural accounts of parting messages are accompanied by the witness of the Holy Ghost. These messages contain the gospel's fundamental teachings. These teachings are real, not imaginary, and in no way are these messages intended to manipulate or control the listener.

Unfortunately, those who were there to hear firsthand the passionate message of a dying prophet may or may not have benefited—everything depending on *if* the individual was teachable. Those leaving their final parting messages most often desired that the younger generation and future generations might avoid common pitfalls and carnal behavior that stunt the ability to learn and halt eternal progression. These righteous men passed the spiritual baton on to the next generation. It is important to note these repeated messages—the fundamentals—all of which are intended to help us prepare for our eternal exam, often referred to in the scriptures as the final judgment. When reading the scriptures, we must listen carefully and learn fundamental lessons as if we were sitting at the prophet's knee, witnessing his final urgent message. These parting messages place an emphasis on fundamentals that are repeated by our modern-day prophets.

Listen to, learn, and stick to the gospel's fundamental principles.

HAVE A GRATEFUL HEART

The Lord loves a grateful heart. In November 2000 President Gordon B. Hinckley urged the youth to "be grateful"—the first of six Bs he counseled the youth to follow. He urged them to walk with gratitude in their hearts and to express gratitude to their parents, friends, and teachers. He also counseled the youth to "thank the Lord for His goodness to you" ("First Presidency Message: A Prophet's Counsel and Prayer for Youth," *Ensign*, January 2001, 4). This inspired advice applies to individuals of all ages, including university students, staff, and faculty.

A grateful heart is an important ingredient in becoming more teachable. When I came to BYU in 1999, I was awestruck by the incredible beauty of the mountains, particularly Mount Timpanogos and the way morning's light struck the edges and angles of the rocky cliffs. Each day as I drove to campus I breathed in a deep, satisfied breath and said a prayer of gratitude for the beauty of these mountains. One day I said to myself, "I will say a prayer of gratitude each day as I soak in the earth's beauty." Several months later I became preoccupied with my to-do list and my responsibilities. As I hurriedly pulled into BYU's parking lot one day and gathered my things, I had a moment of clarity: It had been several days since I had even noticed the mountains, let alone said my prayer of gratitude for the beauty of those mountains. I had developed a spiritual callus. The mountains were still there, but, sadly, and to my detriment, other things clouded my attention. I resolved to daily take time to enjoy the beauty around me and to express my gratitude to Heavenly Father. Feelings of gratitude soften our hearts and open our minds to learning.

The Prophet Joseph Smith spoke frequently of the importance of expressing gratitude to the Lord. Though facing challenging situations, persecution, and the task of carrying the responsibility of opening this dispensation, Joseph Smith was inspired to share these words:

And ye must give thanks unto God in the Spirit for whatsoever blessing ye are blessed with. [D&C 46:32]

And he who receiveth all things with thankfulness shall be made glorious; and the things of this earth shall be added unto him, even an hundred fold, yea, more. [D&C 78:19]

Verily I say unto you my friends, fear not, let your hearts be comforted; yea, rejoice evermore, and in everything give thanks. [D&C 98:1]

In his recent April general conference address titled "Thanks Be to God," Elder Russell M. Nelson commented, "How much better it would be if all could be more aware of God's providence and love and express that gratitude to Him. . . . Our degree of gratitude is a measure of our love for Him." He also quoted Ammon's teaching from Alma 26:8: "Let us give thanks to [God], for he doth work righteousness forever" (*Ensign*, May 2012, 77).

Choosing to have a grateful heart is an important strategy in becoming more teachable because it prepares our hearts to be humble and open to the promptings of the Spirit.

CONQUER PRIDE BY CHOOSING TO BE HUMBLE

In his November 2000 address President Hinckley also urged the youth to "be humble"
—the fifth of the six Bs. He identified the meek and the humble as "those who are teachable" ("Prophet's Counsel," 10). In Doctrine and Covenants 112:10, the Lord counseled Thomas B. Marsh to "be thou humble; and the Lord thy God shall lead thee by the hand, and give thee answer to thy prayers."

When we are humble, we are ready to listen to and follow the Lord's direction. In the April 1989 general conference, President Ezra Taft Benson spoke on a topic that remains especially relevant to me: pride. He described pride as "the great stumbling block to Zion" ("Beware of Pride," *Ensign*, May 1989, 7). Pride makes us deaf to the promptings of the Holy Ghost. Pride takes a heavy toll on our earthly life and on our eternal life. When we allow pride to enter into our lives, we will not and cannot learn the most important things in this life nor in the eternities. We become hard-hearted, stiffnecked, and spiritually blinded. President Benson observed that for those who are infected with pride, "the world shouts louder than the whisperings of the Holy Ghost" ("Beware of Pride," 5).

President Benson identified the core ingredient of pride as enmity, which starts with competitive feelings and a desire to be better than others. Then come feelings of being offended, then contentiousness, and ultimately an intense hatred toward God and mankind. The opposite of humility, enmity is the alluring and controlling power Satan uses. Rather than the Savior's "thy will be done, and the glory be thine," Satan's statement is "my will be done and the glory be mine." It is a battle of the wills (see "Beware of Pride," 4–5).

What characteristics of pride impede learning? For the prideful, the purpose of life narrows down to an obsession with being better than others. One's focus becomes warped, dark, and evil. Pride destroys unity and oneness. It destroys us and those around us. Pride keeps us from confessing our sins; it keeps us from forsaking our sins. Pride literally diverts and squelches the physical and spiritual ability to learn. Pride leads to rebellion, hate, contentiousness, unrighteous dominion, and abusive control of others. Sadly, the prideful are easily offended, they are unforgiving, and they will not take correction and feedback. In other words, their learning and all interpersonal relationships in this life are stunted. Even more tragic is the poor eternal prognosis for those who succumb to pride.

Although pride is potentially a terminal condition, there is an antidote: humility. Choose to be humble. When we are humble we are teachable, opening our minds and hearts to spiritual learning. In Mosiah 3:19 King Benjamin stated:

For the natural man is an enemy to God, and has been from the fall of Adam, and will be, forever and ever, unless he yields to the enticings of the Holy Spirit, and putteth off the natural man and becometh a saint through the atonement of Christ the Lord, and becometh as a child, submissive, meek, humble, patient, full of love, willing to submit to all things which the Lord seeth fit to inflict upon him, even as a child doth submit to his father.

On a personal note, to help me avoid flattery and deception and the end result of sliding down the slippery slope of pride, I have created a realistic and disturbing image: Although flattery feeds our ego, it is nothing more than a lure snatched by a starving rat now writhing on a cheese-less trap. So avoid the cheese! Once the trap snaps shut, it is very hard to escape. In becoming teachable, we must conquer pride by choosing to be humble.

RECALIBRATE AND GET BACK ON TRACK

As we recognize we are off the path and are headed in the wrong direction, we must recalibrate and head back in the right direction. On a recent trip to the Dallas–Fort Worth area, before I left the airport in a rental car, I plugged in my GPS and proceeded to type in my destination. I left the rental-car lot and listened carefully for directions.

"Turn left and proceed 500 feet." I carefully followed those directions. About four turns into the trip, the GPS told me to turn left. But on my left was a barrier blockading a closed road. Luckily it was around 11:00 p.m. and no other traffic was on the road. As I started to panic, the GPS clearly stated, "Merge onto I-15 and head north, traveling toward Salt Lake City." Now I was totally flustered. For some reason my GPS thought I was in Utah! I pulled off the road, turned off the GPS, waited a few seconds, restarted the GPS, and retyped the Texas address. Within a few seconds the correct set of directions was displayed, and I was guided to the intended destination—my targeted goal.

From a spiritual sense, when we realize we are going in the wrong direction, we must stop and get back on the right track—and the sooner the better. From personal experience, I know that the best way to get back on track and keep on track is to stick to those things that I know are right and true. For me this includes daily scripture reading, personal prayer, and attending sacrament meeting. Is this basic and simple? Yes, it is. However, when I fall short in doing those three things, my learning is stunted, because I lose calibration and start to head off in the wrong direction.

A few years ago I attended groups sponsored by the LDS twelve-step addiction recovery program. I attended with a dear friend, and we supported each other. These groups are held every day of the week at various locations throughout the Wasatch Front. Recovering from addiction is a lifelong challenge.

My friend and I learned practical lessons from group members. I learned that successful days of sobriety are never lost. When you slip and fall back into old patterns of addiction, it is critical that you immediately get back on track, repent by following the necessary steps, and move forward to add another day of sobriety to your "new history." You do not lose any of your days of sobriety. Instead, you keep those previous days of sobriety and simply add your new days to the tally. I appreciated the fact that you keep making "new history"—what a positive way to think about getting back on track and staying on track.

Contrary to Satan's voice, which tells us that things are hopeless, that we are worthless, and that we are forever lost, our Savior wants all of us to repent as quickly as possible, get back on track, and come unto Him.

CLOSING

It is my prayer that we strive to become more teachable by knowing and living the gospel's fundamental principles, having a grateful heart, conquering pride by choosing to be humble, and recalibrating and getting back on track. Living these strategies takes courage and honesty, a willingness to submit to the Lord's eternal truths, and a trust in God—that He knows each of us personally and wants us to become more teachable. He wants us to be teachable so that we can learn of Him, make changes to be like Him, and return to Him.

The Holy Ghost bears witness of truth. Listen for that witness. If we are teachable, we will feel and hear that spiritual witness. I bear testimony that God lives and that Jesus is the Christ, our Perfect Example, in the name of our Savior Jesus Christ, amen.

The Simpleness of the Way

———◆———

Stanley A. Johnson

I am definitely humbled by this opportunity to speak to you today. As you can imagine, I have lost a lot of sleep over this responsibility, and I'm guessing that when I am done you will probably say, "He should have slept!"

To begin with, I feel it is important to explain that for most of my life I grew up without a father's influence in the home, so I turned to the leaders of the Church for guidance. I have read over and over the talks given by the General Authorities and other leaders at general conference and other occasions. Their counsel and instruction have guided me throughout my life as a father would, so I will be using many of their quotes today.

Years ago, when I was a young father, I went downstairs one day to our oldest son's bedroom. He was very upset and had been crying. I was there to try to comfort him and find out what was wrong. As he and I talked, he confessed that he had told a fib to his mother. He said, "Dad, it's so hard to be righteous." This caused me to turn my

Stanley A. Johnson was a BYU professor of ancient scripture when this devotional was given on 5 June 2012. © *Brigham Young University.*

head and smile, because he was young, but then he continued to say, "Dad, life is like climbing over a wall, isn't it?" For a moment I was completely stunned. How could he have such insight?

We continued to talk, but the rest of the conversation is a blur. I hope my part of that conversation included teaching him how the Savior made it possible for him to repent of the fib he had told his mother and any other mistakes he had made. I also hope I taught him how very important it is to listen to and follow the promptings of the Holy Ghost each day of his life.

In March 1979 President Marion G. Romney, then second counselor in the First Presidency, gave a BYU devotional titled "Guidance of the Holy Spirit." He stated:

As conditions worsen, it becomes more apparent every day that we are on a collision course with disaster. I am persuaded that nothing short of the guidance of the Holy Spirit can bring us through safely.

He then explained some profound truths. "If you want to obtain and keep the guidance of the Spirit, you can do so by following this simple four-point program":

1. Pray
2. Study and learn the gospel
3. Live righteously
4. Give service in the Church

President Romney continued: "If you will do these things, you will get the guidance of the Holy Spirit and you will go through this world successfully, regardless of what the people of the world say or do."[1] What a wonderful promise that is!

As I read these words, I recall King Benjamin's address to the Nephites and their subsequent conversion:

And they all cried with one voice, saying: Yea, we believe all the words which thou hast spoken unto us; and also, we know of their surety and

truth, because of the Spirit of the Lord Omnipotent, which has wrought a
mighty change in us, or in our hearts, that we have no more disposition to
do evil, but to do good continually. [Mosiah 5:2]

Before we continue, I must share a favorite quote by President
Ezra Taft Benson, given here at a BYU devotional. President
Howard W. Hunter felt it was so important that he later included it
in a general conference talk. President Benson said:

That man is greatest and most blessed and joyful whose life most closely
fits the pattern of the Christ. This has nothing to do with earthly wealth,
power, or prestige. The only true test of greatness, blessedness, joyfulness is
how close a life can come to being like the Master, Jesus Christ. He is the
right way, the full truth, and the abundant life.[2]

It is because of Jesus Christ and through the Holy Ghost that
we can change, that we can change completely, and that we can stay
changed. We do not need to be a part of this world that is on a collision course with disaster. The key is to obtain and keep the Spirit of
the Lord with us continually.

"THAT'S TOO SIMPLE"

While working on my doctoral degree in 1984, I took a course
in education. One day my professor broke from the lecture and
asked the class how one obtains the Spirit of the Lord in his own
life. Many members of the class made comments, and finally I
shared what President Romney had stated in 1979. I recited the
four-point program for obtaining the Spirit. When I had finished,
the professor leaned against the chalkboard, looked down at the
ground, and said, "No, that's too simple—that's too simple."

I have reflected on his comment over and over again, and I keep
thinking about the story of Moses in the wilderness when he raised
the brazen serpent. The rebellious Israelites had been bitten by serpents, and the Lord told Moses to fashion a fiery serpent out of brass

and place it upon a pole. All who would look upon the serpent would live. (See Numbers 21:6–9.)

The Book of Mormon carries on the narrative and explains what happened:

He sent fiery flying serpents among them; and after they were bitten he prepared a way that they might be healed; and the labor which they had to perform was to look; and because of the simpleness of the way, or the easiness of it, there were many who perished. [1 Nephi 17:41]

There you have it—it was too simple, therefore many perished. Remember, President Romney too spoke of the simpleness of the way when he said, "If you want to obtain and keep the guidance of the Spirit, you can do so by following this *simple* four-point program" (emphasis added).

PRAY

The first point is to pray. Even though the idea is simple, the process requires our whole being. President Henry B. Eyring once stated:

[The Lord] *offers us the covenant to always remember Him and the warning to pray always so that we will place our reliance on Him, our only safety. It is not hard to know what to do. The very difficulty of remembering **always** and praying **always** is a needed spur to **try harder.** The danger lies in delay or drift.*[3]

Remember, it is not difficult to know what to do; the difficulty lies in actually doing it.

Years ago Elder Gene R. Cook of the Seventy presided at our stake conference when I was stake president. In the Saturday adult session, he challenged everyone to prayerfully select someone who would not normally attend stake conference and invite them to come to stake conference the following day. He then asked for a raise of hands as a commitment and counseled the congregation to pray themselves through the experience. Then he said something I will always remember: "We should learn to pray ourselves through each day." This has had a lasting impact on me.

Elder Cook also turned to me and asked me to prayerfully select someone whom I could bring to stake conference the following day. I would like to share that experience, with permission from the individual involved. As you can imagine, I immediately started to pray myself through that experience. During the process, the name of one of our neighbors came into my mind. She had been through some challenges, so I thought this would be a good time to challenge her. Elder Cook and I walked across the street, and I asked her if we could visit.

"President," she said, "do you know how many people have already been here?"

"No," I replied.

"Five!" she said, holding up her hand with outstretched fingers.

I remember thinking, "Well, so much for my inspiration!"

Elder Cook didn't miss a beat. He grabbed me by the arm, pulled me in close, and said, "Ask her if we can talk to her." I did, and she invited us downstairs.

As we descended the stairs, Elder Cook turned to me and asked, "Are you praying yourself through this?"

I thought to myself, "What do you think?"

When we were settled on the couch, he started to talk to her, looking her in the eye. He asked her what her maiden name was, and she told him. He then said, calling her by name, "I know your parents really well. Are you from . . . ?" and he named the location.

"Yes," she said.

"I know your dad. He's a stake president."

"Yes," she said.

Elder Cook then proceeded to chasten her firmly, calling her by name again and saying, "You know better."

Tears flowed, and soon commitments followed. At the beginning of that experience I thought I had made a mistake, but the Spirit had guided us there, and by praying through that experience, doors and hearts were opened.

Amulek stated the idea of continual prayer this way: "Yea, and when you do not cry unto the Lord, let your hearts be full, drawn out in prayer unto him continually for your welfare, and also for the welfare of those who are around you" (Alma 34:27).

The Savior said, "Behold, verily, verily, I say unto you, ye must watch and pray always lest ye enter into temptation; for Satan desireth to have you, that he may sift you as wheat" (3 Nephi 18:18).

Recently our youngest daughter was sealed to a fine young man in the temple, and at that time they were admonished to pray next to each other, with their arms and hands intertwined. "Begin and end your day," the temple sealer said, "by giving thanks for another day together." As many of you are at this same stage in life, how important it is to pray for the Spirit of the Lord to protect and guide your little kingdom.

Prayer should be an important part of each and every day. Elder David A. Bednar has said:

Meaningful morning prayer is an important element in the spiritual creation of each day—and precedes the temporal creation or the actual execution of the day. Just as the temporal creation was linked to and a continuation of the spiritual creation [see Moses 3:4–5], so meaningful morning and evening prayers are linked to and are a continuation of each other.[4]

Let me tell you, brothers and sisters, that my morning prayers have changed because of this counsel, and it has had quite an effect upon me.

Years ago President Spencer W. Kimball stated: "Prayer is such a privilege—to speak to our Father in Heaven. It was a prayer, a very special prayer, which opened this whole dispensation! It began with a young man's first vocal prayer."

Then he said this: "I hope that not too many of our prayers are silent, even though when we cannot pray vocally, it is good to offer a silent prayer in our hearts and in our minds."[5]

This little bit of advice really has helped me to commune with our Father in Heaven. It has enabled me to concentrate better and speak "with" instead of "to" our Father in Heaven (see 1 Nephi 3:1). In the same message, President Kimball also suggested that we "do some intense listening"[6] at the end of our prayers.

STUDY AND LEARN THE GOSPEL

The second point in this formula is to study and learn the gospel. As our young family was growing up, like many of your families we would have scripture study early in the morning, and that usually meant our children were not very alert. We sometimes wondered if anyone was listening, let alone learning. My wife and I felt a little relieved when Elder Bednar shared the following statement in general conference about his family:

If you could ask our adult sons what they remember about family prayer, scripture study, and family home evening, I believe I know how they would answer. They likely would not identify a particular prayer or a specific instance of scripture study or an especially meaningful family home evening lesson as the defining moment in their spiritual development. What they would say they remember is that as a family we were consistent.

Sister Bednar and I thought helping our sons understand the content of a particular lesson or a specific scripture was the ultimate outcome. But such a result does not occur each time we study or pray or learn together. The consistency of our intent and work was perhaps the greatest lesson—a lesson we did not fully appreciate at the time.[7]

One day our second son came home from his early years in seminary and gave me a drawing of the plan of salvation. It was well done. He had drawn the premortal existence, mortality, and life beyond the grave, including the celestial, terrestrial, and telestial kingdoms. It was all there. He even had drawn himself holding hands with the Redeemer in the celestial kingdom.

I then asked him how he knew the plan so well, and he said, "I don't know, Dad, but I won a candy bar!" He then said he was the only student in the class who could do it. Hopefully he had learned it in family scripture study or in family home evening, even though we weren't sure they were learning anything at the time.

President Benson once said:

> When **individual members** and families immerse themselves in the scriptures regularly and consistently, . . . other areas of activity will automatically come. Testimonies will increase. Commitment will be strengthened. Families will be fortified. Personal revelation will flow.[8]

I know this promise is real, and I testify that it works.

Paul wrote in 2 Corinthians 4:16 that the "outward man [perisheth], yet the inward man is renewed day by day." I love that scripture.

Elder Jay E. Jensen and I were once traveling together when he shared that scripture with me. He said, "That is of late my favorite scripture." I think it has become one of mine. How important it is to renew ourselves day by day. My experience has been that personal scripture study is a powerful way to renew ourselves day by day. I would encourage you not to miss a day.

Bishop Keith B. McMullin once shared something in our stake conference that I've not forgotten. He said, "You read your scriptures every day, and some days there just isn't time. Simply open the scriptures on those days and read a verse—you can do that. Just read a verse. That way you'll keep the scriptural habit going." I bear witness to that.

President Boyd K. Packer once stated, "When you feel weak, discouraged, depressed, or afraid, open the Book of Mormon and read. Do not let too much time pass before reading a verse, a thought, or a chapter."[9]

Brothers and sisters, make yourselves familiar with the scriptures; apply them to your own lives. They should feel as comfortable in your hands as a well-worn pair of tennis shoes does on your feet. I feel it a real blessing in my life to be able to teach from the scriptures at this university. I know without a doubt they are true. There is power in the scriptures, and they will help us feel the guidance of the Spirit in our lives on a daily basis—of that I am sure.

LIVE RIGHTEOUSLY

How can we live righteously? President Romney answered, "Repent of your sins by confessing them and forsaking them."[10] Living righteously, it seems to me, really could be summarized in one word: *repent!*

Nephi taught his posterity that we are saved by grace "after all we can do" (2 Nephi 25:23). What is all we can do? The king of the Anti-Nephi-Lehis gave us some insight in a sermon he delivered to his people:

> *And now behold, my brethren, since it has been all that we could do, (as we were the most lost of all mankind) to repent of all our sins . . . which we have committed, and to get God to take them away from our hearts, for it was **all we could do to repent sufficiently** before God that he would take away our stain.* [Alma 24:11; emphasis added]

Repenting really is all that we can do.

President Eyring gave a devotional talk here at Brigham Young University that had a powerful effect on me. He told of a young man who needed to repent and had come to him when President Eyring was a bishop. After a lengthy time, Bishop Eyring interviewed him and found him worthy to hold a temple recommend. But the young man was going to be married in the temple to a young lady who was sweet and clean, and he needed to know if his sins had been remitted—if he had forgiveness from the Lord. How could he get that revelation?

Bishop Eyring said it was a good question and that he needed some time, so the young man gave him a deadline—less than two weeks.

During those two weeks Bishop Eyring went to a social function that then Elder Spencer W. Kimball also attended. Elder Kimball found Bishop Eyring and said, "Hal, I understand that you are now a bishop. Do you have anything you would like to ask me?"

President Eyring continued:

I said that I did, but I didn't think that was the place to talk about it. He thought it was. It was an outdoor party. My memory is that we went behind a shrub and there had our interview. Without breaking confidences . . . , I outlined the concerns and the question of this young man. . . . Then I asked Elder Kimball, "How can he get that revelation? How can he know whether his sins are remitted?"

I thought Elder Kimball would talk to me about fasting or prayer or listening for the still small voice. But he surprised me. Instead he said, "Tell me something about the young man."

I said, "What would you like to know?"

And then he began a series of the most simple questions. Some of the ones I remember were:

"Does he come to his priesthood meetings?"

I said, after a moment of thought, "Yes."

"Does he come early?"

"Yes."

"Does he sit down front?"

I thought for a moment and then realized, to my amazement, that he did.

"Does he home teach?"

"Yes."

"Does he go early in the month?"

"Yes, he does."

"Does he go more than once?"

"Yes."

*I can't remember the other questions. But they were all like that—little things, **simple** acts of obedience, of submission. And for each question I was surprised that my answer was always yes. Yes, he wasn't just at all his meetings: he was early; he was smiling; he was there not only with his whole heart, but with the broken heart of a little child, as he was every time the Lord asked anything of him. And after I had said yes to each of his questions, Elder Kimball looked at me, paused, and then very quietly said, "There is your revelation."[11]*

This is repentance: the mighty change of heart. Again, what is all that we can do? It is to repent, as this young man did, not only with our whole hearts but also with a broken heart and a contrite spirit (see 3 Nephi 9:20). The scriptures remind us of the Savior's words:

Repent, and I will receive you. . . .

. . . Come unto me and ye shall partake of the fruit of the tree of life; yea, ye shall eat and drink of the bread and the waters of life freely;

Yea, come unto me and bring forth works of righteousness. [Alma 5:33–35]

By repenting we are living lives of righteousness and allowing the Spirit to help us change.

SERVICE IN THE CHURCH

The fourth point in obtaining the Spirit is service in the Church. The question is, does service bring forth the Spirit or does the Spirit cause one to serve? The answer is yes!

One day in my office at seminary I was speaking with a student when I started to go numb down one side of my body and then the other. For some time I was in a semiconscious state. When I finally regained full consciousness, one of the aftereffects was persistent headaches that nothing seemed to help. I was the bishop of our ward at the time, and the headaches were so intense that I decided to sit down and have a talk with my stake president, William A. Cox.

I explained to him that I was experiencing extreme headaches, and even though I did not ask to be released, he knew why I was there. Finally he leaned over the desk and said, "I'm not going to release you, Bishop." He then continued, "A loaded train doesn't jump the track."

Well, that certainly made no sense to me! Fortunately, President Cox explained what he meant. He had long worked at Geneva Steel, controlling the trains that transported the steel. He said that when a train is loaded down with freight, it will not jump the track. Only when the boxcars are empty is the train liable to leave the track. He then reinforced his statement that he would not release me. I did not fully understand the principle until later. As I went to Church to conduct interviews—still with headaches—I found myself so involved in the work that I soon didn't even notice them. It wasn't long before they lessened in intensity, and I have now all but forgotten about them.

The principle in this for me is that serving others brings the Spirit into our lives and helps us to remain on the straight and narrow way, especially during times of challenge and stress.

Moroni lived during some very challenging times, and Mormon gave him some advice that is helpful for all of us to remember. Let us consider this scripture and how it applies in our lives. Mormon said:

> And now, my beloved son, notwithstanding their hardness, let us labor diligently; for if we should cease to labor, we should be brought under condemnation; for we have a labor to perform whilst in this tabernacle of clay, that we may conquer the enemy of all righteousness, and rest our souls in the kingdom of God. [Moroni 9:6]

Note that his advice was much like President Cox's advice: No matter how difficult it gets, just keep working and serving. Why? The blessings will come!

CONCLUSION

Well, there you have it—four ways to obtain and keep the Spirit in our lives: prayer, gospel study, living righteously, and giving service.

So are we on a collision course with disaster? Yes.

Must we live in fear? No.

Jesus told us, "Be not afraid, only believe" (Mark 5:36) and "see that ye be not troubled" (Joseph Smith—Matthew 1:23). As a watchman on the tower, President Romney told us that if we have the Spirit of the Lord, we can go through this world successfully, regardless of what the people of the world say or do. That is quite a promise, and it is true.

We can learn a lesson from the Israelites in the wilderness. If a prophet of God tells us we can look upon the brazen serpent and be healed, then we can look upon the brazen serpent and be healed. If an apostle of God tells us we can obtain and keep the Spirit of the Lord by following four simple points, then we should believe it! Remember, Alma taught his son Helaman that "by small and simple things are great things brought to pass" (Alma 37:6).

Brothers and sisters, I know these principles are true. I am so grateful that I have had the opportunity to share them with you, and I leave this testimony with you in the name of Jesus Christ, amen.

NOTES

1. Marion G. Romney, "Guidance of the Holy Spirit," BYU devotional address, 20 March 1979; see also Marion G. Romney, "First Presidency Message: Guidance of the Holy Spirit," *Ensign*, January 1980, 2, 5.

2. Ezra Taft Benson, "Jesus Christ—Gifts and Expectations," BYU devotional address, 10 December 1974; see Howard W. Hunter, "Come unto Me," *Ensign*, November 1990, 18.

3. Henry B. Eyring, "Always," CES fireside at BYU, 3 January 1999, emphasis in original; see also Henry B. Eyring, "Always," *Ensign*, October 1999, 9.

4. David A. Bednar, "Pray Always," *Ensign*, November 2008, 41.

5. Spencer W. Kimball, "We Need a Listening Ear," *Ensign*, November 1979, 4.

6. Kimball, "A Listening Ear," 4.

7. David A. Bednar, "More Diligent and Concerned at Home," *Ensign*, November 2009, 19.

8. Ezra Taft Benson, "The Power of the Word," *Ensign*, May 1986, 81; emphasis added.

9. Boyd K. Packer, "The Book of Mormon: Another Testament of Jesus Christ—Plain and Precious Things," *Ensign*, May 2005, 8.

10. Romney, "Guidance," BYU devotional; see also Romney, "Guidance," *Ensign*, 5.

11. Henry B. Eyring, "Come unto Christ," BYU devotional address, 29 October 1989; emphasis added.

The Approachable Master: Life's Critical Relationship

Douglas R. McKinlay

I came to BYU after a career in advertising, and now I'm enjoying my thirteenth year in a "career crescendo." I don't know what that means to those in music, but I've enjoyed every minute of those thirteen years so far.

The field of sports is a wonderful place to find metaphors and analogies for life, and I would like to begin with one this morning: the phrase "leaving it all on the field," which is to say that one gives everything out there on the playing field, the court, or the stage, holding nothing back. There are times in our lives when this analogy makes particular sense. For example, when serving a mission you would want to make sure that you came home with no regrets, that you "left it all" in your field of labor. There is something awfully satisfying about giving 100 percent, whatever the assignment.

But what if your pre-earth assignment was to come to the playing field of mortality, where there would be forces of opposition

Douglas R. McKinlay was an associate teaching professor of advertising in the BYU Department of Communications when this devotional was given on 19 June 2012. © Brigham Young University.

trying to keep you from leaving it all on the field? Such is certainly the case with earth life. But how do we then give our all? What can we do to ensure that we leave this life with the fewest possible regrets? For the next few minutes I will discuss one sure way, and that is to come under the influence of the Master—the one perfect example of someone who indeed left it all on this very playing field.

And so I have titled my remarks this morning "The Approachable Master: Life's Critical Relationship." Let me begin by putting a series of related questions to all of us:

Why is it that we do not befriend with greater intensity our Savior, "The Master of ocean and earth and skies,"[1] at a level that truly affects—perhaps even drives—our own personal behavior?

Said another way, why do we not capitalize on the Spirit of Christ within all of us to more completely comprehend the Master's purpose and the will of the only name under heaven by which we may gain life eternal?[2]

Lastly, why do we not accept more openly the Savior's simple invitation to "come unto me?"

In much the same way President Ezra Taft Benson approached our tendency as a people to undervalue the positive effects of studying the Book of Mormon,[3] may I be bold enough this morning to suggest that the same condition may well apply for us as we come to know the Savior. There is so much more to gain by developing a truly interactive relationship with the Master. To use His own parable, could it be that we are the travelers on the highway and that the master has bid us to his wedding feast? Why would we not come?[4]

We can learn of the Master, even love Him for all He has accomplished on our behalf, and yet still position ourselves beyond our own ability to receive many additional and ennobling blessings. It would be like joining a sports team but not going to practice, not benefiting from the coach's experience, and never actually taking the field.

Listen to the Savior's own injunction:

Come unto me, all ye that labour and are heavy laden, and I will give you rest.

Take my yoke upon you, and learn of me; for I am meek and lowly in heart: and ye shall find rest unto your souls.

For my yoke is easy, and my burden is light.[5]

And in our day, the clarion call from the Brethren is an echo from the corridors of time: "Come unto Christ." The reason this call never goes away is because once we are fully engaged with the Master, we become like the people of King Benjamin. After his landmark speech to his people, King Benjamin sent among them, desiring to know if they believed his message and if it had actually made a difference in their lives. Their unified response is an example to all of us:

Yea, we believe all the words which thou hast spoken unto us; and also, we know of their surety and truth, because of the Spirit of the Lord Omnipotent, which has wrought a mighty change in us, or in our hearts, that we have no more disposition to do evil, but to do good continually.[6]

As professed Christians and practicing Latter-day Saints, we embrace the doctrines set forth in the fourth article of faith: the first principle of the gospel is "faith in the Lord Jesus Christ," something that precedes all else. But, sadly, we sometimes become little more than "Facebook friends" with our Lord and Master, clicking our "like" button on Sunday and then only "visiting His page" when we have a special need or when prompted by another Sunday's arrival.

As we exhibit this symbolic behavior, it is possible for us to become our own version of what the apostle Paul described in his discourse on charity "as sounding brass, or a tinkling cymbal."[7] Perhaps we could change a word or two and make the phrase a more inner-facing interrogative: Have *I* become as a sounding brass or a tinkling cymbal?

So again, why is it that we move closer to the Savior on occasion, then drift away, then move closer, then drift away in an undulating kind of relationship, not unlike the movement of the tides?

Let me share some possible reasons why we might stray from a member of the Godhead who is most anxious to befriend us and most ready to receive us, regardless of our present circumstances.

An obvious place to begin is the sometimes subtle but nevertheless diabolically decreed role of the devil and his everlasting commitment to distance us from the influence of the Master. The devil will do all in his power to keep us from developing a strong personal bond with the Master that would strengthen us and guide us safely through the many vicissitudes of life. And let us remember, the further we are from the influence of the Master, the closer we are to the influence of our most formidable foe.

The adversary knows that if he can make us feel alone, even when we aren't, we become much more vulnerable to his very careful, very strategic advances. Here are two of the many strategies he uses to keep us from the Master:

1. He convinces us that we are unworthy—even through prayer—to enter the presence of the Master. He does this using the tactics of guilt, shame, or embarrassment, knowing that we "all have sinned, and come short of the glory of God."[8] Satan reminds us that the Master is perfect and we are not, thus increasing the distance between us and the Savior.

2. He makes us believe that we can do all things on our own, that we have no need for the Savior's help, just as a small child who responds to parental guidance by saying, "I can do it myself." This is commonly known in LDS parlance as "the pride cycle"—and it's not a good place for us to find ourselves as adults.

Some years ago, while serving with the missionaries in the Arizona Tucson Mission, I created a series of what my bride, Betty Jo, likes to call "doctrinal diagrams." The first diagram deals with what I have termed the Drift Phenomenon, where we drift closer and then farther apart from the Lord.

Say you receive a new calling in the Church and are totally overwhelmed. You need the influence of the Master in order to execute your calling. He, of course, responds with the appropriate inspiration, but, as time goes along, you get more comfortable with the calling and your ability to perform it. What may inadvertently happen is that you begin to drift away from the need for constant inspiration and toward a reliance on your own abilities. The theoretical danger zone is when we begin to depend more on ourselves and less on the Spirit. And now, for just a moment, ponder where you might place yourself on these lines in relation to your present Church assignment.

Not that you would ever plan on, or even notice, this shift happening; it just seems to be a part of what King Benjamin might have called "the natural man syndrome"[9]—that tendency to drift away from the Master and His influence when we are not in personal-crisis mode. Once again we become that proverbial three-year-old, saying, or perhaps indignantly shouting, "I can do it myself." We are exactly where the adversary would like us to be— out there on our own.

On the other hand, if we "lean not unto [our] own understanding"[10] or on "the arm of flesh,"[11] and as we stay close to the Master's influence, it is easy to see a dramatic difference. We might call this the Non-Drift Phenomenon or the Magnifying-Your-Calling Phenomenon, where we stay close to the Lord. Imagine the power that can come as you become increasingly proficient in your calling while enjoying an ever-increasing degree of spiritual influence from the Master. To borrow a word from a famous MasterCard advertising campaign, this power is "priceless"—suggesting a value difference between things we can buy (the temporal) and things we cannot buy (the spiritual).

Speaking of temporal things, consider the time and energy we spend at this and perhaps other institutions preparing for and advancing our careers. Let us remember that—unless I miss my guess—our careers will not rise with us in the Resurrection. Certainly I will be unemployed, since I doubt the existence of or need for billboards, TV sets, YouTube, the Internet, or i-anything on the other side of the veil. I trust that even our two surgeon sons may have to look elsewhere for employment.

A very long time ago, as an undergraduate student at BYU, I memorized this quote from Harvard philosopher James Allen that points out the danger of "going it alone":

Man is the causer (though nearly always unconsciously) of his [own] *circumstances, and that, whilst aiming at a good end, he is continually frustrating its accomplishment by encouraging thoughts and desires which cannot possibly harmonize with that end.*[12]

Making critical life decisions without the aid of the Master's direct spiritual influence is like embarking on a long sea voyage in a craft without a rudder, a helm, or perhaps even a mast.

Here are three more strategies to add to our list of ways in which the adversary keeps us from developing a broader, deeper, and more critical relationship with our Master:

3. He creates doubt about our own self-worth and our God-given abilities.

4. He gives us a feeling of entitlement. Since we are all children of God, we are, somehow—amazingly—due a divine inheritance. Someone with the attitude of entitlement says, "It's never my fault. Surely the blame for my inability to perform to expectations must lie with another. Besides, isn't the Savior supposed to be my all-time safety net?"

5. He helps us develop our powers of procrastination (not that we need help here). After all, there is always and forever tomorrow, right? What could possibly be the rush?

My guess is that at one time or another we have all felt these negative tuggings or feelings in our lives, and we have, to some extent, bought into some of the mortal foibles and frailties with which the adversary is so awfully familiar.

Let me now share a very personal experience from years ago that may serve to illustrate this point. I was set apart as a stake president by two General Authorities, and during the blessing, certain—as I viewed them—promises were mentioned, one of which related to the success of a new business venture I had just undertaken. But things did not go well business-wise. Unbeknownst to me, I had started an advertising agency on the cusp of a serious recession. After weeks of unease, early one morning, with many unanswered questions in my heart, a terrible uncertainty and a feeling of being alone washed over me like a waterfall of doubt. Although going into business for myself seemed like an inspired decision at the time, I had begun to second-guess the rightness of my choice, and I even wondered about the inspired words that had been uttered in that blessing just a few months earlier.

Fortunately I followed a common pattern and went to the scriptures and to the Lord, anxiously looking for answers—*any* answer that would mitigate my vexed state of mind. I was pondering the words in Matthew 28 about the risen Lord, specifically what the angel said to Mary Magdalene and the other Mary who were in search of the Master, searching just as I was on that morning and perhaps as you may be searching today: "He is not here: for he is risen, as he said."[13]

The details of what followed are not important here, except to say that in my scriptures there is written in the margin a little note that says, "Special experience." The Lord blessed me that day with a powerful witness of the reality of the Savior as my personal advocate with the Father, as the Creator of heaven and earth, and as the would-be Friend of all mankind. Today I testify that He lives and that He wants nothing more than to help us perform well on this playing field of life.

Yes, the business survived the recession and, happily, all the words spoken in my blessing were fulfilled. More important, I learned something about the definition of the phrase "in the Lord's own way."

Let's look more closely into the self-doubt scenario we sometimes find ourselves in—that space between our gospel goals and our actual behavior against those goals. There is an interesting space between where we may be performing now and where we'd like to be. Let's just call it the "mortal shortfall gap." This is where many of us get into trouble, allowing self-doubt to creep in and create a series of performance stress risers and debilitative, non-productive thinking. If we are not careful, we succumb to another "flaxen cord"[14] and start to envision the gap widening to the point that we begin to lose faith. Once again we end up exactly where the adversary wants us: solitary and doubtful of our own abilities.

But lest we find this gap troubling, there is good news: the Master also knows full well the challenges of mortality. And, fortunately, He has both the ability and the predisposition to fill that mortal shortfall gap.

When we fully accept Christ as our personal Savior, Advocate, and Redeemer, the gap fills so completely with hope and understanding and promise that the mortal shortfall gap becomes narrower and narrower until that eventual "perfect day."[15] Actually, the diminishing effect of our shortfall is the emancipating and empowering effect of the Savior's Atonement. For our part, a change in attitude or a mighty change of heart[16] to close that gap helps our performance considerably.

Listen to what the ancient and articulate prophet Alma had to say concerning the Atonement:

And he will take upon him [our] *infirmities, that his bowels may be filled with mercy, according to the flesh, that he may know according to the flesh how to succor his people according to their infirmities.*[17]

And in our day the Savior has spoken to us in the Doctrine and Covenants with these reassuring words: "For behold, I, God, have suffered these things for all, that they might not suffer if they would repent."[18]

For a moment now, let's revisit that potentially devastating alone feeling, a feeling I suppose has come over all of us at one time or another, whether we were physically isolated or perhaps within in a supportive group but still very much alone in our thoughts. This feeling of abject loneliness is another key tactic used by the adversary to create distance between us and our Savior.

Satan would have us believe that no one—not even the Master—
can reach us and relate to us on a personal level and feel exactly
how we feel in our terribly unique circumstances. But the Master
knows, and He feels your *precise* pain and anguish, regardless of its
source and intensity. The Savior has vicariously suffered your *exact
same suffering.* Paul's marvelous discourse on this subject in Hebrews
offers "grace to help in [our] time of need."[19] The last few verses
from Hebrews have brought peace and solace to my soul over the
years when I have felt particularly alone in this world, even though
surrounded by friends:

> *For verily he took not on him the nature of angels; but he took on him
> the seed of Abraham.*
>
> *Wherefore in all things it behoved him to be made like unto his
> brethren, that he might be a merciful and faithful high priest in things
> pertaining to God, to make reconciliation for the sins of the people.*
>
> *For in that he himself hath suffered being tempted, he is able to succour
> them that are tempted.*[20]

> *For we have not an high priest which cannot be touched with the feeling
> of our infirmities; but was in all points tempted like as we are, yet without
> sin.*
>
> *Let us therefore come boldly unto the throne of grace, that we may
> obtain mercy, and find grace to help in time of need.*[21]

I love that invitation: "Let us therefore come boldly unto the
throne of grace." Speaking of grace, I for one believe that when it
comes to our individual progress toward our goals, vector almost
certainly trumps velocity. However long it takes, let us not lose our
sense of direction.

Here is one way to look at the Master's limitless ability to connect to us across the entire spectrum of human emotion: As mortals,
we go through life and can experience some pretty low lows and also
some pretty high highs. But even though the Savior's earthly experience was every bit as real and visceral as our own, the Savior is on a

scale that supersedes anything the rest of us can possibly encounter. We simply cannot get outside His ability to relate to us personally and individually. Well-meaning friends may offer their best approximate *sympathy*, but only the Savior offers ultimate and absolute *empathy*.

Though I am a teaching professor and not a scientist per se, I love the way the Lord invites us to participate in the scientific process as described by Alma (who just might have been something of a scientist himself). Alma suggested that we experiment on the word in the crucible of the real world:

> But behold, if you will awake and arouse your faculties, even to an experiment upon my words, and exercise a particle of faith, yea, even if ye can no more than desire to believe, let this desire work in you.[22]

Isn't that the way of the scientist and the researcher? They gather all of the empirical evidence—all the data they can—and develop a theory; then they create a repeatable, predictable experiment that proves or disproves the theory.

The Savior, both in His own recorded words and through the words of His holy prophets, has invited us to come unto Him, to experiment for ourselves on the truthfulness of His gospel, and to claim the attendant blessings.

I appreciate so much the Savior's Intercessory Prayer in which He gives us all a glimpse of the possible glory inherent in a relationship with Him—which is a type of the oneness relationship He has with the Father. Let me share a few verses from John.

First, the Savior prayed for His apostles:

> And now I am no more in the world, but these are in the world, and I come to thee. Holy Father, keep through thine own name those whom thou hast given me, that they may be one, as we are.[23]

And then He prayed for the rest of us:

Neither pray I for these alone, but for them also which shall believe on me through their word;

That they all may be one; as thou, Father, art in me, and I in thee, that they also may be one in us: that the world may believe that thou hast sent me.[24]

We began this morning with the analogy of leaving it all on the field. How is it possible for us to not only "take the field" of this earthly life but to also come away victorious? I suggest two ways: first, by eschewing the strategic advances of the adversary, and, second, by developing that critical, personal, interactive relationship with the Master.

May we not be found undervaluing the role of the Master, whose arms are outstretched still. We have the opportunity here and now to make Him not just a "Facebook friend" but a most personal, powerful, and influential advocate. Let us not buy into the adversary's attempts to keep us away from the everlasting peace, safety, and eventual exaltation available if we but commend our own personal will into the Lord's all-powerful hands.

I testify of the reality of the living Christ, just as the First Presidency and the Twelve Apostles have declared in a modern-day proclamation.[25] I testify that as we boldly approach Him, our own personal performance becomes our own personal legacy. As we engage with the Master, may we leave it all on the playing field of this life, which is my prayer, in the name of Jesus Christ, amen.

NOTES

1. "Master, the Tempest Is Raging," *Hymns,* 2002, no. 105.

2. See Moses 6:52.

3. See Ezra Taft Benson, *A Witness and a Warning* (Salt Lake City: Deseret Book, 1988), 6, 9, 22.

4. See Matthew 22:1–10.

5. Matthew 11:28–30.

6. Mosiah 5:2.

7. 1 Corinthians 13:1.

8. Romans 3:23.

9. See Mosiah 3:19.

10. Proverbs 3:5.

11. 2 Nephi 4:34.

12. James Allen, *As a Man Thinketh* (New York: Crowell, 1913), 18.

13. Matthew 28:6.

14. 2 Nephi 26:22.

15. D&C 50:24.

16. See Alma 5:12–14.

17. Alma 7:12.

18. D&C 19:16.

19. Hebrews 4:16.

20. Hebrews 2:16–18.

21. Hebrews 4:15–16.

22. Alma 32:27.

23. John 17:11.

24. John 17:20–21.

25. See "The Living Christ: The Testimony of the Apostles, The Church of Jesus Christ of Latter-day Saints," *Ensign*, April 2000, 2.

What's in a Name?

D. Gordon Smith

I am grateful for the opportunity to speak today. The weekly devotionals and forums have been a big part of my BYU experience. I attended them when I was a student, and my wife and I still attend them with our children who are students here. I am also grateful to my family, friends, and colleagues who have taken the time to be with us today.

Today is my father's birthday. He is eighty-seven years old. He and my mother are in Wisconsin watching this devotional, and if the volume on the television is turned all the way up, they are listening to it too.

My father's name is Gordon Smith. My mother told me recently—and she reminds me often—that my father never wanted a son named Gordon, but he agreed to give me his first name as my middle name. This is the story about why I took that name upon myself and why I have come to believe that the names we call each other are important.

D. *Gordon Smith was associate dean at BYU's J. Reuben Clark Law School when this devotional was given on 26 June 2012.* © *Brigham Young University.*

WHY I TOOK MY FATHER'S NAME

To understand why I took my father's name as my own, you need to know a bit about my relationship with my father. My father and several generations before him had been dairy farmers in Wisconsin, but in the wake of the Japanese attack on Pearl Harbor, my father, only seventeen years old at the time, joined the navy and was assigned to serve in the South Pacific. He eventually made a career of the military, and I was born in a naval hospital in Bremerton, Washington. Shortly after my birth he was transferred to San Diego, California, where he taught Teletype repair for five years. Following his retirement our family returned to his childhood home of Wisconsin, and that's where I grew up. Many of my earliest memories involve feeding and caring for cows, pigs, and chickens on our small farm, though I was temperamentally not well suited to farming.

My uneasy relationship with farming became apparent to our whole family when our pigs disappeared. Our pigs were named Slurp and Burp. One day they were just gone, and I asked around, "Where did Slurp and Burp go?" Nobody else seemed troubled by their disappearance. They just said that somebody had come and taken them away.

A few weeks later, over a dinner featuring pork chops, my older sister—who introduced so much of life to me—said, pointing at my plate, "Remember Slurp and Burp?"

Lessons about the circle of life were plentiful on that small farm. I saw my father assist in the birthing of a calf, and we drank milk from the calf's mother. I was playing basketball in the yard one day when a rabid raccoon came toward me, and my dad shot the raccoon. (At first I was worried I had been in trouble, and I thought he had just missed.) We learned by observation that chickens do indeed come from eggs, and we also learned by observation what it means to "run around like a chicken with its head cut off."

Despite our humble and remote circumstances, I managed to cultivate big dreams on that farm, in no small part because of my dad. During his last year of service in the navy he traveled the world and sent us souvenirs from Europe, Asia, and Africa. He was gone for a year, and I remember that when he returned, I didn't know what he looked like because I was only four years old when he left and five when he returned. But I treasured those souvenirs that he sent me, and I spent many hours in my room in Wisconsin looking at photos of Rome or pounding on a drum from Africa or playing with toys from the Philippines, imagining what it would be like to visit those faraway lands.

Some of my most treasured memories from childhood involve sitting in the living room or in the backyard listening to stories about my father's childhood or about his adventures in the navy. Like Aesop's fables, these stories almost always came with some moral that we were supposed to take from them. My son Drew and I were recently in Wisconsin for a family reunion, and we again heard stories about the importance of hard work, competence, and integrity.

My father also taught me—more through his reaction to war than through his words—to despise war. Although he could never speak of combat—and he still can't to this day—one navy story inevitably connected to another, and he often found himself led to memories that he would rather suppress. We could discern when he had reached this point because he swallowed hard, his eyes welled with tears, and he looked off into the distance. My mother recently observed, "They don't give Purple Hearts for those wounds."

Another significant lesson—never stated explicitly but reinforced repeatedly in his stories—was that one person could change the world. As far as I know, my dad never changed the course of the war through his naval service, but his stories showed me why the navy always valued one more good man. During the war he was only an enlisted radioman, but I was convinced as a young boy that, aside from Admiral Nimitz, my father was the most important person in the Pacific Fleet. To me he was—and he remains—a great man.

As President Joseph F. Smith wrote over 100 years ago:

Those things which we call extraordinary, remarkable, or unusual may make history, but they do not make real life.

After all, to do well those things which God ordained to be the common lot of all mankind, is the truest greatness. To be a successful father or a successful mother is greater than to be a successful general or a successful statesman. ["Common-Place Things," *Juvenile Instructor,* 15 December 1905, 752]

From my own experience I knew that my dad could fix anything. Whether the problem was mechanical, electrical, or personal, he seemed to always have an answer. Like many young boys I looked up to my dad. He was one of my heroes.

CHANGING MY NAME

During those growing-up years in Osseo, Wisconsin, everyone called me by my first name, Doug. Strangely, my group of friends went through a phase in which we decided to call each other by our fathers' names. Some of those names stuck, but "Gordon Smith" did not seem like a good fit for me at that time. And I was largely content with my name, except when my high school English teacher decided to call me "Dougie." No one in that day was asking me to teach them "how to Dougie."

I was still Doug Smith when I arrived at BYU in August 1980. I was not a member of The Church of Jesus Christ of Latter-day Saints, but my first class in college was Religion 121: The Book of Mormon. My best friend in high school, who had convinced me to attend BYU with him, told me I shouldn't worry about this class. He said the Book of Mormon was just a history of South America, and that was all I knew about the course.

So I showed up on the first day, and the professor introduced the course by saying we would be covering the first half of the Book of Mormon. He started to talk about the events that we would encounter. I wasn't worried until the guy next to me raised his hand and said, "Will we be discussing the sons of Mosiah in this course?"

I did a double take. I thought, "How does he know anything about what's in this book?" And I thought, "Well, the professor will provide us some context for the people who didn't read ahead."

But he just answered the student as if it was a completely natural question.

And then another student raised his hand and said, "How about Samuel the Lamanite? That guy is cool!" Everybody laughed, and I completely missed the joke. Then another person said something, and by this point in the class I was starting to panic.

I wasn't in the habit of praying at the time—I didn't really pray much at all—but I just decided that since I was at BYU, I would bow my head and say a little prayer: "Please, God, make them stop."

Well, it did eventually stop, and at the end of class I approached the teacher and asked, "Did you post an assignment for the first class?"

"No, why do you ask?"

"Well, it just seems like everybody's read ahead."

He looked me up and down and said, "You aren't a member, are you?"

I thought about that for a second, and I responded, "A member of what?"

So we had a nice long talk about the class, and I read the Book of Mormon in my first year at BYU.

The transition from that first day of college to my baptism in the fall semester of my sophomore year did not require a dramatic change in my lifestyle, but my worldview was completely upended. Embracing the gospel impelled me to look outward in a way that I never had before, to place others before myself: "Whosoever will save his life shall lose it: and whosoever will lose his life for my sake shall find it" (Matthew 16:25).

I decided to serve a mission, and one year after my baptism I was called to serve in Vienna, Austria. I became Elder Smith. Over the past few weeks I have read my missionary journals. I don't know if any of you have done that, but it is a horrifying experience. I'm not a great journal writer, but I was impressed by the effort I expended in trying to create a new identity for myself as Elder Smith. I wanted to become a powerful missionary. I knew that Austria was not a high-baptizing mission, but, I thought, England wasn't a high-baptizing mission before Wilford Woodruff got there either. Unfortunately my motives were entirely self-interested: I felt like I had a debt to pay, and I wanted to pay it. I hadn't internalized the lesson taught by King Benjamin that even if we serve God with our "whole souls," we remain "unprofitable servants" (Mosiah 2:21).

I worked hard in Austria, and I was frustrated at my inability to reduce my debt. Every sacrifice that I made, every extra effort that I made, was repaid many times over, and early in my mission I wrote about my frustration in my journal:

I have been so blessed by the Lord . . . , and I wanted to go on a mission, in part, to show the Lord how much I love Him. To think of my mission as just something else by which I can make myself better is offensive to me. That implies that the biggest attempt I've made in my life to be selfless has turned into the most selfish endeavor that I have ever undertaken.

By the end of my mission I had come to terms with God over my indebtedness, and I had learned that the most valuable lesson of my mission was to love the people. As King Benjamin said, "When ye are in the service of your fellow beings ye are only in the service of your God" (Mosiah 2:17). During my last week in Austria I wrote the following entry in my journal while riding on a train from Vienna to Linz:

Austria is a beautiful land, dotted with small villages. One of the most common sights from the train is the steeple of a Catholic church against the background of rolling green hills. We are sitting with a lady from Vienna who is dressed in a traditional Austrian hat, blouse, and skirt. Tradition prevents most Austrians from hearing our message. And, yet, after being rejected by thousands of people, I have learned to love these people with a love that I have felt for no others. Somehow, I pray for them, cry for them, and hope for them as I do my own family.

You can perceive in these entries a journey taken by many young people—a transition from inward-looking, self-centered teenagers to outward-looking, empathetic adults.

When I returned to Osseo after my mission, I shed the title of Elder Smith, and, like many returned missionaries, including my son Drew, who just came home from Ukraine, I went through that awkward phase of adjusting to being called by my first name. In my case, however, my pre-mission name evoked thoughts about a confused young boy who had arrived at BYU three years before. "Doug" just didn't seem to fit anymore, but I didn't do anything about it until I met a young woman at BYU the following year who was changing her name. She just decided one day to ask people to call her by her middle name. And they did!

I thought, "Is that really all there is to it? Just tell people, 'Call me [Whatever],' and they do it?" This was a revelation to me. I didn't have to be Doug Smith anymore. I could be anything I wanted! After much contemplation I decided that using my middle name would not only be the simplest change—after all, I wouldn't have to make a legal change to my name—but it would also honor my father. What I did not fully comprehend was how that change would affect me.

Changing my name was a tremendous hassle. My wife, Sue, was supportive, and I didn't ask our families to call me Gordon, so when we visit relatives I'm still Doug. But the real challenge was among my friends. In my first accounting class of the fall semester, legendary accounting professor Jay Smith called on me by my first name, and I asked, "Would you mind calling me Gordon?"

By that time I was well into my major, and both he and my classmates looked at me quizzically, wondering, "What's the punch line?"

But I didn't have a punch line. "Um . . . I changed my name to Gordon."

In another class so many people knew me by the name Doug that they simply wouldn't allow me to change my name to Gordon. They insisted, over my protests, that I was joking. My coworkers and supervisors in the Reading and Writing Center split about evenly between those who made the adjustment and those who couldn't, and that just caused confusion. It was hard on people.

Several times during the first few months I considered abandoning my project. In conversation I stumbled over my new name. More than once I failed to acknowledge people who called me Gordon. I experimented with new signatures. I changed my driver's license. I learned to fill out forms that had blanks for "First Name, Middle Initial, Last Name."

At the same time I was surprised to discover that when people called me Gordon, it felt different than being called Doug. In the beginning, each reference to Gordon caused me to think about my father. I was clothing myself in his name, and I felt obliged to wear it honorably. I didn't want to become my father, but I wanted to become a person who would make him proud. Over time I came to associate the name Gordon with my Mormon identity and the name Doug with my pre-Mormon life.

TAKING CHRIST'S NAME UPON US

I have sometimes thought of the experience of changing my name in relation to my baptism—an ordinance in which I took upon myself the name of Jesus Christ. In both instances the name was given to me by another, but I was asked to embrace the name as my own. Now each week in taking the sacrament I reaffirm my willingness to take upon myself the name of Jesus Christ (see D&C 20:77). What is the significance of this representation?

When I took upon myself the name of my father, I was not using his name as a description of my character. I was not saying, "I am my father." Rather, I was using the name to honor him and to inspire myself to develop attributes like him. Similarly, taking upon ourselves the name of Christ is not a recognition of an achievement but rather a nudge toward improved behavior.

King Benjamin gave his people the name of Christ only after the Spirit had changed their hearts, but he gave them the name not because they had reached some threshold and not because they had "no more disposition to do evil, but to do good continually" (Mosiah 5:2). Rather, he gave them the name so that they could remember that moment and remain "steadfast and immovable, always abounding in good works" (Mosiah 5:15).

When faithful people take upon themselves the name of Jesus Christ, they assume a name that is imbued with meaning. President Spencer W. Kimball once said, "The name Jesus Christ and what it represents has been plowed deep into the history of the world, never to be uprooted" ("Why Call Me Lord, Lord, and Do Not the Things Which I Say?" *Ensign*, May 1975, 4). This feature of the name is useful in transmitting large quantities of information. Rather than saying that we should have "faith, virtue, knowledge, temperance, patience, brotherly kindness, godliness, charity, humility, diligence" (D&C 4:6)—or any of the other myriad of attributes that we associate with Jesus Christ—we can say more simply that we take upon ourselves the name of Christ. Moreover, because we have stories of His life, Christ's name has a richness and texture that is impossible to convey merely by listing the attributes of His character.

NAME-CALLING AND JUDGING

I have spoken about the positive power of naming, but naming also has a dark side. Just as naming can inspire and direct, it can also discourage or obstruct. This is a phenomenon that we all recognize as name-calling or labeling. The line between labeling for the purpose of providing information and labeling for the purpose of marginalizing others can be subtle, but I will strive to illustrate a few guiding principles from my experiences as a law professor.

Each year BYU Law School attracts some of the brightest law students in the country. I have taught at six law schools in the United States and in several programs abroad, and I know from law students. When I came to BYU five years ago, some of my colleagues at other law schools wondered aloud whether law could be taught effectively at a school whose students who share so many religious values.

While an outsider might imagine legal education at BYU Law School as a form of indoctrination, my experience has been quite the contrary. The fairly high degree of religious homogeneity we experience here has actually enabled or encouraged discussions in class that are more vigorous than those discussions that typically occur at other law schools. While students at other law schools often pass off their disagreements on the simplistic grounds that they belong to different value groups, students at BYU's law school often feel compelled to examine the implications of their assumed shared beliefs. This is real learning, not indoctrination.

For example, in my Contracts class, students express a range of views about the social implications of contracting. (The following discussion draws in part on Stewart Macaulay, Jean Braucher, John Kidwell, and William Whitford, *Contracts: Law in Action*, 3rd ed. [New Providence, New Jersey: LexisNexis Matthew Bender, 2010], 491–93.) Some students enter the class with a bias in favor of market transactions, believing that economic efficiency and respect for the liberty of individuals should compel courts to enforce almost all contracts, regardless of the consequences. The students who hold this view sometimes invoke the gospel principle of agency, arguing that we all benefit if people are encouraged to take responsibility for their own risk.

Other students enter the course with a bias in favor of social control, believing that respect for the dignity of individuals should compel courts to protect the weakest members of our society. The students who hold this view sometimes appeal to the gospel principle of charity, arguing that legal rules should ensure that contracts are fair and that people with more wealth, talent, or bargaining skill should not be allowed to use those advantages to prey upon the weak.

Former Yale law professor Arthur Allen Leff recognized both of these impulses and described in poetic prose why we cannot have our cake and eat it too:

> *In effect, we want to have the world so arranged that everyone will be motivated to get as good a deal for himself as possible by being as informed and efficient as he can be, but that no one will have to get a bad deal in*

the process. But the payoff for the former necessitates, indeed entails, the latter. Hence doing both is not a technical problem . . . but a cultural one: we cannot have perfect freedom and perfect fairness at once. What we have, instead, [are] . . . legal device[s] that [allow] us, inconsistently and with only symbolic impact, an occasional evasive bow in the direction of our incoherent hearts' desires. ["Thomist Unconscionability," *Canadian Business Law Journal* 4 (1979–1980): 428]

Sometimes in the course of our class discussions the students will square off in these two camps—even identifying members of the rival camp with a derogatory name—but I strive to be sensitive about the formation of viewpoint cliques in the classroom. If students caricature their classmates—if they attempt to marginalize someone in the class as an "other"—then learning suffers and we have to talk about the importance of empathy in learning law. We truly understand our own views only when we understand the views of those who disagree with us. In seeking to understand those who disagree with us, my own experience has been that views evolve. This is not only acceptable but praiseworthy.

In the April 2012 general conference, President Dieter F. Uchtdorf reminded us to "stop judging others and replace judgmental thoughts and feelings with a heart full of love for God and His children" ("The Merciful Obtain Mercy," *Ensign*, May 2012, 75). Name-calling and labeling are forms of judgment, and the problem with judgment is its finality. As disciples of Jesus Christ we should encourage people to change and improve. If we believe that others have taken a wrong turn, one of the greatest acts of charity that we can perform is to give them room to repent.

As observed by President Uchtdorf:

We must recognize that we are all imperfect—that we are all beggars before God. Haven't we all, at one time or another, meekly approached the mercy seat and pleaded for grace? Haven't we wished with all the energy of our souls for mercy—to be forgiven for the mistakes we have made and the sins we have committed?

Because we all depend on the mercy of God, how can we deny to others any measure of the grace we so desperately desire for ourselves? My beloved brothers and sisters, should we not forgive as we wish to be forgiven? ["The Merciful Obtain Mercy," 75]

Thus, if we are to be like Jesus Christ—if we have truly taken upon ourselves His name—we should avoid name-calling and labeling and stand ever ready to receive those who have strayed. My own experience has been that when we exercise influence "by persuasion, by long-suffering, by gentleness and meekness, and by love unfeigned" (D&C 121:41), we not only bless the lives of others but we also elevate ourselves.

I pray that we may all come closer to that ideal, in the name of Jesus Christ, amen.

Persistence, Patience, and Posies

Patricia Ravert

We all have individual plans for our lives. Some of your plans may be very detailed; others may only be brief outlines. What I do know is that part of your plan was to come to BYU for your education.

My plan also included BYU for my undergraduate education. My father was not a member of the Church, but he was very supportive of education. He would often help us with science projects or on a variety of our homework assignments, particularly math—he was really good at math. My mother was a member of the Church, and each week she took us to Sunday meetings and made sure we had rides to the weekly youth meetings, which at that time were Primary for the children and Mutual for the teenagers. From my teachers in these Church programs I learned the basic gospel principles.

As a teenager I also learned about BYU. When the time came I applied to the colleges in my hometown of San Diego, California, as well as BYU. My plan included the study of medical laboratory

Patricia Ravert was associate dean of the BYU College of Nursing when this devotional was given on 10 July 2012. © *Brigham Young University.*

science so that I could work as a technologist in a hospital setting. My plan was pretty set in stone, I thought. I actually put in my high school yearbook that I was going to go to BYU and that I was going to be a medical technologist. I do not know where this desire to be a medical technologist stemmed from. My father was a pharmacist, so there was a bit of the medical profession influence in my home, but I did not know anyone who worked as a medical technologist.

When I came to BYU I began my classes for the medical laboratory science major. Several semesters of chemistry were required, and I soon learned that I did not really love chemistry as much as a medical laboratory science major should. It was then that I realized my plan would need to change. I visited many colleges on campus and explored a variety of majors. Many were of interest to me. Each week I wrote handwritten letters home to my parents—this was before cell phones, email, and texting—and each week each letter contained a different idea regarding a possible major. I'm not sure what my parents told people I was studying, because I didn't know what I was studying either.

This situation reminds me of a poem by Robert Frost:

Two roads diverged in a yellow wood,
And sorry I could not travel both
And be one traveler, long I stood
And looked down one as far as I could
To where it bent in the undergrowth.

The last stanza reads:

I shall be telling this with a sigh
Somewhere ages and ages hence:
Two roads diverged in a wood, and I—
I took the one less traveled by,
And that has made all the difference.[1]

I did not know which road to take, and when I finished my freshman year I returned home to San Diego, discouraged because I had not settled on a major. Near the end of the summer I received a letter with a BYU return address. It was an acceptance letter from the College of Nursing for the fall semester. In my search for a major I had visited the College of Nursing, but I didn't realize I had applied. In today's world I can assure you that would not happen, but what an opportunity that was for me. My plan was changing!

After consulting with my parents I decided to change my major to nursing. This change in my plan has had life-altering effects for forty years. I've been a nurse for more than thirty-eight years—now don't start counting how old I am, but yes, that's a long time—and I've done a variety of other things with my major. I've enjoyed the profession of nursing, and I've thoroughly enjoyed my time here at BYU. I'm anxious to begin serving in a new role as the dean of the College of Nursing, and I'm sure that after I finish this talk, being dean will cause more anxiety than speaking does right now. But I know I can be of service, and I'm greatly appreciative of the opportunity to do so.

OF POSIES AND MAKING PLANS

Another part of my plan is always to enjoy the beauty of the world, particularly flowers. I enjoy flowers in many ways: as posies, which is a small bouquet of flowers; in flower gardens; and in artwork such as paintings and sculptures of flowers. The BYU campus has outstanding floral displays throughout the year. When I walk across campus I often stop and admire the flowers. Wherever I am and wherever I travel, I strive to take advantage of the opportunities to visit gardens, take pictures, and admire God's creations.

I have special feelings for some flowers. Daffodils in the spring remind me of the renewing of life and new beginnings. They have always been a favorite of mine. When I was a young woman in Mutual we earned felt seals, or emblems, to mark our progress in the program. The felt seals were sewn onto blue bandalos, or sashes, which we wore each week. I created a felt daffodil to add to my bandolo to remind me of renewal and new beginnings. There are also two flowers that remind me of my mother: purple pansies and poinsettias. My mother would sing the Primary song "Little Purple Pansies" to us, and she often had pansies in her garden. Her birthday was in December, and whenever I see poinsettias I am reminded of her.

I would also like to share another favorite flower. Clematis flowers grow on climbing vines that twist and curl around supporting structures to anchor the plant as it climbs. I took a picture in France not far from Giverny, where the French impressionist painter Claude Monet lived and maintained beautiful gardens. The clematis vines were thick with gorgeous blossoms and covered the building. A few years ago I searched for a home to purchase, and one of my requirements was a nice yard with flower beds. That year I closed on a home in November and was excited to find two clematis vines in the backyard. I thought the plan included two gorgeous vines on either side of the back steps the next spring and summer. The plant on the left side has many blossoms, but the right vine has not done well. Some of the leaves have died, yet the plant is persistent and occasionally has a few small blossoms. These blossoms are purple—a little bit of a different color from the other vine's flowers. I am sure when the previous owner planted these vines, the plan was to have full, beautiful vines on each side of the steps. There has been a bump in this plan.

PERSISTENCE, PERSEVERANCE, AND PROGRESS

Most of our plans have bumps along the way. Your plan may include an education program that because of limited resources cannot admit all applicants. Your bump may be that you are not able to get into your program or that you have to apply to it more than once. Maybe you will find some of your courses especially challenging. This is when persistence and patience are particularly helpful.

Persistence is a stick-to-it attitude, even when things are difficult. Consistent individual actions show persistence. As you practice persistence, such as by daily studying for that challenging course or by completing the necessary tasks to reapply to a program, your daily persistence develops into perseverance.

Elder Joseph B. Wirthlin spoke regarding perseverance:

> Perseverance *means to continue in a given course until we have reached a goal or objective, regardless of obstacles, opposition, and other counter-influences.* . . .
>
> *Perseverance is a positive, active characteristic. It is not idly, passively waiting and hoping for some good thing to happen.* . . .
>
> *. . . Perseverance is vital to success in any endeavor, whether spiritual or temporal, large or small, public or personal. Think seriously of how important perseverance, or the lack of it, has been in your own endeavors, such as Church callings, schooling, or employment. I believe that essentially all significant achievement results largely from perseverance.* . . .
>
> *. . . Perseverance is essential to us in learning and living.*[2]

Sometimes persistence is needed for the short term in completing a difficult assignment or course. At the time it may feel overwhelming, yet with patience and sincere effort we can complete the goal. Sometimes we need to be persistent and persevere over a long period of time—maybe over a lifetime.

A woman I know—I will call her Suzanne—has persisted daily in a very different plan than she ever imagined as a young woman. She has an optimistic and positive attitude, finding joy in the ups and downs of life. She completed her degree in nursing, married, and began her family, which eventually included three daughters. As her second daughter began to grow, Suzanne realized she was not developing normally. After a period of time her daughter was diagnosed with a form of autism that severely affected her social and communication skills. The plan for Suzanne's family was altered. A few years later Suzanne delivered her third daughter, who eventually was also diagnosed with autism. Suzanne's husband was a supportive, involved father, and together they altered their plan, knowing that they could handle this challenge. When the girls were ages eleven, thirteen, and eighteen, their father unexpectedly passed away from a heart attack while out on his daily run. Again Suzanne's plan was greatly altered. She continues to find joy as she has realized that life doesn't have to be perfect to be wonderful. She is persistent and will continue to persevere over her lifetime.

We often are admonished to endure to the end, as in Matthew 24:13, "But he that shall endure unto the end, the same shall be saved"; and in Doctrine and Covenants 50:5, "Blessed are they who are faithful and endure, . . . for they shall inherit eternal life." For many years I struggled with the word *endure* because "to the end" seemed so far off and overwhelming. I came to realize that what I really needed was persistence as I worked on my daily to-do list.

In the last general Young Women meeting President Thomas S. Monson offered this suggestion:

Seek heavenly guidance one day at a time. Life by the yard is hard; by the inch it's a cinch. Each of us can be true for just one day—and then one more and then one more after that—until we've lived a lifetime guided by the Spirit, a lifetime close to the Lord, a lifetime of good deeds and righteousness.[3]

As we strive to live our lives by the inch we must examine the contents of our daily to-do lists. We all want to be successful, but continuing to focus on the wrong to-do items puts us on the wrong plan or road and will only slow our progress. C. S. Lewis wrote:

We all want progress. . . . If you are on the wrong road, progress means doing an about-turn and walking back to the right road; and in that case the man who turns back soonest is the most progressive man.[4]

If life is not what you would like, this is where the concepts of Alma 5 come into play. Alma 5 is the "personal inventory" chapter:

And now behold, I ask of you, my brethren of the church, have ye spiritually been born of God? Have ye received his image in your countenances? Have ye experienced this mighty change in your hearts?

Do ye exercise faith in the redemption of him who created you? Do you look forward with an eye of faith, and view this mortal body raised in immortality, and this corruption raised in incorruption, to stand before God to be judged according to the deeds which have been done in the mortal body?

I say unto you, can you imagine to yourselves that ye hear the voice of the Lord, saying unto you, in that day: Come unto me ye blessed, for behold, your works have been the works of righteousness upon the face of the earth? [Alma 5:14–16]

So I ask myself, and I ask all of you: Are the right things on our to-do lists? Are we focusing on the tasks that will have the outcomes we desire so that our behavior is an example of who we desire to be? Do the expressions on our faces show that we have His image on our countenances? If we need to make changes, President Dieter F. Uchtdorf reminded us that it is much easier to make minor course corrections along the way. But if we are way off course, there is a way back. President Uchtdorf said:

No matter how terribly off course you are, no matter how far you have strayed, the way back is certain and clear. Come, learn of the Father; offer up a sacrifice of a broken heart and a contrite spirit. Have faith, and believe in the cleansing power of the infinite Atonement of Jesus the Christ.[5]

I urge you to strive to stay focused on a plan that is in line with the basic gospel principles. The gospel principles sound so simple. We know them from Primary and Sunday School:

• Read and study the scriptures and conference talks.
• Consistently pray.
• Obey the commandments.
• Attend and be actively engaged in Church meetings and callings.
• Keep your covenants.
• Attend the temple.

The gospel principles are foundational to happiness in our individual plans. Elder M. Russell Ballard said:

The Church is a mooring in this tempestuous sea, an anchor in the churning waters of change and division, and a beacon to those who value and seek righteousness. The Lord uses this Church as a tool in pulling His children throughout the world toward the protection of His gospel.[6]

THE PATIENCE TO REACH YOUR GOALS

Another important thing to remember is to not allow your enthusiasm to be stifled by the discouragement that will inevitably come to you. As we are persistent and persevere in living the gospel principles, we also must trust Heavenly Father and His timing. We don't always know His plan for us. We must be patient and continue in faith to understand.

President Uchtdorf spoke of patience:

Brigham Young taught that when something came up which he could not comprehend fully, he would pray to the Lord, "Give me patience to wait until I can understand it for myself." And then Brigham would continue to pray until he could comprehend it.

We must learn that in the Lord's plan, our understanding comes "line upon line, precept upon precept." In short, knowledge and understanding come at the price of patience.[7]

The principles of persistence and patience have served me well in my life. After I changed my major to nursing, I first obtained an associate degree and then continued on to complete my bachelor's degree in my early married life. I had a goal to return to school for a master's degree. When I had five children I began the nursing administration master's program at BYU. I took one class a semester. People often would say, "How can you take one class per semester? You may never finish." Well, I knew that if I continued I would. I was persistent and patient, and after five years I finished the degree. Twenty-five years after beginning my college education at BYU, I again returned to school, this time at the University of Utah to earn a doctorate degree. My plan has been different than that of many others, but with persistence, patience, and faith I have enjoyed the journey—the hard times and especially the easy and rewarding times.

Now, back to the posies. Of the two clematis vines in my backyard, even with persistence and patience the one has not prospered. I have added fertilizer and water; it has not flourished, but I still have enjoyed the few flowers it has produced. The vine is not perfect, but it is still wonderful in its own way. I urge you to be persistent and persevere and exercise patience to find your plan and reach your goals.

I have a testimony of the truthfulness of the gospel. I know that Joseph Smith served as the Lord's instrument to restore the true gospel to the earth. The Book of Mormon is the word of God, and it contains the gospel principles that, if followed, will lead us back to Heavenly Father. I am very grateful for Jesus Christ, who is my Redeemer and Savior. I say these things in the name of Jesus Christ, amen.

NOTES

1. Robert Frost, "The Road Not Taken" (1916).

2. Joseph B. Wirthlin, "Never Give Up," *Ensign*, November 1987, 8, 9, 10.

3. Thomas S. Monson, "Believe, Obey, and Endure," *Ensign*, May 2012, 129.

4. C. S. Lewis, chapter 5, paragraph 2, in *Mere Christianity* (New York: HarperOne, 2001), 28.

5. Dieter F. Uchtdorf, "A Matter of a Few Degrees," *Ensign*, May 2008, 60.

6. M. Russell Ballard, "That the Lost May Be Found," *Ensign*, May 2012, 98–99.

7. Dieter F. Uchtdorf, "Continue in Patience," *Ensign*, May 2010, 58; quoting *DBY*, 224, and D&C 98:12.

Angels, Chariots, and the Lord of Hosts

Donald W. Parry

T he title of my presentation is "Angels, Chariots, and the Lord
of Hosts."[1] Please know that I have, through various means,
sought for the Spirit of the Lord. Please know also that the Lord's
angels exist and are empowered by Jesus Christ through His infinite
Atonement.

THE MINISTRY OF ANGELS

Since the days of Adam and Eve angels have had significant
responsibilities in the Lord's great plan of happiness. Angels figure
prominently in ancient and modern scripture. Angels have minis-
tered to or communicated with such notables as Adam, Hagar (see
Genesis 16:7–11), Manoah's wife (see Judges 13:3, 6, 19–21), Daniel,
Mary the mother of Jesus (see Luke 1:26–38), Mary Magdalene,
Salome, Joanna, Mary the mother of James, other women (see
Mark 16:4–6; Luke 24:2–4; John 20:11–12), Peter, Paul, John the
Revelator, and many others. Angels have also ministered to Book of

*Donald W. Parry was a professor of the Hebrew Bible in the BYU Department
of Asian and Near Eastern Languages when this devotional was given on 31 July
2012. © Brigham Young University.*

Mormon characters, including Nephi (see 1 Nephi 11:14; 2 Nephi 4:24), King Benjamin (see Mosiah 3:2), Alma the Younger (see Mosiah 27:10–11; Alma 8:14), Amulek (see Alma 10:7), Samuel the Lamanite (see Helaman 13:7), and others.

Furthermore, in our own dispensation prophets and apostles have testified of the eminence and considerable standing of angels. In fact, our dispensation has been a period of extraordinary angelic activity. Joseph Smith received dozens of communications from angels. Additional Church authorities and others have been recipients of angelic communications.

The Church of Jesus Christ of Latter-day Saints was restored, in part, when angels imparted revelations and truths to the Prophet Joseph Smith. A passage in the Doctrine and Covenants summarizes:

The voice of Michael, the archangel; the voice of Gabriel, and of Raphael, and of divers angels, from Michael or Adam down to the present time, all declaring their dispensation, their rights, their keys, their honors, their majesty and glory, and the power of their priesthood. [D&C 128:21]

Elder Jeffrey R. Holland reminded us that it is appropriate to speak about angels. He wrote, "I believe we need to speak of and believe in and bear testimony of the ministry of angels more than we sometimes do."[2]

For a definition of angels, see the Bible Dictionary. In this presentation I will refer to the Lord's angels unless otherwise stated.

THE ANGELS OF THE LORD OF HOSTS

How many angels are there? There are *hosts* of angels. The Old Testament expression "Lord of hosts" sometimes refers to the Lord of hosts of angels. The Bible Dictionary states: "The Lord of Sabaoth was a title of Jehovah; the hosts were the armies of Israel (1 Sam. 17:45), but also included the angelic armies of heaven."[3] Hebrew lexicons agree with this interpretation. One prominent Hebrew lexicon states that the term *Lord of hosts* sometimes refers to "the heavenly beings" of the Lord[4] or "the heavenly entourage" of the Lord.[5] Another Hebrew lexicon agrees with this definition, referring to a host as an "(organized body) of angels."[6]

The title "Lord of hosts" is so important that it is found some 250 times in the Old Testament; Isaiah alone used the term about fifty times. This title, then, is a frequent reminder that the Lord has hosts of angels. How many angels belong to the Lord of hosts of angels? The singular *host*, by definition, refers to "a large number of people or things."[7] The plural, *hosts*, multiplies this number. The Lord of hosts of angels refers to immense numbers.

Other passages of scripture also indicate that there are great numbers of the Lord's angels. For example, Lehi envisioned "God sitting upon his throne, surrounded with numberless concourses of angels" (1 Nephi 1:8). Two passages of scripture—Hebrews 12:22 and Doctrine and Covenants 76:67—use the expression "an innumerable company of angels." Furthermore, John the Revelator recorded:

> *And I beheld, and I heard the voice of many angels round about the throne . . . : and the number of them was ten thousand times ten thousand, and thousands of thousands.* [Revelation 5:11]

Indeed, ten thousand times ten thousand angels, which equals 100 million, symbolizes a great number. To sum up, there are numberless concourses of angels, an innumerable company of angels, and hosts of angels—all of whom are in the service of our Lord and God.

ANGELS AS AGENTS OF POWER

Angels are agents of power. Each of the Lord's angels possesses extraordinary capabilities and powers, making them formidable beings. Their power ultimately exists because of Jesus Christ and His Atonement. Consider the following examples of the power of angels:

When Daniel was cast into the lions' den, a stone was placed over the den's opening to prevent Daniel's escape. Then, to ensure that possible coconspirators with Daniel would not remove the stone without detection, the king and his officers used their signets to seal the stone (see Daniel 6:17). Had the seals been broken during the night, the king and his officers could have claimed deception or trickery on the part of Daniel. But neither the rock nor the seals prevented the angel from entering the den and stopping the lions' mouths. We note that the angel was not only empowered to save Daniel but that the angel himself was also immune from the lions' destruction. Because of Daniel's faith and righteousness, the angel saved him from a horrific death. Daniel would later testify, "My God hath sent his angel, and hath shut the lions' mouths, that they have not hurt me: forasmuch as before him innocency was found in me" (Daniel 6:22).

We live during a day of wars and rumors of wars. News organizations regularly report conflicts taking place in various parts of the world. However, we as Latter-day Saints should have a high degree of comfort in knowing the power of the Lord's angels with regard to such conflicts. The Bible sets forth the following account of a powerful angel.

During the reign of King Hezekiah the Assyrian army was advancing toward Jerusalem with the intent of conquering it. With scores of thousands of enemy soldiers camped outside of Jerusalem's gates, waiting to destroy the city's inhabitants, Hezekiah petitioned the Lord through prayer in the temple. In response to Hezekiah's humble prayer, the Lord sent his prophet Isaiah to the king, promising deliverance from the Assyrian army. Soon thereafter "the angel of the Lord went forth, and smote in the camp of the Assyrians a hundred and fourscore and five thousand" (Isaiah 37:36; see also Isaiah 37:33–35; 2 Chronicles 32:21). It is sometimes difficult to comprehend such extraordinary dominance: one angel versus some 185,000 disciplined soldiers—and the angel was victorious. Such an angelic operation is permitted only according to the Lord's divine will.

In addition to these two examples of angels operating as agents of power during the Old Testament period, I will provide a modern example of a powerful heavenly messenger in the life of President Harold B. Lee. When President Lee was serving as the president of the Church, he shared an experience that occurred while he and his wife were traveling on an airplane. They had been visiting a mission, and both were impressed to return home earlier than they had planned. As President and Sister Lee were sitting in the airplane, homeward bound, President Lee received a blessing from an unseen person. He related:

As we approached a certain point en route, someone laid his hand upon my head. I looked up; I could see no one. That happened again before we arrived home, again with the same experience. Who it was, by what means or what medium, I may never know, except I knew that I was receiving a blessing that I came a few hours later to know I needed most desperately.

. . . Shortly [after we arrived home], *there came massive hemorrhages which, had they occurred while we were in flight, I wouldn't be here today talking about it.*

I know that there are powers divine that reach out when all other help is not available. . . . Yes, I know that there are such powers.[8]

The unseen person who gave President Lee a blessing demonstrated extraordinary powers: he remained invisible, he knew where to find President Lee, he knew of President Lee's physical condition and of his need for a blessing, and he blessed the prophet with priesthood power. Additionally, it is my opinion that this unseen person did not board the plane as did other passengers, obtaining a passport, ticket, and boarding pass; showing his photo ID; dealing with airport security; and so forth. It is entirely possible, knowing of the vast power of angels, that this unseen person entered the plane through miraculous means. Such is the way of heavenly beings.

ANGELS AS PROTECTORS OF THE RIGHTEOUS

Not only are angels agents of power, but they also serve as protective and reassuring forces for the righteous, as shown by the symbol of chariots of fire. During my research on angels I have collected a number of accounts that feature angels, horses, and chariots of fire. I will now provide a few examples.

We recall from the Old Testament the attempt of Syria's king to capture Elisha. During the night the king surrounded Dothan with soldiers, horses, and chariots. When Elisha's assistant awakened early in the morning, he saw the armies that surrounded the city and cried out to Elisha, "Alas, my master! how shall we do?"

Elisha replied by saying:

Fear not: for they that be with us are more than they that be with them.

[After this reply,] *Elisha prayed, and said, Lord, I pray thee, open his eyes, that he may see. And the Lord opened the eyes of the young man; and he saw: and, behold, the mountain was full of horses and chariots of fire round about Elisha.* [2 Kings 6:15–17]

This account signifies a demonstration of great power and supremacy—a mountain full of horses and chariots of fire providing courage and protection to Elisha and his servant.

Church authorities and others often liken this account to us. President Henry B. Eyring, for example, provided us with the following encouragement:

I know that the promise of angels to bear us up is real. You might want to bring to memory the assurance of Elisha to his frightened servant. That assurance is ours when we feel close to being overwhelmed in our service. Elisha faced real and terrible opposition. . . .

Like that servant of Elisha, there are more with you than those you can see opposed to you. Some who are with you will be invisible to your mortal eyes.[9]

Elder Jeffrey R. Holland related the account of Elisha and then applied this important story to each of us:

In the gospel of Jesus Christ we have help from both sides of the veil. When disappointment and discouragement strike—and they will—we need to remember that if our eyes could be opened, we would see horses and chariots of fire as far as the eye can see, riding at great speed to come to our protection. They will always be there, these armies of heaven, in defense of Abraham's seed.[10]

The account of Elisha reminds us also of when Elijah and Elisha were walking and talking near the Jordan River, and "there appeared a chariot of fire, and horses of fire, and parted them both asunder; and Elijah went up by a whirlwind into heaven." When Elisha witnessed this scene, he cried out, "My father, my father, the chariot of Israel, and the horsemen thereof" (2 Kings 2:11–12). For multiple reasons this is a marvelous and incredible show of power: a chariot of fire, horses of fire, and Elijah ascending to heaven in a whirlwind create a magnificent scene.

On April 3, 1836, this same Elijah visited Joseph Smith and Oliver Cowdery in the Kirtland Temple. Joseph wrote, "Another great and glorious vision burst upon us; for Elijah the prophet, who was taken to heaven without tasting death, stood before us" (D&C 110:13).

The protective theme of horses and chariots of fire continues in our day. Some individuals who attended the dedication of the Kirtland Temple beheld angels, horses of fire, and chariots. The Prophet Joseph Smith recorded: "The heavens were opened unto Elder Sylvester Smith, and he, leaping up, exclaimed: 'The horsemen of Israel and the chariots thereof.'"[11]

Additionally, Joseph Smith wrote that

Elder Roger Orton saw a mighty angel riding upon a horse of fire, with a flaming sword in his hand, followed by five others, encircle the house [temple], *and protect the Saints, even the Lord's anointed, from the power of Satan and a host of evil spirits, which were striving to disturb the Saints.*[12]

This account makes it unmistakable that the angels who encircled the temple did so to protect the Saints from Satan's host of evil spirits. This account also features angels with swords in their hands—a demonstration of angels' power to protect us from harm and danger.

Angels with swords are found in the Old Testament as well as in accounts during the Restoration. We are reminded, for instance, that Joseph Smith envisioned

Elder Brigham Young standing in a strange land, in the far south and west, in a desert place, upon a rock in the midst of about a dozen men . . . , who appeared hostile. He was preaching to them in their own tongue, and the angel of God standing above his head, with a drawn sword in his hand, protecting him, but he did not see it.[13]

ANGELS IN THIS DISPENSATION

Many of the accounts of angels that I have shared today are exceptional or unique. Most of us will never be protected by an angel in a lions' den, nor will the majority of us be privileged to see horses and chariots of fire. But we should bear in mind that angelic communications are not reserved for those who lived during the ancient periods of the Old Testament or the Book of Mormon, nor are such communications reserved only for prophets, apostles, or notable women such as Hagar or Mary the mother of Jesus. Indeed, several of our Church authorities have clearly taught that we who are laypersons may receive angelic communications according to the divine will of our loving Heavenly Father. To this end I will cite President Boyd K. Packer and Elder Dallin H. Oaks.

President Packer provided the following significant statement:

Angels attend the rank and file of the Church. . . .
Who would dare to say that angels do not now attend the rank and file of the Church who—
answer the calls to the mission fields,
teach the classes,
pay their tithes and offerings,
seek for the records of their forebears,
work in the temples,

raise their children in faith,
and have brought this work through 150 years?[14]

This statement of President Packer's clearly shows that angels attend the Church's rank and file as they raise children in faith, pay tithing, conduct sacred temple work, teach classes, and more.

It is my understanding—based on more than twenty years of research—that operations and ministrations of angels are largely unknown to mortals. Angels can move about the earth conducting the Lord's divine work, and they serve, minister, and mingle among mortals, usually without our awareness. Most of us in mortality will never see an angel. As Parley P. Pratt instructed, angels can "be present without being visible to mortals."[15] And Paul wrote, "Be not forgetful to entertain strangers: for thereby some have entertained angels unawares" (Hebrews 13:2).

Before I cite Elder Oaks, I want to share a personal item. During the 1990s my parents had a landline telephone that was state of the art, high tech, and ultramodern. It was so technologically advanced that it had an internal memory that would remember up to twenty phone numbers. After my parents entered the phone numbers of friends or family into the phone's memory, all my parents had to do was lift the receiver and push the appropriate button, and the phone would automatically dial any of their children. What an amazing miracle! Dad and Mom could be in contact with any one of their children in seconds.

I will now refer to Elder Dallin H. Oaks' conference talk. Elder Oaks presented specific teachings on how angels may communicate to us who are mortals. His teachings apply to you and to me:

The ministering of angels can also be unseen. Angelic messages can be delivered by a voice or merely by thoughts or feelings communicated to the mind. . . .

Nephi described three manifestations of the ministering of angels when he reminded his rebellious brothers that (1) they had "seen an angel,"
(2) they had "heard his voice from time to time," and (3) also that an angel

had "spoken unto [them] in a still small voice" though they were "past
feeling" and "could not feel his words" (1 Ne. 17:45). . . . Most angelic
communications are felt or heard rather than seen.[16]

Compared to the aforementioned telephone, which is now a relic
of the past, angelic communications are astounding and remarkable.
They are wonderful gifts from a loving Heavenly Father: visitations
from beyond the veil—unseen angels communicating to mortals
by thoughts or by feelings—are spectacular gifts. As the Book of
Mormon teaches, "It is by faith that angels appear and minister unto
men" (Moroni 7:37). The telephone, of course, does not work by
faith.

My research has uncovered instances in which angels have
provided temporal assistance to mortals. An angel, for example,
provided food and water to the prophet Elijah when he fled for his
life from Jezebel (see 1 Kings 19:1–7). And here is a modern example
of an angel providing temporal assistance: Elder Heber C. Kimball
related an occasion when he and Brigham Young traveled together,
conducting the Lord's work. They started out with only $13.50, but
along the way they paid for a number of items, including travel,
lodging, and meals. In fact, they paid out over $87.00, although they
had only had $13.50. Elder Kimball stated:

Brother Brigham often suspected that I put the money in his trunk or
clothes, thinking I had . . . money which I had not acquainted him with,
but this was not so. The money could only have been put in his trunk by
some heavenly messenger who administered to our necessities daily, as he
knew we needed.[17]

ANGELS AS AGENTS OF LOVE

All angels minister with heavenly love, and every angelic
communication to the Saints is a message of love. Oliver Cowdery
personally witnessed the love of John the Baptist when John
appeared to him and Joseph Smith. Sometime after John's visitation
Oliver wrote that this angel's "love enkindled upon our souls."[18]

Decades later, in the April 1916 general conference, President Joseph F. Smith spoke of the love of heavenly messengers:

I believe we move and have our being in the presence of heavenly messengers and of heavenly beings. We are not separate from them. . . . I claim that we live in their presence, they see us, they are solicitous for our welfare, they love us now more than ever. . . . Their love for us and their desire for our well being must be greater than that which we feel for ourselves.[19]

I will now share two stories wherein angels communicated love to mortals. At one point in his life Parley P. Pratt remained captive for months in a Missouri dungeon. He was very discouraged. After fasting and praying for a number of days, Elder Pratt experienced a powerful answer to his prayer. He wrote:

A personage . . . stood before me with a smile of compassion in every look, and pity mingled with the tenderest love and sympathy in every expression of the countenance. . . . A well known voice saluted me, which I readily recognized as that of the wife of my youth, who had for near two years been sweetly sleeping where . . . the weary are at rest.[20]

This personage, as an angelic messenger, delivered her message to Elder Pratt and then departed.

While on the subject of female angels, I will share an important statement by President Brigham Young:

Suppose that a female angel were to come into your house and you had the privilege of seeing her, how would she be dressed? . . . She would be neat and nice, her countenance full of glory, brilliant, bright, and perfectly beautiful, and in every act her gracefulness would charm the heart of every beholder. There is nothing needless about her.[21]

The second account of an angel who communicated love comes from President Ezra Taft Benson, who recounted an eternal love story of his wife's parents. His father-in-law, Carl Christian

Amussen, a convert from Denmark, was a watchmaker and jeweler in Utah. He passed away in 1902, leaving his wife, Barbara, a widow for forty years. In 1942 the deceased Carl came to his wife to inform her of her approaching death. What a great blessing it was for her to see her eternal companion for the first time in so many years. Carl appeared to Barbara and informed her that she would pass away on the following Thursday. Barbara had no doubt that her husband had appeared to her, nor did she doubt that she only had less than a week to live; in fact, she began to make concrete plans for her death. On Sunday at church she bore her testimony and bid the ward members good-bye. During the coming days she withdrew her savings from the bank, ordered her casket from a local mortuary, paid her bills, and even had the power and water turned off at her home. Then she went to her daughter Mabel's home to await her passing.

President Benson concluded:

> On the day of her passing, Mabel came into the room where her mother was reclining on the bed. Her mother said, "Mabel, I feel a little bit drowsy. I feel I will go to sleep. Do not disturb me if I sleep until the eventide."
>
> Those were her last words, and she peacefully passed away.[22]

It is my testimony that angels are agents of love, light, and power. The Lord's angels exist because of Jesus Christ and His infinite Atonement. I testify that angels appeared to the Prophet Joseph Smith. I also testify that the sacred work of angels continues in our day. In the name of Jesus Christ, amen.

NOTES

1. For those who wish to pursue a study of angels, there are hundreds of passages of scripture that deal with the topic. Additionally, latter-day prophets and apostles have provided hundreds of statements on the subject.

2. Jeffrey R. Holland, "For a Wise Purpose," *Ensign*, January 1996, 17.

3. Bible Dictionary, s.v. "Sabaoth," 764.

4. Ludwig Koehler and Walter Baumgartner, *The Hebrew and Aramaic Lexicon of the Old Testament*, 2 vols. (Leiden: Brill, 2001), 2:996; citing the following passages: 1 Kings 22:19; 2 Chronicles 18:18; Psalm 103:21; 148:2.

5. Koehler and Baumgartner, *The Hebrew and Aramaic Lexicon*, 2:995.

6. Francis Brown, S. R. Driver, and Charles A. Briggs, eds., *A Hebrew and English Lexicon of the Old Testament*, trans. Edward Robinson (Oxford: Clarendon, 1977), 839; "host (organized body) of angels," which cites 1 Kings 22:19; 2 Chronicles 18:18; Nehemiah 9:6; Psalm 103:21; 148:2; and Joshua 5:14–15, which refers to a "theophanic angel."

7. *New Oxford American Dictionary*, 3rd ed., s.v. "host," 841.

8. Harold B. Lee, "Stand Ye in Holy Places," *Ensign*, July 1973, 123.

9. Henry B. Eyring, "O Ye That Embark," *Ensign*, November 2008, 58.

10. Jeffrey R. Holland, *However Long and Hard the Road* (Salt Lake City: Deseret Book, 1985), 13–14.

11. *HC* 2:383.

12. *HC* 2:386–87.

13. *HC* 2:381.

14. Boyd K. Packer, *Mine Errand from the Lord: Selections from the Sermons and Writings of Boyd K. Packer* (Salt Lake City: Deseret Book, 2008), 385.

15. Parley P. Pratt, *Key to the Science of Theology*, 10th ed. (Salt Lake City: Deseret Book, 1973), 113.

16. Dallin H. Oaks, "The Aaronic Priesthood and the Sacrament," *Ensign*, November 1998, 39.

17. Heber C. Kimball, "One York Shilling," in *Best-Loved Stories of the LDS People*, vol. 1, ed. Jack M. Lyon, Linda Ririe Gundry, and Jay A. Parry (Salt Lake City: Deseret Book, 1997), 375; from Helen

Mar Whitney, "Life Incidents, No. II," *Woman's Exponent* 9, no. 4 (15 July 1880): 26.

18. In B. H. Roberts, *A Comprehensive History of The Church of Jesus Christ of Latter-day Saints, Century One*, 6 vols. (Salt Lake City: Deseret News, 1930), 1:178, note 5; from Oliver Cowdery, First Communication on the Rise of the Church, *Latter Day Saints' Messenger and Advocate* 1, no. 1 (October 1834): 15.

19. Joseph F. Smith, *CR*, April 1916, 2–3.

20. *PPP*, 1874, 261.

21. *JD*, 16:21. Beyond this explicit quote by Brigham Young, there is other evidence for the existence of female angels.

22. Ezra Taft Benson, *Come unto Christ* (Salt Lake City: Deseret Book, 1983), 20–22.

Our Identity and Our Destiny

Tad R. Callister

In keeping with the theme of this week, I would like to discuss with you a vision of who we are and what we may become. At a recent training session for General Authorities, the question was asked: "How can we help those struggling with pornography?"

Elder Russell M. Nelson stood and replied, "Teach them their identity and their purpose."

That answer resonated with me, not only as a response to that specific question but as an appropriate response to most of the challenges we face in life. And so today I speak of the true nature of our identity and a correct vision of our divine destiny.

First, our identity. There is a sentiment among many in the world that we are the spirit creations of God, just as a building is the creation of its architect or a painting the creation of its painter or an invention the creation of its inventor. The scriptures teach, however, a much different doctrine. They teach that we are more than creations of God; they teach that we are the literal spirit offspring

Tad R. Callister was a member of the Presidency of the Seventy of The Church of Jesus Christ of Latter-day Saints when this devotional address was delivered on 14 August 2012 during Campus Education Week. © *Intellectual Reserve, Inc.*

or children of God our Father.[1] What difference does this doctrinal distinction make? The difference is monumental in its consequence because our identity determines in large measure our destiny. For example, can a mere creation ever become like its creator? Can a building ever become an architect? A painting a painter? Or an invention an inventor? If not, then those who believe we are creations of God, rather than His spirit offspring, reach the inevitable conclusion that we do not have the capacity to become like our creator, God. In essence, their doctrine of identity has defined and dictated a diminished destiny.

On the other hand, as members of The Church of Jesus Christ of Latter-day Saints, we believe that we are the spirit offspring of God with inherited spiritual traits that give us the divine potential to become like our parent, God the Father. As to this identity, President Packer has written:

You are a child of God. He is the father of your spirit. Spiritually you are of noble birth, the offspring of the King of Heaven. Fix that truth in your mind and hold to it. However many generations in your mortal ancestry, no matter what race or people you represent, the pedigree of your spirit can be written on a single line. You are a child of God![2]

It is this doctrine of identity that defines our potential destiny of godhood. If one does not correctly understand his divine identity, then he will never correctly understand his divine destiny. They are, in truth, inseparable partners.

What, then, has God revealed to us about our destiny? He has spoken clearly and frequently and forthrightly on this subject from the very beginning. When Adam and Eve were in the Garden of Eden, they lived in a state of innocence—meaning they only had a limited knowledge of good and evil. Lehi described their condition as follows: "Wherefore they would have remained in a state of innocence, having no joy, for they knew no misery; doing no good, for they knew no sin" (2 Nephi 2:23).

Suppose for a moment my wife and I invited one of you good Saints from California to drive to our home in Utah. Further suppose I asked you to drive in neutral.

You might smile and respond, "That's not possible."

What if I further replied, "Just push the accelerator all the way to the floor—you know, as they say, 'Push the pedal to the metal.'"

You might respond, "That would make no difference. I cannot reach your destination until I put my car in gear."

So it was with Adam and Eve. They were in a state of spiritual neutral and could not progress toward their divine destiny until they were cast out of the garden and thus put in spiritual gear.

When Adam and Eve were cast out of the Garden of Eden, they traded their innocence, meaning a lack of knowledge of good and evil, for the prospect of perfection—that was the deal. Innocence and perfection are not the same. An infant may be innocent but certainly not perfect in the sense that he or she has acquired all the attributes of godliness. Once Adam and Eve were cast from the garden, we read in the book of Genesis that God Himself said, "Behold, *the man is become as one of us* [meaning like the gods]" (Genesis 3:22; emphasis added). How could that be? God then tells us why this new destiny was possible—because men now "know good and evil." Being immersed in a world of good and evil, having the capacity to choose, and being able to draw upon the powers of the Atonement resulted in man having unlimited opportunities to progress toward his destiny of godhood.

We learn a great doctrinal truth in these series of events surrounding the Garden of Eden: unfallen man would have remained in a state of innocence—safe, but restricted in his progress. On the other hand, fallen man ventured into a heightened arena of risk, but, blessed with the Atonement of Jesus Christ, he gained access to unlimited possibilities and powers and potential. Speaking of the effect of the Atonement on fallen man, C. S. Lewis remarked:

*For God is not merely mending, not simply restoring a **status quo**. Redeemed humanity is to be something more glorious than unfallen* *humanity would have been, more glorious than any unfallen race now is. . . . And this super-added glory will, with true vicariousness, exalt all creatures.*[3]

Through the Atonement of Jesus Christ, God can exalt all His children—meaning empower them to become like Him.

But one might ask, "Why does God want us to become like Him?" In order to answer that question, one must first understand why man exists. Lehi gave the short and simple answer: "Men are, that they might have joy" (2 Nephi 2:25). President David O. McKay confirmed that fundamental doctrinal truth: "Happiness is the purpose and design of existence."[4] If I were to ask you who is the happiest being in all the universe—the one with the most joy—you would no doubt respond, "God." Accordingly, God wants us to become perfect like Him so we can experience His quality of joy and thus best fulfill the measure of our existence. That is why His plan for us is sometimes called "the plan of happiness" (see Alma 42:8, 16).

OUR QUEST FOR GODHOOD

In spite of God's altruistic aims on our behalf, perhaps no doctrine, no teaching, no philosophy has stirred such controversy as has this: that man may become a god. It is espoused by some as blasphemous, by others as absurd. Such a concept, they challenge, lowers God to the status of man and thus deprives God of both His dignity and divinity. Others claim this teaching to be devoid of scriptural support. It is but a fantasy, they say, of a young, uneducated schoolboy, Joseph Smith. Certainly no God-fearing, right-thinking, Bible-oriented person would subscribe to such a philosophy as this.[5] While some of these advocates are hardened critics, others are honest and bright men who simply disagree with us on this doctrine. So wherein lies the truth? Hopefully the following will invite the Holy Ghost to whisper the quiet but certain truth to all those who honestly seek it.

For our search of truth, we will turn to five witnesses—first and foremost to the testimony of the scriptures; second, to the witness of the early Christian writers; third, to the wisdom of those poets and authors who drink from the divine well; fourth, to the power of logic; and fifth, to the voice of history.

Scriptures

First, the scriptures. Did not an angel appear unto Abraham and extend to him this heavenly mandate: "Walk before me, and be thou perfect" (Genesis 17:1)?

"That is true," interjects the critic. "Perfect as compared to other men, other mortals—certainly not perfect as compared to God. The word was used in its relative, not absolute sense."

"Is that so?" comes the reply. "Let us then pursue the use of the word *perfect* as used by the Savior Himself."

It was in the Sermon on the Mount when the Savior declared, "Be ye therefore perfect, *even as your Father which is in heaven is perfect*" (Matthew 5:48; emphasis added).[6] Was the Savior inviting men to be perfect as compared to other men—other mortals—or as compared to God Himself? This command was consistent with the Savior's high priestly prayer. Speaking of the believers, He petitioned the Father:

That they may be one, even as we are one:
I in them, and thou in me, that they may be made perfect in one.
[John 17:22–23]

In accord with that request for perfection, Paul taught that a critical purpose of the Church was "for the perfecting of the saints . . . till we all come . . . unto a perfect man, *unto the measure of the stature of the fulness of Christ*" (Ephesians 4:12–13; emphasis added). Note the measuring rod: not man, not some form of mini-Christ or quasi-God, but rather that we should become "a perfect man, [and then he gives us the standard we should strive for] unto the measure of the stature of the fulness of Christ." Does that sound relative to you?

The critic is momentarily quiet. Sheepishly he responds, "Certainly those scriptures must mean something else."

The scriptures supporting this doctrine, however, continue to roll forth with repeated and powerful testimony. At one point the Savior was about to be stoned by the Jews for blasphemy. He reminded them of His good works and then asked, "For which of those works do ye stone me?"

They replied that they were not stoning him for good works "but for blasphemy; and because that thou, being a man, *makest thyself God.*"

To this He readily acknowledged that He was and declared that they should be likewise: "Is it not written in your law, I said, Ye are gods?" (John 10:32–34; emphasis added). In other words, He said not only am I a god, but all of you are potential gods. He was referring to His own Old Testament declaration, with which the Jews should have been familiar: "Ye are gods; and all of you are children of the most High" (Psalm 82:6). The Savior was merely reaffirming a basic gospel teaching that all men are children of God, and thus all might become like Him.

Paul understood this principle, for, when speaking to the men of Athens, he said: "Certain also of your own poets have said, For we are also his offspring" (Acts 17:28). Paul knew the consequences of being the offspring of God, for, while speaking to the Romans, he declared:

> *The Spirit itself beareth witness with our spirit, that we are the children of God:*
> *And if children, then heirs; heirs of God, **and joint-heirs with Christ.*** [Romans 8:16–17; emphasis added; see also 1 Corinthians 3:21–23 and Revelation 21:7]

Not subordinate heirs, not junior, not contingent, but joint, equal heirs with Christ Himself, to share in all that He shall share. After all, is not that the same promise made by the Lord to the Apostle John? "To him that overcometh will I grant to sit with me in my throne, even as I also overcame, and am set down with my Father in his throne" (Revelation 3:21).

Is it any wonder that Paul should write to the Saints of Philippi, "I press toward the mark for the prize of the high calling of God in Christ Jesus" (Philippians 3:14). Paul, who understood so very well our destiny, was striving for the reward of godhood. Peter, who also understood this doctrine, pled with the Saints that they might become "partakers of the divine nature" (2 Peter 1:4), meaning recipients of godhood. That is exactly what Jesus ordered when speaking to the Book of Mormon Saints: "Therefore, what manner of men ought ye to be? Verily I say unto you, even as I am" (3 Nephi 27:27; see also 1 John 3:2). And it is exactly what the Savior promised in this dispensation for all faithful Saints: "Then shall they be gods, because they have all power, and the angels are subject unto them" (D&C 132:20; see also verse 19; see also D&C 76:58–60).

The critic, still shaking his head, responds, "But such a concept lowers God to the status of man and thus robs Him of His divinity."

"Or, to the contrary," comes the reply, "does it elevate man in his divine-like potential?"

Paul well knew this argument of the critic and silenced it once and for all ages ago. Speaking to the Saints of Philippi, he said:

> Let this mind be in you, which was also in Christ Jesus:
> Who, being in the form of God, **thought it not robbery to be equal with God.** [Philippians 2:5–6; emphasis added]

The Savior knew that for Him to be a god and for us to be thus minded would not rob God of His divinity. That makes good sense. After all, who is greater: that being who limits or that being who enhances man's eternal progress?

One might ask, Who can give greater honor and glory to God—a creature of lower or more exalted status? Can an animal offer the same honor or worship with the same passion and intensity as a human? Can a mere mortal express the empyreal feelings or exercise the spiritual fervency of a potential god? One's capacity to honor and worship is magnified with one's intellectual, emotional, cultural, and spiritual enlightenment. Accordingly, the more we become like God, the greater our ability to pay Him homage. In that process of lifting men heavenward, God simultaneously multiplies His own honor and glory and thus is glorified more, not less.

Brigham Young addressed this issue:

> [Man's godhood] *will not detract anything from the glory and might of our heavenly Father, for he will still remain our Father, and we shall still be subject to him, and as we progress, in glory and power it the more enhances the glory and power of our heavenly Father.*[7]

That is the irony of the critic's argument—godhood for man does not diminish God's status; to the contrary, it elevates it by producing more intelligent, more passionate, more spiritual Saints who have enlarged capacities to understand, honor, and worship Him.

The Savior's soul-stirring and thought-provoking injunction to "be ye therefore perfect" was more than the sounding of brass or tinkling of cymbals (see 1 Corinthians 13:1). It was a divine-like invitation to rise up to our full potential and become like God our Father. C. S. Lewis, as a rampant advocate of this simple but glorious truth, wrote:

> *The command* Be ye perfect *is not idealistic gas. Nor is it a command to do the impossible. He is going to make us into creatures that can obey that command. He said (in the Bible) that we were "gods" and He is going to make good His words. . . . The process will be long and in parts very painful; but that is what we are in for. Nothing less. He meant what He said.*[8]

Could it be any clearer?

Early Christian Writers

Second, early Christian writers likewise wrote of our divine destiny.[9] As early as the second century, Irenaeus (A.D. 115–202) noted: "We have not been made gods from the beginning, but at first merely men, then at length gods."[10] On another occasion Irenaeus clarified that exalted man would not be relegated to some type of glorified angel but literally become a god: "Passing beyond the angels, and be made after the image and likeness of God."[11]

Clement of Alexandria (A.D. 160–200), a contemporary of Irenaeus, spoke of the reward of godhood that followed long preparation: "Being destined to sit on thrones with the other gods that have been first put in their places by the Saviour."[12] This same Clement of Alexandria then added this unequivocal statement about the man who lives a righteous life: "Knowing God, he will be made like God. . . . And *that man becomes God, since God so wills.*"[13]

Hippolytus (A.D. 170–236), bridging the second and third centuries, spoke of the unlimited potential of faithful Saints in this life: "And thou shalt be a companion of the Deity, and a *co-heir* with Christ. . . . For thou hast become God: . . . thou hast been deified, and begotten unto immortality."[14]

Cyprian (A.D. 200–258), a well-known Christian leader of the third century, reaffirmed that men can become like Christ: "What Christ is, we Christians shall be, if we imitate Christ."[15]

Origen (A.D. 185–255), also of the third century, wrote: "The true God [referring to the Father], then, is 'The God,' and those who are formed after Him are gods, images, as it were, of Him the prototype."[16]

And in the fourth century St. Athanasius of Alexandria (A.D. 295–373) explained that "[God] was made flesh in order that we might be enabled to be made gods."[17]

For several centuries this doctrinal truth survived, but eventually the Apostasy took its toll, and this doctrine in its purity and expansiveness was lost. The doctrine of man's potential for godhood as taught by the Prophet Joseph Smith was not his invention—not his creation, not conjured up by some fertile mind. It was simply and solely a restoration of a glorious truth that had been taught in the scriptures and by many early Christian writers of the primitive Church.

Poets and Authors

The third witness—inspired poets and authors. We may look to the wisdom of selected poets and authors who are men of integrity and spiritual insight. It was C. S. Lewis who again and again reaffirmed this divine proposition:

> *It is a serious thing to live in a society of possible gods and goddesses, to remember that the dullest and most uninteresting person you talk to may one day be a creature which . . . you would be strongly tempted to worship. . . . There are no ordinary people.*[18]

How right he was. There are no ordinary people, only potential gods and goddesses in our midst.

It was Victor Hugo, that masterful author, who said, "The thirst for the infinite proves infinity."[19] What a powerful and sublime thought. Perhaps the thirst for godhood likewise proves godhood. Would the God you and I know plant the vision and desire for godhood within a man's soul and then frustrate him in his ability to attain it? Shakespeare had a flash of this insight, for, when speaking through the lips of Hamlet, he said:

> *What a piece of work is a man! How noble in reason! how infinite in faculty! in form, in moving, how express and admirable! in action how like an angel! in apprehension how like a god!*[20]

Robert Browning's vision that so often pierced the mortal veil did so once again in these lines from his poem *Rabbi Ben Ezra:*

> *Life's struggle having so far reached its term,*
> *Thence shall I pass, approved*
> *A man, for aye removed*
> *From the developed brute—a god, though in the germ.*[21]

This insightful poet saw the seeds and germ of godhood in every man.

Logic

The fourth witness is the power of logic. Do not the laws of science teach us that like begets like, each after its kind? Science has taught us that a complex genetic code transferred from parent to child is responsible for the child attaining the physical attributes of his parents. If this be so, is it illogical to assume that spirit offspring receive a spiritual code giving to them the divine characteristics and potential of their parent—God—thus making them gods in embryo? No, it is but a fulfillment of the law that like begets like. This is the same truth taught by the prophet Lorenzo Snow:

> *We were born in the image of God our Father; He begat us like unto Himself.* **There is the nature of Deity in the composition of our spiritual organization.** *In our spiritual birth, our Father transmitted to us the capabilities, powers and faculties which He possessed, as much so as the child on its mother's bosom possesses, although in an undeveloped state, the faculties, powers and susceptibilities of its parent.*[22]

President Boyd K. Packer told of coming home one day and helping his children gather new chicks in the barn. As his little four-year-old daughter held a baby chick in her hands, he said something like, "Won't that be a beautiful dog when it grows up?"

His daughter looked at him in surprise.

And then he said something like, "Or perhaps it will be a cat or even a cow."

His little daughter wrinkled her nose, as if to say, "Daddy, don't you know anything? It will grow up exactly like its parents."

Then he observed how this little four-year-old girl knew, almost instinctively, that the chick would grow up to follow the pattern of its parentage.[23]

The Gospel of Philip, an apocryphal book, makes this simple statement of logic: "A horse sires a horse, a man begets man, a god brings forth a god."[24] The difference between man and God is significant—but it is one of degree, not kind. It is the difference between an acorn and an oak tree, a rosebud and a rose, a son and a father. In truth, every man is a potential god in embryo, in fulfillment of that eternal law that like begets like.

Voice of History

Fifth, and finally, the voice of history will likewise verify this truth. I recall the story of the large milk truck that drove past the pasture of cows. Written on the side of the vehicle in large letters were the words "Homogenized, Pasteurized, Vitamins A and D Added."

One cow looked at the sign, turned to the other, and said, "Makes you feel kind of inadequate, doesn't it?"

I admit that is how I feel when I look at the distance between God and me, but I take comfort when I contemplate what is accomplished in the short space of a mortal life. I paraphrase these thoughts of B. H. Roberts: From the cradle have risen orators, generals, artists, and workers to perform the wonders of our age. From a helpless babe may arise a Demosthenes or Lincoln to direct the destinies of nations. From such a babe may come a Michelangelo to fill the world with beauty. From such a beginning may come a Mozart, a Beethoven to call from silence the powers and serenity of music. From such a helpless babe may arise a Joseph Smith to give light in a world of darkness.[25]

Contemplate for a moment what can be accomplished in the short space of a mortal life. Suppose now that you were to remove from man the barriers of death and grant him immortality and God for his guide. What limits would you then want to ascribe to his mental, moral, or spiritual achievements? Perhaps B. H. Roberts expressed it best when he said:

If within the short space of mortal life there are men who rise up out of infancy and become masters of the elements of fire and water and earth and air, so that they well-nigh rule them as Gods, what may it not be possible for them to do in a few hundreds or thousands of millions of years?[26]

A glimpse beyond the veil tells us that the records of history do not end at death but continue to mark man's unlimited achievements. Victor Hugo, with an almost spiritual X-ray, saw the possibilities after death:

The nearer I approach the end, the plainer I hear around me the immortal symphonies of the worlds which invite me. . . . For half a century I have been writing my thoughts in prose and verse; history. . . . I have tried all. But I feel I have not said a thousandth part of what is in me. When I go down to the grave, I can say, like so many others, "I have finished my day's work," but I can not say, "I have finished my life." My day's work will begin again the next morning. The tomb is not a blind alley; it is a thoroughfare. . . . My work is only beginning.[27]

Perfection is a quest on both sides of the veil. The scriptures remind us, "Wherefore, continue in patience until ye are perfected" (D&C 67:13).

THE DIVINE POSSIBILITY BECOMES A DIVINE REALITY

The scriptures, early Christian writers, poetry, logic, and history testify not only of the divine possibility but of the divine reality that man may become as God. The Doctrine and Covenants refers to Abraham, Isaac, and Jacob, declaring, "And because they did none other things than that which they were commanded, they have entered into their exaltation, . . . and sit upon thrones, and are not angels but are gods" (D&C 132:37). For these men the divine possibility became the divine reality. This does not mean they became gods who replaced our Father in Heaven but rather exalted men who have enlarged capabilities to honor and glorify Him. Our Father in Heaven will forever stand supreme as our God, whom we will love and revere and worship, worlds without end.

But how is it possible that you and I, with all our faults and weaknesses and shortcomings, could ever become a god? Fortunately, a loving Heavenly Father has given us resources to lift us above our mortal restraints and propel us to divine heights. I mention but two such resources, both made possible because of the Atonement of Jesus Christ, whose crowning aim is to assist us in our pursuit of godhood—so that we might be "at one"—not only with Him but also "at one" like Him. First, I mention the saving ordinances of the kingdom.

Joseph Smith received a revelation that explained the relationship between ordinances and godhood:

> *Therefore, in the ordinances thereof, the power of godliness is manifest.*
> *And without the ordinances thereof, and the authority of the priesthood, the power of godliness is not manifest unto men in the flesh.* [D&C 84:20–21]

In other words, participation in the saving ordinances unlocks and unleashes certain powers of godliness in our lives that are not available in any other way. These powers help refine us and perfect us. The five saving ordinances and the corresponding powers of godliness are as follows:

First, baptism by immersion (and the corollary ordinance of the sacrament). Because of the Atonement of Jesus Christ, this ordinance cleanses us from our sins and helps make us holy, thus aligning our life more closely with the Savior's.

Second, the gift of the Holy Ghost. This gift helps us know "the will of the Lord [and] the mind of the Lord" (D&C 68:4) and thus makes possible our acquisition of a more godlike mind.

Third, the priesthood. This ordinance transfers to a mere mortal the power to act for God on earth as though He Himself were present. In essence, it is a spiritual power of attorney to be God's agent and to invoke His power, thus helping us learn how to exercise divine powers in righteousness.

Fourth, the endowment. This ordinance is a gift of knowledge from God as to how we might become more like Him, accompanied by covenants to inspire us in that endeavor. There is an old saying, "Knowledge is power." Accordingly, the righteous use of this knowledge received in the endowment ordinance results in more godly power in our own lives. That is why the Doctrine and Covenants says, "I design to endow those whom I have chosen with power from on high" (D&C 95:8).

Fifth, the sealing ordinances. Death, with all its mighty power, cannot destroy those relationships sealed in a temple—which relationships can now continue beyond the grave and allow us, like God, to have eternal increase.

The saving ordinances are much more than a checklist of actions we must satisfy to gain entrance to the celestial kingdom—they are the keys that open the doors to heavenly powers that can lift us above our mortal limitations.

The second resource to assist us in our pursuit of godhood is the gifts of the Spirit. What are the gifts of the Spirit? We know them as love, patience, knowledge, testimony, and so on.[28] In essence, each gift of the Spirit represents an attribute of godliness. Accordingly, each time we acquire a gift of the Spirit, we acquire a potential attribute of godliness. In this regard Orson Pratt taught:

One object [of the Church] *is declared to be "For the perfecting of the Saints." . . . The . . . plan . . . for the accomplishment of this great object, is through the medium of the spiritual gifts. When the supernatural gifts of the Spirit cease, the Saints cease to be perfected, therefore they can have no hopes of obtaining a perfect salvation. . . .*

. . . In every nation and age, where believers exist, there the gifts must exist to perfect them.[29]

No wonder the Lord commands us to "covet earnestly the best gifts" (1 Corinthians 12:31); "seek ye earnestly the best gifts" (D&C 46:8); and to "lay hold upon every good gift" (Moroni 10:30).

President George Q. Cannon spoke of man's shortcomings and the divine solution. Recognizing the link between spiritual gifts and godhood, he fervently pleaded with the Saints to overcome each manifested weakness through the acquisition of a countermanding gift of strength known as the gift of the Spirit. He spoke as follows:

If any of us are imperfect, it is our duty to pray for the gift that will make us perfect. . . . No man ought to say, "Oh, I cannot help this; it is my nature." He is not justified in it, for the reason that God has promised to give strength to correct these things, and to give gifts that will eradicate them. . . . He wants His Saints to be perfected in the truth. For this purpose He gives these gifts, and bestows them upon those who seek after them, in order that they may be a perfect people upon the face of the earth, notwithstanding their many weaknesses, because God has promised to give the gifts that are necessary for their perfection.[30]

What was the Lord's response to Solomon's prayerful request for the gift of an understanding heart? The scriptures record, "The speech pleased the Lord, that Solomon had asked this thing," and then the Lord noted, "Behold, I have done according to thy words: lo, I have given thee a wise and an understanding heart" (1 Kings 3:10, 12).

When was the last time we prayed for a gift of the Spirit that would lift us above our mortal weakness and further our pursuit of godhood? Again and again the Lord has both invited and promised, "Ask, and it shall be given you" (Matthew 7:7).

Why is it so critical to have a correct vision of this divine destiny of godliness of which the scriptures and other witnesses so clearly testify? Because with increased vision comes increased motivation. Elder Bruce R. McConkie wrote, "No doctrine is more basic, no doctrine embraces a greater incentive to personal righteousness . . . as does the wondrous concept that man can be as his Maker."[31] And why not possible? Do not all Christian churches advocate Christlike behavior? Is that not what the Sermon on the Mount is all about? If it is blasphemous to think we can become as God, then at what point is it not blasphemous to become like God—90 percent, 50 percent, 1 percent? Is it more Christian to seek partial godhood than total godhood? Are we invited to walk the path of godhood—to "be ye therefore perfect, *even* as your Father which is in heaven is perfect"—with no possibility of ever reaching the destination?

As we better understand our potential destiny, our level of self-worth and confidence and motivation is greatly heightened. Youth will understand that it is shortsighted at best to take easy classes and easy teachers rather than ones that will stretch them toward godhood. They will catch the vision that it is godhood, not grades, for which they are striving.

And what of our more elderly members? They will understand there is no such thing as a retirement farm, no day when the work is done. Like Victor Hugo, they know their work has only begun. There are yet thousands of books to read and write, paintings to enjoy, music to score, and service to render. They understand the Lord's revelation to the Prophet Joseph: "Whatever principle of intelligence we attain unto in this life, it will rise with us in the resurrection" (D&C 130:18).

What about those of us who feel weaknesses in our life? We can take renewed hope in the words of the Lord to Moroni: "For if they humble themselves before me, and have faith in me, then will I make weak things become strong unto them" (Ether 12:27).

And what about those who believe they have sinned beyond Christ's redeeming grace? They can take comfort in His promise: "Though your sins be as scarlet, they shall be as white as snow" (Isaiah 1:18). Or perhaps there are some who believe their lives are shattered beyond repair. Can they not have renewed hope in these words of the Savior: "[I will] give unto them beauty for ashes" (Isaiah 61:3)? There is no problem, no obstacle to our divine destiny, for which the Savior's Atonement does not have a remedy of superior healing and lifting power. That is why Mormon said, "Ye shall have hope through the atonement of Christ" (Moroni 7:41).

How could we not have increased faith in God and in ourselves if we knew He had planted within our souls the seeds of godhood and endowed us with access to the powers of the Atonement? "*Godhood?*" If not, the critic must answer, "Why not?"

Perhaps we could suggest three answers for the critic's consideration: Maybe man cannot become like God because God does not have the power to create a divine-like offspring. It is beyond his present level of comprehension and intelligence.

"Blasphemous," responds the critic. "He has all knowledge and all power."

Perhaps then He has created a lesser offspring because He does not love us.

"Ridiculous, absurd," is his reply. "For God so loved the world, that he gave his only begotten Son" (John 3:16).

Well, perhaps God has not planted within us the divine spark because He wants to retain godhood for Himself; He is threatened by our progress. He can only retain His superiority by asserting man's inferiority.

"No, no," laments the critic. "Have you ever known a loving, kindly father who didn't want his children to become all that he is and more?"

And so it is with God, our Father.

I testify there are no ordinary people, no ciphers, no zeros—only potential gods and goddesses in our midst. While many witnesses testify of this truth, the most powerful of all are the quiet whisperings of the Spirit that confirm both to my mind and to my heart the grandeur and truth of this glorious doctrine. As Jacob so taught, "The Spirit speaketh the truth and lieth not. Wherefore, it speaketh of things as they really are, and of things as they really will be" (Jacob 4:13).

I pray we will recognize our true identity as literal sons and daughters of God and grasp a vision of our divine destiny as it really may be. I pray we will be grateful to a loving Father and Son who made it so. In the name of Jesus Christ, amen.

NOTES

1. See Acts 17:28–29; Romans 8:16–17; and Hebrews 12:9.

2. Boyd K. Packer, "To Young Women and Men," *Ensign*, May 1989, 54.

3. C. S. Lewis, "The Grand Miracle," *Miracles: A Preliminary Study* (New York: Macmillan, 1978), 122–23; emphasis added.

4. David O. McKay, *Pathways to Happiness* (Salt Lake City: Bookcraft, 1957), xi.

5. While I was serving as a mission president, we discussed at a zone conference man's potential for godhood. In so doing we referred to an oft-cited scripture of the critics, Isaiah 43:10, which states, "Before me there was no God formed, neither shall there be after me." Therefore the critics conclude that if there is no God before or after the Father, then man certainly could not become a god.

As fate would have it, several days thereafter one of our younger missionaries was knocking on a door. A distinguished man invited him in. The missionaries soon learned he was a theological professor at a local university. The man was polite but stated adamantly that Mormon doctrine was incorrect because it taught that a man might become a god, and, after all, the Bible teaches there is no god before or after the Father.

This fine young missionary was not taken back one bit. He simply replied, "Sir, do you know where that scripture is found?"

The man hesitated, "I can't recall exactly, but it is in the Bible."

The young missionary replied, "It is in Isaiah 43:10, but it is also found in Isaiah 44, 45, and 46." He further asked, "Do you recall the context in which it was given?"

The professor could not remember.

"Then," said the young missionary, "let me help you. God was reprimanding the Israelites because they were worshipping graven images and statues made with man's hands. On repeated occasions the Lord declared in these chapters that none of these images or statues, whether formed in the past or in the future, would ever be a god." In essence this young missionary explained that these verses had everything to do with the incapacity of graven images to become gods and absolutely nothing to do with man's capacity to become a god. He invited the professor to learn more about the truth concerning man's potential, but the invitation was declined.

6. The word *perfect* as used in this scripture comes from the Greek word *telios*. Some have suggested this might be translated as

"finished" or "completed," resulting in a connotation other than moral perfection—perhaps meaning a complete or mature Saint. While this might be one interpretation, the scripture does not preclude a reference to moral perfection. In fact, when read in context, this passage seems to require moral perfection. It specifically delineates the type of completeness or perfection to which it is referring when it makes the comparison "*even* as your Father which is in heaven is perfect" (emphasis added). God is not perfect like a mature Saint or in a relative sense. He is absolutely perfect. It is of interest to note that both the King James Version and the New International Version of the Bible translate the word *telios* as "perfect."

7. *JD* 10:5.

8. C. S. Lewis, "Counting the Cost," *Mere Christianity* (New York: Macmillan, 1960), 174–75.

9. Some might contend that some references by early Christian writers to man's potential for godhood were simply alternative phrases for man's immortality, and in some cases this interpretation may be correct, but there are certainly multiple references by the early Christian writers to also evidence that these references to godhood were qualitative, not just quantitative, statements.

10. Irenaeus, *Adversus Haereses* (Irenaeus Against Heresies), book 4, chapter 38, in *The Apostolic Fathers, Justin Martyr, Irenaeus,* vol. 1 of *Ante-Nicene Fathers: The Writings of the Fathers Down to A.D. 325,* ed. Alexander Roberts and James Donaldson (Peabody, Massachusetts: Hendrickson Publishers, 1994), 522.

11. Irenaeus, *Adversus Haereses* (Irenaeus Against Heresies), book 5, chapter 36, in vol. 1, *The Apostolic Fathers,* 567.

12. Clement of Alexandria, *Stromata* (Miscellanies), book 7, chapter 10, in *Fathers of the Second Century: Hermas, Tatian, Athenagoras, Theophilus, and Clement of Alexandria (Entire),* vol. 2 of *Ante-Nicene Fathers,* ed. Alexander Roberts and James Donaldson (Peabody, Massachusetts: Hendrickson Publishers, 1994), 539.

13. Clement of Alexandria, *Paedagogus* (The Instructor), book 3, chapter 1, in vol. 2, *Fathers of the Second Century,* 271; emphasis added.

14. Hippolytus, *Philosophumena* (The Refutation of All Heresies), book 10, chapter 30, in *Fathers of the Third Century: Hippolytus, Cyprian, Caius, Novatian, Appendix*, vol. 5 of *Ante-Nicene Fathers*, ed. Alexander Roberts and James Donaldson (Peabody, Massachusetts: Hendrickson Publishers, 1994), 153; emphasis added.

15. Cyprian, "On the Vanity of Idols," *The Treatises of Cyprian*, 6:15, in vol. 5, *Fathers of the Third Century*, 469.

16. Origen, *Commentary on John*, 2:2, in *The Gospel of Peter, the Diatessaron of Tatian*, vol. 9 of *Ante-Nicene Fathers*, ed. Alexander Roberts and James Donaldson (Peabody, Massachusetts: Hendrickson Publishers, 1994), 323.

17. See Athanasius, *Orationes Contra Arianus* (Four Discourses Against the Arians), 1.39, 3.34, in *St. Athanasius: Select Works and Letters*, vol. 4 of *A Select Library of Nicene and Post-Nicene Fathers of the Christian Church: Second Series*, ed. Philip Schaff and Henry Wace (Grand Rapids, Michigan: Eerdmans, 1978–79), 329, 413; see also Athanasius, *De Incarnatione Verbi Dei* (On the Incarnation), 54.3, in *St. Athanasius*, 65. No doubt Athanasius gained this insight from Irenaeus, who earlier had said: "If the Word has been made man, it is so that men may be made gods" (*The Westminster Dictionary of Christian Theology*, ed. Alan Richardson and John S. Bowden [Philadelphia: Westminster Press, 1983], s.v. "deification," 147; see Irenaeus, *Adversus Haereses* [Irenaeus Against Heresies], book 5, preface, in vol. 1, *The Apostolic Fathers*, 526).

Martin Luther taught this same truth in his Christmas sermon of 1514: "Just as the word of God became flesh, so it is certainly also necessary that the flesh may become word. In other words: God becomes man so that man may become God. . . . He takes what is ours to himself in order to impart what is his to us" (quoted in Jonathan Linman, "Martin Luther: 'Little Christs for the World'; Faith and Sacraments as Means to *Theosis*," in *Partakers of the Divine Nature: The History and Development of Deification in the Christian Traditions*, ed. Michael J. Christensen and Jeffery A. Wittung [Grand Rapids, Michigan: Baker Academic, 2007], 191). Luther further taught: "Aye, through faith we become gods and partakers of the divine nature and name, as Psalm 82:6 says: 'I have said, Ye are gods; and all of you are children of the Most High'" (Martin Luther, as quoted in Linman, "Martin Luther," 198).

18. C. S. Lewis, "Love Thy Neighbor," *The Joyful Christian* (New York: Touchstone, 1996), 197.

19. As related by Arsène Houssaye, "Victor Hugo on Immortality," in Samuel Gordon Lathrop, ed., *Fifty Years and Beyond; or, Gathered Gems for the Aged* (Chicago; New York: Fleming H. Revell, 1881), 325; quoted by Hugh B. Brown in *CR*, April 1967, 50.

20. Shakespeare, *Hamlet*, act 2, scene 2, lines 323–27.

21. Robert Browning, *Rabbi Ben Ezra* (1864), stanza 13; in *The Individual and Human Values*, vol. 1 of *Out of the Best Books: An Anthology of Literature*, ed. Bruce B. Clark and Robert K. Thomas (Salt Lake City: Deseret Book, 1964), 463.

22. Lorenzo Snow, in Eliza R. Snow, *Biography and Family Record of Lorenzo Snow: One of the Twelve Apostles of The Church of Jesus Christ of Latter-day Saints* (Salt Lake City: Deseret News, 1884), 335; emphasis added.

23. See Boyd K. Packer, *Let Not Your Heart Be Troubled* (Salt Lake City: Bookcraft, 1991), 289.

24. "The Gospel of Philip (II, 3)," in *The Nag Hammadi Library: In English*, trans. members of the Coptic Gnostic Library Project of the Institute for Antiquity and Christianity (New York: Harper and Row, 1977), 145.

25. See B. H. Roberts, *The Mormon Doctrine of Deity* (Salt Lake City: Deseret News, 1903), 33–34.

26. Roberts, *The Mormon Doctrine of Deity*, 35.

27. Houssaye, "Victor Hugo on Immortality," *Fifty Years*, 324–25; quoted in Sterling W. Sill, *Thy Kingdom Come* (Salt Lake City: Deseret Book, 1975), 222–23.

28. See 1 Corinthians 12 and 13; Galatians 5:22–23; D&C 46; Moroni 10.

29. Orson Pratt, chapter 4 of "Kingdom of God," *Orson Pratt's Works* (Salt Lake City: Deseret News Press, 1945), 97; emphasis added.

30. George Q. Cannon, "Discourse by President George Q. Cannon," *Millennial Star* 56, no. 17 (23 April 1894): 260–61; emphasis added; quoted in Marvin J. Ashton, *The Measure of Our Hearts* (Salt Lake City: Deseret Book, 1991), 24–25.

31. Bruce R. McConkie, *The Promised Messiah: The First Coming of Christ* (Salt Lake City: Deseret Book, 1978), 133.

Beware the Dragons

Sharon G. Samuelson

Greetings! And welcome to fall semester 2012. This assembly is a wonderful sight, and I always enjoy greeting Brigham Young University students at the beginning of a new school year. You bring your talents, goals, experiences, and perceptions from your homes—some merely a few blocks away from campus and others in faraway places across the globe. Your classmates come from all fifty states, the District of Columbia, six territories, and 106 countries. Your desire to learn in an environment of faith will afford you many opportunities to teach and support each other as you become classmates, roommates, neighbors, leaders, listeners, mentors, and friends. Discover the world and all its wonders from each other. Contribute in as many positive ways as you can during your time here. When you leave, take all you have experienced and go forth into the world prepared to bless others with your acquired spiritual and temporal knowledge.

Sharon G. Samuelson, wife of BYU President Cecil O. Samuelson, delivered this devotional address on 4 September 2012. © Brigham Young University.

One learns about so many varied aspects of life from different cultures and countries as well as their inhabitants. Mankind has always been filled with curiosity concerning unfamiliar peoples and territories. I can recall watching in awe as Neil Armstrong took his first steps on the moon over forty-three years ago. Recently we witnessed a rover landing millions of miles away on Mars—a planet that has continually fueled the imaginations of science-fiction writers as well as serious scientists. Now we await the pictures it will send to earth to show what the Red Planet looks like and possibly find the answer to the question, "Could there be life or some form of intelligence on Mars?"

We are all fascinated by stories about the unknown and the dangers it may hold. Men and women throughout history have sought— often at peril to their lives—to explore mysterious and strange lands and places of which they had little or no information. These individuals would marvel at the use of a GPS, Google Earth, and MapQuest today.

Historically, cartographers used their skills and limited knowledge to produce maps of their time period. These maps were not necessarily very accurate but were archaic prototypes of those we use today. Found among myths and legends are stories of medieval European mapmakers placing the phrase "Here Be Dragons" on the edges or other locations of their maps to indicate unknown, strange, and/or dangerous areas—in other words, the end of the known world. Areas beyond their geographical knowledge contained the warning "Here Be Dragons."

Dragons, sea serpents, and other mythical and frightening creatures were placed on later maps to warn people of areas to be avoided or entered into at their own risk. Sometimes the phrase might be included and written in Latin or English.

Why most often dragons? A dragon is a fearsome creature that appears in folklore in most countries. Haven't you all grown up with stories of brave and courageous knights fighting dragons to save the hapless princesses or dragons prowling the earth destroying villages and cities? I would surmise that some of your childhood nightmares included fire-breathing dragons chasing you through dense forests. Even though you have met timid, reluctant, and huggable dragons, such as Puff in children's literature and movies, the fearful ones are those you probably remember the most and would want to give a wide berth to at all costs.

Today you are making decisions and choosing courses to take on the many maps and pathways presented to you. We read in the scriptures that Isaiah declared, "Woe unto them that call evil good, and good evil; that put darkness for light, and light for darkness; that put bitter for sweet, and sweet for bitter!" (Isaiah 5:20; see also 2 Nephi 15:20). Our society seems to exemplify what is described in this scripture. The paths your lives take today have areas that could be marked by the phrase "Here Be Dragons" as a warning that you should and must avoid them. A firm testimony of the truth of the gospel of Jesus Christ is so necessary to maintain the proper perspectives and withstand the buffetings of the adversary that can and often will bombard you from all directions.

What are some of the "dragons" that can have harmful effects if you venture into their territories of influence? The early explorers often lacked the insight and knowledge about what they would find in the areas marked by dragons, but you young people have knowledge they didn't. You are warned by loved ones as well as by prophets and other leaders concerning what may await you in these lairs. Let me just mention some dragons I believe are tempting forces of destruction for each of you.

The Internet and social and other media can be dragons if they are not used properly. Speaking to a group of BYU–Hawaii students, Elder M. Russell Ballard gave this warning:

> Now some of these tools—like any tool in an unpracticed or undisciplined hand—can be dangerous. The Internet can be used to proclaim the gospel of Jesus Christ and can just as easily be used to market the filth and sleaze of pornography. Computer applications like iTunes can be used to download uplifting and stirring music or the worst kind of antisocial lyrics full of profanity. Social networks on the Web can be used to expand

healthy friendships as easily as they can be used by predators trying to trap the unwary. That is no different from how people choose to use television or movies or even a library. Satan is always quick to exploit the negative power of new inventions, to spoil and degrade, and to neutralize any effect for good. Make sure that the choices you make in the use of new media are choices that expand your mind, increase your opportunities, and feed your soul.[1]

You live in a world of technology and cannot avoid it with all the laptops, iPhones, iPads, iPods, and so forth that you find essential in your lives. I had a friend recently text me that she had just acquired an iPhone and hoped she could figure out how to use it. I sent her a picture of three of our grandchildren playing children's games on their parents' iPhones and iPad. I sent her the message "If these youngsters can do it, you can too." Now when our grandchildren come to visit us, and after we share hellos, hugs, and kisses, they inevitably ask, "May I use your iPhone?" This is not only our world today, but it is also a glimpse into the future in which there will be inventions you cannot now envision. How will you use technology to bless your lives and also avoid the dragons it can represent? That is for you to decide.

There is also the dragon of immorality. President Thomas S. Monson once stated:

You live in a world where moral values have, in great measure, been tossed aside, where sin is flagrantly on display, and where temptations to stray from the strait and narrow path surround you. Many are the voices telling you that you are far too provincial or that there is something wrong with **you** *if you still believe there is such a thing as immoral behavior.*[2]

The teachings and admonitions you have received up to this point in your lives are very clear on the importance of acceptable behavior. Beware of being tempted into a dragon's lair in this area of your life.

In our culture today it seems that the traits of honesty and integrity are often lacking or absent in individuals, governments, politics, businesses, and even athletics. Unfortunately, honor, trustworthiness, and incorruptibility are traits that take a backseat to winning and aspirations of high position and/or wealth. You have the choice to be honest and ethical or not. Remember the thought "Here Be Dragons" when you enter the realm in which choices can lead to a path of dishonesty and a lack of integrity. You have made covenants with your Heavenly Father to be honest. President James E. Faust once taught:

Honesty is a principle, and we have our moral agency to determine how we will apply this principle. We have the agency to make choices, but ultimately we will be accountable for each choice we make. We may deceive others, but there is One we will never deceive. From the Book of Mormon we learn, "The keeper of the gate is the Holy One of Israel; and he employeth no servant there; and there is none other way save it be by the gate; for he cannot be deceived, for the Lord God is his name." [2 Nephi 9:41][3]

My dear friends, be examples of honesty and integrity wherever and in whatever you do. Brigham Young University students are known for being examples of these attributes. Once when my husband had an important decision to make concerning a change in his professional path, he sought the advice of an individual he admired and respected concerning the matter. The counsel received was very short and concise. It was that at all costs he should protect his integrity. Once lost, your integrity and reputation for honesty are very difficult to regain. Steer clear of the dragons that would take them from you.

You are blessed to have the teachings of the gospel to help you shy away from the areas in which dangers and forces of evil can enter and put you in peril of losing your faith and testimony. Sometimes you may think that you can get close to a dragon and escape in time because you are strong enough to fight him when necessary and can easily ignore any temptation he might place before you. Your curiosity and questions about the unknown may lead you to say to yourself, "I can always choose when to stop and turn around. I know I can." Do not be fooled. The adversary is deceptive and will seek to ensnare you with such thoughts.

There is an oft-told story of three men who applied for the job of driving the coaches for a transportation company. The successful applicant would be driving over high, dangerous and precipitous mountain roads. Asked how well he could drive, the first one replied: "I am a good, experienced driver. I can drive so close to the edge of the precipice that the wide metal tire of the vehicle will skirt the edge and never go off."

"That is good driving," said the employer.

The second man boasted, "Oh, I can do better than that. I can drive so accurately that the tire of the vehicle will lap over, half of the tire on the edge of the precipice, and the other half in the air over the edge."

The employer wondered what the third man could offer, and was surprised and pleased to hear, "Well, sir, I can keep just as far away from the edge as possible." It is needless to ask which of the men got the job.[4]

You should be like the third driver. Just as he wisely chose to avoid danger, you should too. Hold on to the iron rod—the teachings of the gospel of Jesus Christ. It is your only way to have sure footings as you make your way on the roadways of life. Releasing your firm grip on the iron rod will surely put you in danger of being entangled in the river of water, the mist of darkness, or the great and spacious building as described by Lehi and Nephi (see 1 Nephi 8). Their dragons, which were not too different from yours in this century, included the temptations of the adversary and the pride, wisdom, and vain imaginations of the world. Do not be fooled and lured by the dragons that will confront you as you make choices and decisions each day. It can be too easy to fall over the edge if you are not diligent in safely shunning it.

If you find that you have indeed fallen over the edge or have become burned by the fires of a dragon, you are blessed with the knowledge that your Savior has given you His gift of the Atonement.

It is a message of love, hope, and mercy. He has provided a way for you to overcome any sins or their consequences. If you have entered an area in which you were warned there were dragons, you do have a way to find the correct path out, and that is God's plan of salvation, which includes repentance and forgiveness. His love for you is boundless and provides a way for you to return to Him.

I have a testimony of the significance of the Atonement and know that the Lord loves each one of you. He desires that you remain unwavering and firm in your testimonies of Him and steadfast and immovable in your choices and behavior. I say this in the name of Jesus Christ, amen.

NOTES

1. M. Russell Ballard, "Sharing the Gospel Using the Internet," *Ensign*, July 2008, 60.

2. Thomas S. Monson, "May You Have Courage," *Ensign*, May 2009, 125; emphasis in original.

3. James E. Faust, "Honesty—A Moral Compass," *Ensign*, November 1996, 42.

4. Spencer W. Kimball, *The Miracle of Forgiveness* (Salt Lake City: Bookcraft, 1969), 217–18.

Character

---◆---

Cecil O. Samuelson

Good morning, brothers and sisters. I appreciate this opportunity to add my welcome to all gathered today as we begin the new fall semester. It is a season of anticipation, planning, excitement, and perhaps even a little trepidation for those adjusting to all that goes on in this special place. We are very glad that you have chosen BYU and are qualified to be here.

At Brigham Young University we must always remember, reflect upon, and recall our fundamental purposes for being at this unique institution. As the semester progresses, all of us will likely be increasingly consumed with the demands and details of our daily tasks, which, at least superficially, are similar to or even much the same as we would encounter at another serious university. If we are not careful, papers, presentations, examinations, and other expectations will crowd out the higher or greater purposes for which BYU was established and the reasons for which we each decided to come and devote our time and energy.

Cecil O. Samuelson was BYU president when this devotional address was delivered on 4 September 2012. © *Intellectual Reserve, Inc.*

Over the years I and many others have spoken at length and in some detail about the Aims of a BYU Education. I hope and expect we will continue to do so. I think virtually everyone seriously committed to BYU and our view of education will be able to recite without difficulty the expected outcomes of the BYU experience, which are that it should be spiritually strengthening, intellectually enlarging, and character building, and then leading to a lifetime of learning and service.

Without apology, I recognize that I have frequently emphasized the spiritually strengthening aspect of our efforts because it is unique in the world of higher education. Likewise, I have taken seriously and publicly the charge from our prophet leaders to make sure our academic and intellectual pursuits are of the highest order and quality. In addition, it is my perception that in our devotional services we are frequently reminded of the responsibilities and opportunities to provide meaningful service now and in the future. I continue to endorse and commend these initiatives and efforts.

Today I wish to focus my remarks on the importance of our individual character and on what we need to do to build and strengthen it as envisioned by the Savior and His duly selected prophet leaders. There are many definitions of character, but one simple idea articulated by someone long ago seems most satisfactory to me: "A man's reputation is the opinion people have of him. His character is what he [or she] really is" (Jack Miner).

I hope in our time together this morning we can think carefully and seriously about what we really are and, more important, what we desire and need to become. I am satisfied that this aim of a BYU education—to build character—cannot be neglected or diminished because all of the aims and the mission of this great university are so intimately related to one another.

While growing up I remember the rather constant counsel from parents, teachers, Church leaders, and others to guard one's reputation. Most of us learned rather early that it was not a good thing to have a bad reputation about anything. While I still think this is good advice, I also believe that character—real character—is more important than just a good reputation. The reason for this assertion is that each of us is in complete control of our actual character while public opinion, slander, and misrepresentation on the part of others may influence one's reputation.

For example, it is not too rare to learn in the media of someone with an apparently stellar reputation who has been found involved in a large variety of unsavory activities that usually demonstrate that the person has taken advantage of another in ways unfair and often illegal. On the other side, there are those like the Prophet Joseph Smith and others even in our day who have impeccable character but suffer regular unfair and untrue assaults on their reputation. Such, for example, might occur during a political campaign.

In a similar vein, I have always liked the observation made in various settings by Elder Neal A. Maxwell that it is better to have character than to be one (see "The Disciple-Scholar," in Henry B. Eyring, ed., *On Becoming a Disciple-Scholar* [Salt Lake City: Bookcraft, 1995], 21; also "Sharing Insights from My Life," BYU devotional address, 12 January 1999). I admit that some of my favorite people are both.

As a young man, I was impressed by the comments often made by President David O. McKay about the importance of good character. Let me share just a couple of examples. First, in answer to the question "What do you consider is the most important purpose of life?" he responded, "To develop a noble character" (quoted in Gregory A. Prince and Wm. Robert Wright, *David O. McKay and the Rise of Modern Mormonism* [Salt Lake City: University of Utah Press, 2005], 11). Second is a statement very close to home as we think about the Aims of a BYU Education. Said he:

Character is the aim of true education; and science, history, and literature are but means used to accomplish this desired end. Character is not the result of chance, but of continuous right thinking and right acting. True education seeks to make men and women not only good mathematicians, proficient linguists, profound scientists, or brilliant literary lights, but also, honest men [and women], with virtue, temperance, and brotherly love. It seeks to make men and women who prize truth, justice, wisdom, benevolence, and self-control as the choicest acquisitions of a successful life. [David O. McKay, quoted in *Rise of Modern Mormonism*, 160]

I believe it fair to say that President McKay felt character building was of equal rank with spiritually strengthening and intellectually enlarging as primary educational goals for both individuals and institutions. From the very beginning this attitude has also prevailed with the administration and faculty of BYU. Karl G. Maeser was known for his deep, unswerving commitment to all three legs of the BYU stool that are now known as our Aims. As was the case then, and so it remains today, our students, staff, and faculty do not arrive as blank pages, and so we must always give great credit to families, preparatory schools, and the Church for the quality of people who come and so readily adopt the Aims of a BYU Education, including the necessity of character building.

One such product of the early Brigham Young Academy was James E. Talmage. He was recognized quickly for his great intellect, spiritual strength, and outstanding character. As he concluded his studies at BYA, he became a member of the faculty and then left for a few years to obtain his graduate education at Lehigh University and Johns Hopkins University before returning to BYA and the Church Educational System. Of course his crowning appointment was to serve as a member of the Quorum of the Twelve Apostles, and his many contributions are widely known and appreciated throughout the Church. *Jesus the Christ* and *The Articles of Faith* are two books that continue to be classics in Church literature and deserve our careful and regular study in our libraries of "best books" (D&C 88:118).

Two accounts of his character (perhaps showing that he also was a character) are found in *The Talmage Story*, the biography written by his son, John. These accounts have been favorites of mine for many years, and some of you are likely familiar with these experiences. I believe they deserve retelling because they not only reveal much about Brother Talmage but also give significant insights into important dimensions of character.

Let me go directly to the experiences as the younger Brother Talmage recorded them. Both occurred when James Talmage was a mature man. The first was shortly after he left the Church Educational System and became president of the University of Utah at the encouragement of the First Presidency. He had obtained a bicycle, which was then the newest fad in transportation during the 1890s. These are his son's words:

James acquired one of the new machines, not as a hobby or physical conditioner but as a practical means of transportation. . . .

Some time after James had achieved reasonable proficiency in handling his machine on standard roads, he showed up at the front door one evening a full hour late for dinner and scarcely recognizable.

May [his wife] nearly went into shock, for her husband was a frightening sight. Battered, bruised, and bleeding profusely, clothes torn in a dozen places and covered with dust and mud, James looked as though he had been caught in a riot, or at least a fight of unusual violence. Neither, it developed, had been the case.

Half a block from the Talmage home a single-plank footbridge crossed the ditch of running water that separated the street from the footpath. Until now, James had dismounted when he reached this point in a homeward journey, and crossed the narrow bridge on foot. Today, he had decided that he had reached the point in his development as a cyclist where he should no longer resort to this prudent maneuver, but rather ride over the bridge in the manner of an accomplished veteran of the two-wheeler.

Having so decided, James approached the bridge resolutely, confident that he would negotiate the tricky passage in a manner to be proud of and to impress neighbors, if any should chance to be watching, with his skill and casual daring. He turned sharply from the road toward the bridge with scarcely any diminution of speed. The result was spectacular, and observers, if any there were, must indeed have been impressed, but in a very different way from that intended. The professor's bicycle went onto the plank at an oblique angle and quickly slid off the side, throwing its rider heavily into the ditch bank.

Dazed, bruised, bleeding, and humiliated, Dr. Talmage was not convinced that the difficult maneuver was beyond his skill. Rather, he was stubbornly determined to prove that he could and would master the difficulty.

For the next hour, [James] might have been observed trundling his bicycle fifty yards or so down the road from the bridge, mounting and riding furiously toward the plank crossing, turning onto it with grim-lipped determination—and plunging off it in a spectacular and bone-shaking crash into the rough ditch bank. Uncounted times this startling performance was repeated, but in the end mind triumphed over matter, willpower over faltering reflexes, and the crossing was successfully made. Not just once, but enough times in succession to convince James that he was capable of performing the feat without mishap at any time he might desire to do so. From then on, he never again dismounted to cross the bridge, albeit he never made the crossing without experiencing deep-seated qualms which he kept carefully concealed from any who might be watching. [John R. Talmage, *The Talmage Story: Life of James E. Talmage— Educator, Scientist, Apostle* (Salt Lake City: Bookcraft, 1972), 138–40]

This is an interesting insight into a man who believed something likely trivial to most people was not only worth doing but worth doing well. This same unfailing determination was demonstrated much later in a more widely recognized sense when Brother Talmage literally lived in the Salt Lake Temple as he wrote his famous and beloved book *Jesus the Christ* at the direction of the First Presidency. His absolute commitment to completing a task he determined to be important, whatever anyone else might think, served him very well throughout his life and, in turn, blessed and continues to bless countless others.

The other account I will share—which most will also likely find amusing—occurred while he was serving as a member of the Quorum of the Twelve. Although usually a strength, his dogged determination and almost complete focus on his work was also a cause for worry on occasion not only for his family but also for the top leadership of the Church. Let me again return to the account recorded by John Talmage:

> In later years, James' long hours of work, unrelieved by periods of recreation, were cause for real concern among family, friends, and associates. President Heber J. Grant [the president of the Church], for one, repeatedly urged Dr. Talmage to take up some form of sport, if only for its therapeutic value. Himself an enthusiastic golfer, President Grant tried to get his friend to try that sport, confident (as are all golfers) that if anyone were once thoroughly exposed to golf he would be captivated by its subtle but powerful attractions.
>
> As President Grant's urgings increased in frequency and intensity, so did Dr. Talmage's demurrers on the grounds of lack of interest and lack of ability to master a complicated skill so late in life. President Grant was certain the skill could be mastered and that interest would automatically follow. Finally a compromise was reached, and a test agreed upon: James would give the game of golf an honest trial, and work at it until he was able to hit a drive which President Grant would rate as satisfactory, "a real golf shot."
>
> "If you hit just one really good drive, nature will do the rest," President Grant assured his pupil-to-be. "You won't be able to resist the game after that."
>
> It was agreed that James would make his own choice after he had acquired the skill to hit the specified shot. If he felt the fascination of the game, as President Grant was certain he would, he would take up golf and play with reasonable regularity. If, after giving the game a fair trial, James still felt no interest, President Grant would cease his efforts to get Dr. Talmage to play.
>
> On an appointed day, the two, accompanied by a number of others of the General Authorities who played golf and who had joined the friendly argument on the side of President Grant, proceeded to Nibley Park for James' first session in what was expected to be a series of lessons.
>
> James removed his coat and was shown how to grip the club and take his stance at the ball. The coordinated movements involved in making a

*golf stroke were carefully explained and then demonstrated by President
Grant and by others. Finally it came James' turn to try it himself.*

*What followed astonished all those who watched, and probably James
himself. Instead of missing the ball completely, or weakly pushing it a few
feet along the grass, James somehow managed to strike the ball cleanly and
with substantial force. It took off in a fine arc and with only a minimum
amount of slice. Some who saw it described it later as "a truly magnificent
drive," which was probably a considerable exaggeration. However, there
was consensus that the ball went close to 200 yards and stayed in the fair-
way. It was a drive that would have gladdened the heart of any golfer short
of the expert class, and it bordered on the phenomenal for a novice.*

*The spectators were momentarily struck dumb, then burst into
enthusiastic applause.*

*"Congratulations," said President Grant, rushing forward, beaming,
with outstretched hand. "That was a fine shot you will remember for the
rest of your life."*

*"You mean **that** was a fully satisfactory golf shot?" James asked,
cautiously.*

"It certainly was!" said President Grant.

"Then I have fulfilled my part of the agreement?"

*"You have—and don't you feel the thrill of excitement? Now you'll be
playing regularly. As a matter of fact, we can go into the clubhouse now
and I will help you select a set of clubs."*

*"Thank you," said James, putting on his coat. "If I have carried out
my part of the agreement, then I shall call on you to live up to yours. You
promised that if I hit a satisfactory drive and did not feel the spontaneous
desire to play, you would stop urging me to do so. Now I should like to get
back to the office, where I have a great deal of work waiting."*

*So far as is known, James never again struck a golf ball, or made the
attempt.* [*The Talmage Story,* 226–28; emphasis in original]

It is very clear that Brother Talmage was always absolutely
supportive and obedient to the prophet on matters of doctrine,
principle, and Church practice or procedure, but he did not consider
his loyalty to the Brethren to extend to their love of golf!

Brother Talmage was his own man, but he was also a man of impeccable character. He decided to do what he considered was really important and deflected those things of lesser or no priority. Perhaps there is a lesson here for us with respect to video games, social media, television, and other activities you might think about.

At BYU we have the good fortune of being surrounded by many impressive examples of people with genuine, sterling character. Might we each do what we must to ensure that our own personal character comes as close as possible to that of the Savior, whom we know to be of perfect character, even the Lord Jesus Christ, of whom I testify, in His sacred name, Jesus Christ, amen.

Stepping-Stones and Stumbling Blocks

Steven E. Snow

During the westward migration, early pioneers encountered landmarks that marked the progress of their journey
west. Prominent rock formations such as Chimney Rock and
Independence Rock are examples of such landmarks.

Such features have special prominence in our own Church history. Rocky Ridge and Rock Creek Hollow have deep meaning
for the handcart pioneers who struggled across the high plains of
Wyoming in early snowstorms that terrible winter of 1856.

Hole-in-the-Rock and Dance Hall Rock bring to mind the
tenacious faith of those called to settle southeastern Utah. Their
expedition stymied by towering cliffs overlooking the Colorado
River, these courageous settlers built a road through a cleft in the
cliff wall, which even today seems to defy possibility.

My remarks today involve other kinds of rocks. I would like to
speak of the stepping-stones and stumbling blocks that define our
own spiritual journey through life.

*Steven E. Snow was a member of the Quorum of the Seventy of The Church
of Jesus Christ of Latter-day Saints when this devotional address was given on
11 September 2012. © Intellectual Reserve, Inc.*

On October 19, 1856, nearly two weeks before the terrible days at Martin's Cove, the Martin Handcart Company faced the prospect of making their last crossing of the Platte River. Extremely low on food and supplies, they also faced the prospect of crossing the icy river during a fast-approaching storm. Because of the weakness of the teams that pulled wagons accompanying the handcart company, all of the sick who were able to walk were required to enter the icy water. Thomas Durham recorded, "All the sick that could walk at all had to get out of the wagons and walk through the river, some of them falling down in the river several times, not being able to stand up in it being so weak" (Thomas Durham journal, 1854–1871, 15).

While the place of crossing was a known location to ford the river, the freezing water was at least waist deep to most of the 200 to 300 souls who waded and swam the river.

Josiah Rogerson recalled the experience years later by writing, "I rolled up my trousers and waded that cold river, six or eight rods wide, slipping betimes off the smooth stones and boulders into deeper water" ("Strong Men, Brave Women and Sturdy Children Crossed the Wilderness Afoot," in *Salt Lake Tribune*, 4 January 1914, n.p.).

Between the last crossing of the Platte River and the arrival of the advance party of rescuers, fifty-six members of the handcart company perished. Many more lost their lives during those horrible days at Martin's Cove as they waited for the main rescue party.

Because of the horrible suffering experienced by the Willie and Martin handcart companies, a few of the survivors lost their faith and left the Church. But to many who suffered, this experience proved to be the refiner's fire.

Forty-eight years later, in a Sunday School class in Cedar City, Utah, class members were offering criticism of the Church and its leaders for permitting the handcart companies to cross the plains so poorly equipped and so late in the season. Francis Webster, now an old man, listened as long as he could and then stood and said the following:

I ask you to stop this criticism for you are discussing a matter you know nothing about. . . . Mistake to send the handcart company out so late in the season? Yes. But I was in that company and my wife was in it. . . . We suffered beyond anything you can imagine and many died of exposure and starvation. But did you ever hear a survivor of that company utter a word of criticism? . . . Every one of us came through with the absolute knowledge that God lives, for we became acquainted with him in our extremities. . . .
Was I sorry that I chose to come by handcart? No. Neither then nor one moment of my life since. The price we paid to become acquainted with God was a privilege to pay, and I am thankful that I was privileged to come to Zion in the Martin Handcart Company. [William R. Palmer, "Pioneers of Southern Utah: VI. Francis Webster," *Instructor*, May 1944, 217–18; see also David O. McKay, "Pioneer Women," *Relief Society Magazine*, January 1948, 8]

How can there be such different responses from individuals who undergo difficult and trying circumstances in this mortal existence? Why do some wander off and become lost? Why are some ashamed and fall away into forbidden paths and become lost? (See 1 Nephi 8:23, 28.) Others, however, like Francis Webster, find their faith strengthened and their devotion increased.

How do we turn adversity into a stepping-stone and not a stumbling block? How can we make a bad experience become a learning experience? Part of the answer lies in perspective. How we choose to lead our lives and how we make faith part of our lives ultimately helps us face the challenges that come to everyone in this earthly existence.

In Hebrews 11:1 we read: "Now faith is the substance of things hoped for, the evidence of things not seen."

The Joseph Smith Translation gives us further insight into this scripture. The Prophet teaches us that faith leads to an assurance. This assurance begins with a belief, or, as Alma described it in the Book of Mormon, a "desire to believe" (Alma 32:27). In order for belief to become assurance, it requires action on our part. Every missionary knows an investigator must take action before obtaining a testimony, even if that investigator has a strong desire to believe. Someone who hears the gospel for the first time must not just believe but must take action for there to be a witness or assurance. For a new investigator this means study, prayer, and attending Church. Only after making commitments and acting upon them does an investigator obtain a testimony of the restored gospel. These actions become a series of stepping-stones leading to a testimony.

The pattern is the same with those of us who have been in the Church for many years. We must continue to step forward on the stepping-stones that will increase our faith. As our study and prayer continue, we accept new callings in the Church that cause us to stretch and grow. We serve others through home or visiting teaching. We prepare for and keep covenants made in the temple. As we continue on this path of learning, serving, and growing, we touch on the stepping-stones that strengthen our faith and ultimately lead us to an assurance or witness of truth.

From this spiritual growth we are then more prepared to face and overcome the adversity that is part of our mortal probation. President Boyd K. Packer has said:

[Today's children] *will see many events transpire in the course of their lifetime. Some of these shall tax their courage and extend their faith. But if they seek prayerfully for help and guidance, they shall be given power over adverse things. Such trials shall not be permitted to stand in the way of their progress, but instead shall act as stepping-stones to greater knowledge.* ["Do Not Fear," *Ensign*, May 2004, 77]

So, in a marvelous way, by using the stepping-stones of faith, prayer, study, and service, we prepare ourselves to overcome the challenges and trials life undoubtedly holds in store.

The scriptures often refer to these challenges and trials as stumbling blocks. In Isaiah we read: "Cast ye up, cast ye up, prepare the way, take up the stumblingblock out of the way of my people" (Isaiah 57:14).

As we contemplate the straight and narrow path that returns to the presence of our Heavenly Father, invariably that path will contain stumbling blocks that can, if ignored, become trials, even crises in our lives. Now, please understand: the trail of life is strewn with stumbling blocks placed there to test us and to try us. Sometimes it seems we are literally stumbling through life as we deal with the challenges and trials of this mortal existence. The stumbling blocks of which I speak are those that we can avoid if we are obedient, plan ahead, and remain vigilant.

My list is only a short one and does not begin to include the many stumbling blocks the adversary has stored in his quarry of sin and misery. The ways he can trip us up are limited only by our imaginations. Nonetheless, here is a list of stumbling blocks you will want to avoid.

First, beware of the stumbling block of pride. While we are proud of you and we hope you take pride in your accomplishments, it is important to not be prideful.

Pride can blind us from danger. If we are caught up in ourselves and our own well-being, we become more susceptible to the enticements of the adversary. Pride prevents us from serving and giving and causes us to become self-centered and demanding. Pride interferes with relationships between husbands and wives, parents and children, friends and loved ones. No one cares to be around a truly selfish person.

Nephi wrote:

And the Gentiles are lifted up in the pride of their eyes, and have stumbled, because of the greatness of their stumbling block, that they have . . . put down the power and miracles of God, and preach up unto themselves their own wisdom and their own learning, that they may get gain and grind upon the face of the poor. [2 Nephi 26:20]

Nephi taught 2,500 years ago that the prideful forget the poor, fail to serve, and only seek gain.

In our time, Elder Neal A. Maxwell wrote:

Meekness helps us to surmount the stumbling blocks so that we are prepared to receive a deeper and wider view. Obviously, Philip had such meekness when he recognized Jesus as the Messiah of whom Moses had spoken. (John 1:45.) Obviously, Paul had the broad view when he described Moses as having, by choice, forgone life in Pharaoh's court for a life of service to Jesus. (Hebrews 11:24–27.) Nevertheless, the stones of stumbling are real. In fact, these offending rocks prove insurmountable unless we have the attribute of meekness. [*Meek and Lowly* (Salt Lake City: Deseret Book, 1987), 76]

Second, be aware of the stumbling blocks of negativity and pessimism. While there are challenges and difficulties we all face, it is important to maintain an eternal perspective. Life is sometimes hard because it is supposed to be. The great plan of happiness provides for a mortal existence in which we can come to learn to overcome hard things. If we tend to focus on only those things in our lives that do not go as we intend, we will miss the marvelous blessings we otherwise would enjoy.

Be optimistic. The glass really is half full. President Gordon B. Hinckley said it best: "Save your fork. The best is yet to come!"

The story is told of a traveler in the Ozarks who passed by a general store. A hound dog was sitting out front howling his head off. The traveler stopped and asked, "Why's that ol' hound dog howling so much?"

The man standing by the store said, "Because he's sitting on a thistle."

The traveler asked, "Well, why doesn't he just sit somewhere else?"

The man answered, "Because he'd rather howl."

Don't howl and whine. Choose to be optimistic. Being optimistic is good for you. Dr. Martin E. F. Seligman, a psychologist from the University of Pennsylvania, did more than a quarter-century of research on this subject. Among his conclusions: Optimistic people are happier, healthier, and more successful than those with a negative outlook on life. Optimism results in less depression, higher achievement, and a stronger immune system.

The gospel of Jesus Christ teaches these same principles. When we say, "It's impossible," the Lord says, "The things which are impossible with men are possible with God" (Luke 18:27).

When we say, "I'm too tired," the Lord says, "I will give you rest" (Matthew 11:28; see also verses 29–30).

When we say, "Nobody really loves me," the Lord says, "I love you" (see John 13:34).

When we say, "I can't do it," the scriptures teach us, "I can do all things through Christ which strengtheneth me" (Philippians 4:13).

When we say, "It's not worth it," the Lord reminds us it will be worth it: "And we know that all things work together for good to them that love God, to them who are the called according to his purpose" (Romans 8:28).

When we say, "I'm not smart enough," the scriptures remind us that God gives us wisdom (see 1 Corinthians 1:30).

When we say, "I can't forgive myself," we are reminded that He does forgive us (see 1 John 1:9).

When we say, "I don't have enough faith," He reminds us in scripture, "God hath dealt to every man the measure of faith" (Romans 12:3).

The gospel of Jesus Christ is the "good news." It is for good reason we often refer to the plan of salvation as the plan of happiness. In spite of the challenges and trials of life, we must look forward with hope. As members of the Church of Jesus Christ, we have within us the hope Peter refers to in the New Testament: "But sanctify the Lord God in your hearts: and be ready always to give an answer to every man that asketh you a reason of the hope that is in you with meekness and fear" (1 Peter 3:15).

So choose to be optimistic. Choose to look on the bright side. As you go about your day's activities, expect the best.

This is perhaps best illustrated by the following anecdote.

A little boy was overheard talking to himself as he strode through his backyard, baseball cap in place and toting ball and bat. "I'm the greatest baseball player in the world," he said proudly.

Then he tossed the ball in the air, swung, and missed. Undaunted, he picked up the ball, threw it into the air, and said to himself, "I'm the greatest player ever!"

He swung at the ball again, and again he missed. He paused a moment to examine the bat and ball carefully. Then once again he threw the ball into the air and said, "I'm the greatest baseball player who ever lived."

He swung the bat hard and again missed the ball. "Wow!" he exclaimed. "What a pitcher!"

Choose to look on the bright side.

Before I move on, let me leave a word of caution and advice. Today's events have focused a great deal of attention on the Church. The Broadway musical *The Book of Mormon* and especially the Republican primary campaign have created what *Newsweek* magazine has coined "the Mormon moment." This unprecedented attention on our Church and our beliefs has also had a downside. Never before have we received such scrutiny. Some of our beliefs, which to some may seem peculiar, have been ridiculed by a few. The ability to transmit information through the Internet and the media is unparalleled. The words of a bitter or disrespectful critic are magnified many times through the use of social media. This was a platform not available to our critics just a generation ago.

Our responsibility is to appropriately filter this rhetoric and attempt to understand why such things are said. For some critics, their crude utterances are made for political gain or entertainment. But please understand, the followers of the Savior have always been in the minority and often in history have suffered more than the simple sting of unkind and cruel words.

For a few, these verbal assaults on our religion have created a crisis of faith. They wonder if such things are true and, if so, how this could possibly be. Our history as a Church is a rich tapestry woven with beautiful threads of sacrifice, service, and devotion. The stories of early Church leaders and members are motivating and compelling. Their accounts of the remarkable and the mundane inspire us to accomplish difficult tasks. But, like all of us, they were not perfect. It is important to view the entire tapestry of our history and not just individual threads that may seem to strike us as too peculiar if not viewed in the context of time and place.

I can testify that the more I learn of our Church, its doctrine, and its history, the stronger my testimony becomes. To achieve a proper balance, I encourage you to continue to pay attention to your spiritual well-being by praying, studying the scriptures, and keeping the commandments. Touch upon the stepping-stones that will build your faith. Then, when the winds of discontent blow, you will be protected from the storm.

While there are many stumbling blocks along our path, I will conclude with just one more. Stumbling blocks are often cleverly disguised. Let the advancements of today's modern technology be a springboard in your lives, not a stumbling block. Never have we been blessed with so many tools to perform the purposes of the Church. Social media can be an effective way to share the gospel. The new Family Search has revolutionized our ability to do family history. Instantaneous communication is achieved around the world with members and non-members alike with tools like LDS.org and Mormon.com.

Unlike even a generation ago, it is impossible for you to successfully complete your studies without ownership or easy access to a computer. Cell phones and texting have changed the way we communicate. Based on its membership, Facebook is now the third-largest country in the world. The Internet, with its use of social media, has contributed to revolutions in the Middle East. It is an absolutely fascinating time, and we are just seeing the beginning of this information revolution.

Unfortunately, all of this technology does have a downside. We should not be surprised Satan has figured that out so quickly. Resist the urge to spend too much time on video games, and avoid violent and inappropriate games altogether. This kind of entertainment can become strangely addictive. In ten years we do not want to find some of you bright young people living in your parents' basements playing video games and surviving on Cheetos. Life does have greater meaning than the latest and greatest game.

Avoid online pornography at all costs. There has been a clarion call from our prophets on this matter, and you will be wise to pay careful heed to their warnings. To not do so can lead you to become ensnared in your own personal hell. Stay away from pornography.

While I appreciate the economy and efficiency of texting, don't give up on personal face-to-face communication. You don't need a battery, you don't need a signal, and you don't need a handheld device. You will be surprised what can come from a real, live conversation. Let's embrace the technology, but let's not forget the importance of personal communication. Try it. You might like it.

Well, brothers and sisters, there are many other stumbling blocks that will undoubtedly threaten your future progress. Some of you will need to maneuver around them or laboriously push them from your path. You will avoid many stumbling blocks by living wise, obedient lives and by paying attention to the stepping-stones that will build your faith. But the challenges and trials will nonetheless come. When they do, if you have prepared they will become seasons of learning in your life. Rather than times of setback and loss of faith, these experiences themselves will become stepping-stones of spiritual strength for your eternal progression.

Be meek, humble, strong, and wise. The future is bright, and you, the rising generation, will determine our course. It has ever been so. Being with you today convinces me that our future has never been in better hands.

I wish you the Lord's choicest blessings as you continue forward on this magnificent journey known as mortality. This I say in the name of Jesus Christ, amen.

Optimism and Joy in the Gospel of Jesus Christ

T. Jeffrey Wilks

I have imagined for the past two months what this would feel like, and my imagination doesn't begin to compare with reality. I stand before you in amazement and awe at who you are. I can't help but look at you and think of the days when I was a student at BYU. In fact, it was twenty years ago this month that I first met my dear sweetheart, Melinda.

I had been home from my mission for about four months, and I was attending my BYU ward for the first time. As the opening hymn began, I looked up at the person leading the music (as I should, right?), and she was the most beautiful young woman I had ever seen. That evening I saw her again at ward prayer, but I was way too scared to go up and introduce myself to her. Fortunately for me, Heavenly Father took care of that little detail by inspiring our bishop to assign us to the same family home evening group. They announced the new groups that very evening. We flirted for a few

T. Jeffrey Wilks was a professor in the BYU School of Accountancy when this devotional address was given on 25 September 2012. © Brigham Young University.

months before we finally started dating, and we were married the following June.

Since that time, every significant blessing that has come into my life I have shared with my best friend and eternal companion. I love every moment we get to spend together, and there are never enough of those moments!

Well, I know many of you are hoping for similar experiences sometime this year or maybe in the next few years. In fact, the beginning of a new semester or school year is filled with all kinds of hope and excitement for many different reasons. But, sadly, by the time we get to the end of the semester, with final projects and final exams, a lot of that hope has just plain vanished. I still remember the nightmare I used to have at the end of each semester in which I dreamed that I had forgotten to attend one of my classes for the entire semester. It was horrible! Funny enough, I had that same nightmare years later when I first became a professor, but that time I dreamed that I had forgotten to teach one of my classes for the entire semester. I just knew I was going to be fired.

What is it that happens between the beginning and end of a semester that drains us of our hope and excitement? Why is it so hard sometimes to be positive and upbeat? Well, I don't know all the answers, to be sure, but I was accused at a very young age of being too positive, too upbeat, and even naïve sometimes about life. I can't remember exactly when those accusations began, but when I was sixteen years old, an inspired patriarch placed his hands on my head and said the following:

Jeffrey, this is a good world. You will be positive in your thinking. You will think positively, you will speak positively, you will act positively. With all the negativism in the world today, you will sort it out and you will be happy because you will do the things which are pleasant and worthwhile.

I have seen this blessing come true countless times in my life, and I can testify that this world is a good world. There is so much to be happy about in this world. And when we fail to see the world around us for the wonder and joy that it has to offer and when we refuse to see the hope and the light everywhere around us, we are not seeing the world as it truly is. We are not seeing the world as Heavenly Father sees it.

I have to tell you about something that happened to me just last Tuesday afternoon when I was writing down this very idea of needing to see the good in the world. I stood up for a moment to take a break from my writing, and I looked out my fifth-floor window in the Tanner Building, which has a perfect view of the walkway that rises from Helaman Halls up past the Tanner Building. As I looked down, I saw a young man in a wheelchair who was wheeling himself up that long, steep walkway. And just as I started thinking about how much effort that must take, I saw another young man just slightly ahead on the walkway turn around and notice this young man in the wheelchair. I don't know if they knew each other or if they were complete strangers, but in that moment the one young man walked quickly around and behind the wheelchair, and he pushed the other young man up the rest of that long walkway. In fact, he practically ran as he pushed him up that hill.

This simple moment in time—1:30 p.m. on a Tuesday afternoon—witnessed to me again how much light and goodness are everywhere around us if we will just look. So today I want to share with you five lessons that I have learned in my life about how to be positive in a world filled with negativism. Each of these lessons is based on experiences I have had as a husband and a father. Now, I am fully aware that Elder Steven E. Snow spoke two weeks ago from this very pulpit about optimism, but as much as I tried to steer my thoughts to another topic, the Spirit kept bringing me back to this one. So I can only trust that Heavenly Father thinks we could use a double dose of this particular topic—and perhaps even more at times.

RIGHTEOUSNESS DOES NOT MEAN PERFECTION

The first lesson about being positive in a negative world is that righteousness does not mean perfection. A humorous experience

from when our family was younger taught me this lesson. I say
humorous—it is now, but it wasn't then. When my oldest daughter,
Ashlyn, was almost ten years old, we were camping at Palisade State
Park in the mountains above Manti, Utah. With my kids so young,
they weren't a whole lot of help setting up our massive tent with
those flexible, fiberglass poles that you have to push through the
sleeves in the tent and then try to lift all at once to get the tent to
rise. While my wife was unloading our vehicle and setting up the
rest of camp, I was struggling to get the tent off the ground on my
own. Then, suddenly, with one of my pushes on the poles to get the
tent to rise, I snapped the pole. I am ashamed to admit that at that
moment I let slip from my mouth a colorful word that I dare not
repeat here. Oh, it wasn't a horrible word, but my daughter clearly
recognized it to be a swear word. I continued on in my battle to set
up the tent and eventually succeeded with the help of some duct tape
and other makeshift efforts to get the tent up.

Unbeknownst to me at the time was the conversation that
followed between my daughter and my wife. Melinda later told me
that my daughter approached her with a troubled look on her face
and said, "Mommy, I thought Daddy was perfect."

My immediate reaction was to feel horribly ashamed for having
crushed my daughter's perception of me. My second reaction was to
think, "Wow, I managed to get my daughter all the way to ten years
old convinced that I was perfect!"

But all humor aside, I felt pretty bad for what I had done. And
then came the teaching moment. My dear wife said simply to my
daughter, "Daddy is not perfect, but he is righteous." It was one of
those moments when I was profoundly reminded that I had married
an angel, for who else could have come up with such a simple teaching in that moment?

Perfection can sometimes be the enemy of righteousness. When
we get so caught up worrying about being perfect—about being a
perfect spouse, a perfect son or daughter, a perfect parent, a perfect teacher, or a perfect friend—it's easy to become discouraged,
because none of us will ever be perfect in this life. Even though

our Savior commanded us to be perfect like Him and our Heavenly Father (see 3 Nephi 12:48), He has no expectation that we will accomplish that in this life. It's impossible. Remember, He taught Moroni that He gives unto us weaknesses so that we can be humble. And if we humble ourselves, His grace is sufficient to make those weaknesses become strengths (see Ether 12:27) but not perfections.

KEEP TRYING ANYWAY

The second lesson about being positive in a negative world is that life really is hard sometimes, and you've got to keep trying anyway. My son Tanner taught me this one day when he was eight years old. Tanner had decided to switch from skiing to snowboarding that year, and it was his first day on the slopes. Now, those of you who have snowboarded know that the first day is typically horrible and painful. In fact, most instructors say that you can't make a decision about whether you like snowboarding unless you've tried it three days, because most people still hate it after the first two days. I still haven't tried snowboarding, and I'm not sure I ever will. But if I do, I will have to rent one of those giant sumo costumes with all the extra padding just to protect myself from all the falls! I haven't done it yet.

Well, Tanner's first day on the snowboard proved to be like most first days—very painful and frustrating. Initially he started down the mountain with his older brother, who knew how to snowboard. But every two or three feet Tanner would fall down, catching a toe and landing on his stomach or sliding his heels too far and landing on his rear end. He was crying and yelling the entire way down the mountain! He got to the point where he didn't even want to try standing up anymore; instead he just slid down the mountain on his bum. And after what seemed like two hours, he finally reached the bottom of the hill. He was exhausted physically and mentally. He was in pain, and I was very tired of dealing with my cranky son.

Fortunately we were staying in a lodge at the base of the resort, so we decided to take a break. I figured Tanner was done for the day anyway. So, after a good lunch and sitting around a bit, I was surprised when Tanner said he wanted to go out again. I asked him if he remembered what the morning had been like. But he said he wanted to try again anyway. I don't know what happened, but that afternoon his attitude was completely different. He kept getting up every time he fell, and by the end of the day he could butter down the hill pretty well. And today he can carve a line down any hill his older brothers can ride.

Life sometimes really is hard, and all we can do is get back up on the snowboard, even though we know perfectly well how easily that snowboard can slide out from under us. Some of you know what it's like to struggle with addictions, and getting back up after falling off those particular snowboards can be very frustrating. You may wonder if you will ever be able to overcome that addiction. When you feel this frustration—the physical and mental anguish from trying and failing and trying again—please remember this wonderful counsel recorded in Doctrine and Covenants 123:

> *Therefore, dearly beloved brethren, let us cheerfully do all things that lie in our power; and then may we stand still, with the utmost assurance, to see the salvation of God, and for his arm to be revealed.* [D&C 123:17]

When you're sitting there wondering if you can stand back up again, remember that sometimes the test is not about overcoming but about whether we will keep trying no matter how hard things seem to be. Never give up. Do all things cheerfully that lie in your power, and then stand still with the assurance that God will help you.

KEEP YOUR FOCUS ON HEAVENLY FATHER

The third lesson about being positive in a negative world is to keep your eyes focused on Heavenly Father. When my youngest daughter, Maleah, was nearly two years old, she was playing in the cultural hall of our church in New Canaan, Connecticut. You know those doors that open up under the stage where we store chairs and tables? Maleah was playing with those doors and accidentally closed both doors at the same time really hard with her thumb in between them. She just cried and cried, our sweet little girl. When she finally settled down, we noticed that her thumb was stuck in a bent position. After visiting the emergency room and then a hand specialist a week later, we learned that Maleah had what is called congenital trigger thumb, in which the tendon that flexes the thumb is stuck in its sheath, holding the thumb in a bent position. We waited a few weeks at the doctor's recommendation to see if it might heal itself. And when that didn't happen, we scheduled a time for surgery.

Early that morning at the hospital, our little girl—who normally bounces off walls, wrestles with her older brothers, and generally causes havoc wherever she goes—was pretty subdued. We dressed her in the cutest yellow hospital clothes they had and found some fluffy red socks to keep her feet warm. Then the nurse took us down to a closet where Maleah chose a cute pillow-soft teddy bear to take with her into the surgery prep room. Then I put on some scrubs, we said good-bye to Melinda, and I carried my sweet little girl down the hall to the prep room, her arms tightly around my neck.

I was so worried that she might not let go and that she would be scared to go into surgery. But when we arrived in the room, I gave her a big hug and then gently laid her down on the table onto a nice warm blanket. The nurse put another warm blanket over Maleah while I talked with her, kept her calm, and placed her little teddy bear—which she snuggled closely—under her arm. I looked at her right in the eyes, and she looked at me while I explained that the doctor was going to put a mask over her face and that she was going to fall asleep. While holding my hand and looking into my eyes, she watched the doctor place the mask over her mouth and nose. Shortly after, I whispered to her that I loved her, and I watched her little lips inside the mask speak the words "I love you too." Then her little lips started to quiver, and she closed her eyes to sleep. My sweet little girl who bounces off walls had calmly gone into surgery listening to my voice and looking deeply into my eyes. It was one of the most sacred experiences of my entire life.

From this and many other experiences as a father and as a bishop, I have learned how deeply Heavenly Father loves each one of us. He is always nearby when we are going through tough times, but it's up to us whether we will look into His eyes and listen to His voice. We look into His eyes and we listen to His voice when we immerse ourselves in the scriptures and we converse with Him in daily, meaningful prayer. I testify to you that by keeping our focus on Him and listening to His voice, we will see the goodness and wonder that surrounds us, even in the most difficult of circumstances.

HEAVENLY FATHER'S APPROVAL MATTERS MOST

The fourth lesson about being positive in a negative world is that Heavenly Father's approval is the only approval that matters. I was reminded of this lesson this past spring when I took my boys to a place called Snogression—an indoor practice facility in Salt Lake City for skiers and snowboarders. It has trampolines everywhere and a massive foam pit so that skiers and snowboarders can practice their tricks without having to worry about landing perfectly. The coolest feature of this facility is the practice ramp. A person stands up at the top, holds onto a bar, and, when ready, clicks a button. The bar pulls them down the ramp, accelerating them into the jump so they can go flying out into the foam pit. This foam pit is pretty huge too—it's about fifty by fifty feet. It's an enormous place. You're not going to get hurt, but you'll have a hard time getting out of it. It's really deep.

Dallin, my thirteen-year-old son, was the most excited to go to this facility. He wants to be a professional free skier someday, and he could probably spend every day at Snogression and never get bored. But on this first day he was a little bit timid. He'd probably be the first to tell you that he was worried about looking foolish to all the other cool kids who were there. Their approval mattered a lot to him. As a result, he hadn't tried anything really hard during the whole session. Then, on his last chance of the day, I yelled up to him from by the foam pit (where I was filming) that he should try a backflip. I knew he could do it because I'd seen him do much more difficult tricks on our trampoline, but I wasn't sure he'd have enough courage to try with so many others watching him. Well, watch and listen carefully to this video clip to see what happened next. [A video of Dallin doing a backflip was shown.]

What you see here is Dallin jumping up and down, trying his best to relax and loosen up. Then he grabbed the bar and hit the button. I couldn't believe my eyes as Dallin completed a near perfect backflip. Everyone there was cheering with excitement—and no one louder than me. Dallin floated around on cloud nine for the rest of the day.

Why do we care so much about the approval of others? Why do we "aspire to the honors of men" (D&C 121:35) and forget that Heavenly Father's approval is all that matters in the end? When we allow our decisions to be influenced by the approval of others, we put ourselves at the mercy of fickle mobs, ever-changing fashions, and the devil's whirlwinds. If instead we seek our Heavenly Father's approval only, we build our foundation upon a rock that cannot be moved (see Helaman 5:12). And I can think of nothing that will bring us more stability and optimism than building our foundation upon the rock of our Redeemer.

When we got home from our trip to Snogression, we took out the video camera and watched Dallin's flip forward and backward, in fast and slow motion. And we listened as well. It was then that I realized what I nut I had been when Dallin threw that trick. I was a little embarrassed at first, but later I thought to myself, "This has to be how Heavenly Father feels when we stop worrying about what others think of us and try to use the talents He has given us." I think He is just as excited in celebrating our accomplishments as I was with Dallin's jump. I testify to you that Heavenly Father and Jesus Christ are our greatest cheerleaders and fan section. We will feel more joy and hope in this world when we do our best to seek and obtain Their approval.

LOOK FOR AND REMEMBER THE JOY IN OUR LIVES

The last lesson about being positive in a negative world is that we must look for and remember the joy in our lives. When was the last time you felt true joy? How long ago was it? Do you remember the details of that moment, and do you think of it often? As my final story today, I want to tell you about a time this summer when I felt true joy, brimming over and impossible to contain.

My son Tate is fifteen years old, and he practices the piano about three to four hours per day on school days and closer to six hours per day during the summer. This past spring he set a goal to play with the Utah Symphony in their Salute to Youth Concert, which is held each fall. It is a statewide competition that draws some of the best young pianists each year. Tate spent countless hours practicing and refining a fifteen-minute Chopin concerto and eventually submitted his best recording to the judges in late June in hopes that he would be selected to play in the final round of the competition later that summer. The finalists were to be announced the morning of July 20, which happened to be the day that our youth would be pulling handcarts up Rocky Ridge in Wyoming.

Time went by slowly, and we prayed as a family every day that Tate would make it to the final round of the competition. Eventually the youth trek began, and Tate seemed to forget the impending announcement amidst the excitement of pulling a handcart in the 95-degree Wyoming sun, crossing rivers, square dancing, and singing songs with his handcart brothers at the tops of their lungs.

On that Friday morning, soon after we sent our handcart company off toward Rocky Ridge, I received an unexpected text message from Melinda out in the middle of nowhere in Wyoming. Tate had been selected to play in that final round of the competition. I couldn't wipe the smile from my face, and I couldn't prevent the tears that came with it. That has to be one of the greatest emotions in the world—tears and smiling at the same time. I still remember the sweetness of how that moment felt and how I couldn't wait until noon, when I would be able to tell Tate personally. Here's what I recorded in my pioneer journal that evening about the events of that day:

*Because I was taking lunches to the trekkers today, I got to catch up to
Tate after he hiked Rocky Ridge. He looked so good coming into the break
area, so strong and pure. After he had eaten [lunch], I asked him to come
talk with me. I walked with him just a little ways from everyone so we
could be alone, and I asked him if he was ready to hear the decision. He
looked [very] concerned, and he said he wasn't sure he wanted to know
because he didn't want to ruin the rest of his trek. I just looked at him
in the eye, and I said, "You won't be disappointed." His look registered
complete disbelief at what he had just heard. So I clarified, "Tate, you get
to play in the final round of the competition." His face was an expression
of pure joy, and he couldn't contain it. He reached out to me and hugged
me like he has never hugged me before. He was in tears with joy. He even
picked me up and swung me around, he was so excited. He walked off a
little ways and just looked over the plains. He couldn't contain all that joy.
He was so adorable to watch with his friends as they found out. Tate just
kept smiling and crying. I experienced true joy for those precious minutes.*

All of the stories I have shared with you today came from my
personal journal. I have learned from my own experience that I
feel greater joy and optimism in my life when I am keeping a daily
journal. Now, I know that keeping a journal is an overwhelming
challenge for most people. As one of my friends told me, he doesn't
like keeping a journal because he writes too much about each day,
and that ends up taking too long, and eventually he stops again.
So, I have a recommendation for you to help you with this fifth and
final lesson.

In October 2007 President Henry B. Eyring told of how he kept
a journal for years by asking himself a single question every day. He
said:

*I wrote down a few lines every day for years. I never missed a day no
matter how tired I was or how early I would have to start the next day.
Before I would write, I would ponder this question: "Have I seen the hand
of God reaching out to touch us or our children or our family today?" As
I kept at it, something began to happen. As I would cast my mind over the*

day, I would see evidence of what God had done for one of us that I had not recognized in the busy moments of the day. As that happened, and it happened often, I realized that trying to remember had allowed God to show me what He had done. ["O Remember, Remember," *Ensign,* November 2007, 67]

This final lesson is perhaps the most important lesson of them all. To look for joy in our lives we need only look for the ways in which God's hand has touched us or our family or our friends that day. Sometimes He touches us through tender mercies. Other times He touches us with wonderful humor. And frequently we will see His hand in our lives by the way in which He prompts us to serve someone that day or to lift someone else who is struggling. We don't have to write lengthy, mundane journal entries about our days. Instead, we can simply write one or two lines in which we identify the hand of God in our lives that day. As we do this, we will see more clearly how blessed our lives really are. We will be filled with gratitude and optimism. We will see the world more in the way our Heavenly Father sees the world. We will see the world as it really is and be filled with joy and hope.

CONCLUSION

I testify to you that this world is a good world and that Heavenly Father sees it that way. He is a God of hope, of joy, of excitement, of enthusiasm, and of optimism. With all the negativism in the world, we can sort it out and see the world as Heavenly Father sees it. Let us not confuse righteousness with perfection. Let us get back up every time we fall. Let us keep our focus on Heavenly Father and listen to His voice. Let us seek His approval and not the approval of the world. And let us look for and remember the joy and the touch of God's hand in our lives every day. After all, the gospel is good news. The Savior has overcome the world, and He has prepared the way for us to do the same. That we may we feel the optimism and joy of His gospel every day of our lives is my prayer, in the name of Jesus Christ, amen.

A Grateful Heart

———◆———

Ray L. Huntington

G ratitude unlocks the fullness of life. It turns what we have into enough, and more. It turns denial into acceptance, chaos to order, confusion to clarity. It can turn a meal into a feast, a house into a home, a stranger into a friend. . . . Gratitude makes sense of our past, brings peace for today, and creates a vision for tomorrow.[1]

President Samuelson, members of the administration, students, and faculty, I appreciate the opportunity of being with you today. I am especially grateful to have my wife, Sandra, and my family with me today as well.

In the latter part of the 19th century, Johnson Oatman Jr., a Methodist preacher, penned the following words, which we know as the hymn "Count Your Blessings." I quote from the second verse:

Are you ever burdened with a load of care?
Does the cross seem heavy you are called to bear?

Ray L. Huntington was a professor in the BYU Department of Ancient Scripture when this devotional was given on 2 October 2012. © Brigham Young University.

Count your many blessings; ev'ry doubt will fly,
And you will be singing as the days go by.[2]

I know those words are familiar, and I believe you accept them at face value: Counting our blessings and being grateful for them has a positive impact—not just upon our lives but upon the lives of those to whom we show our gratitude. Remember what Mark Twain said: "I can live for two months on a good compliment."[3]

THE STUDY OF GRATITUDE

It now appears that some psychologists have arrived at the same conclusion. Being mindfully grateful for our blessings and expressing gratitude has a strong correlation with increasing our personal happiness and well-being. For example, Dr. Robert Emmons, a professor at the University of California, Davis, and one of the leading scholars in the scientific study of gratitude, said the following:

It is possible that psychology has ignored gratitude because it appears, on the surface, to be a very obvious emotion, lacking in interesting complications: we receive a gift—from friends, from family, from God—and then we feel pleasurably grateful. But while the emotion seemed simplistic even to me as I began my research, I soon discovered that gratitude is a deeper, more complex phenomenon that plays a critical role in human happiness. Gratitude is literally one of the few things that can measurably change people's lives.[4]

Dr. Emmons and his colleagues found scientific proof that people who practice gratitude through activities such as keeping a gratitude journal are more loving, forgiving, and optimistic about the future. They exercise more frequently, report fewer illnesses, and generally feel better about their lives.[5]

For example, in a ten-week study Dr. Emmons randomly assigned participants into one of three groups. One group of participants was encouraged to briefly record five things they were grateful for each week; a second group was asked to describe five hassles or negative events that had happened to them each week;

and the third group was simply asked to list five events, but they were not told to emphasize the positive or the negative. Before each participant wrote about their blessings or hassles, they completed a daily journal in which they rated their moods, their physical health, and their overall well-being. The moods they rated included feelings like distress, excitement, sadness, stress, and happiness, while their physical health included ratings such as headaches, sore muscles, stomach pain, nausea, coughing, sore throat, and poor appetite. The participants also rated how they felt about their lives, selecting from descriptions ranging from terrible to delighted.

The results of the ten-week study are impressive for the gratitude group. The gratitude participants felt better about their lives and were more optimistic about the future than people in the other two groups. The gratitude group also reported fewer health concerns, like headaches, and spent significantly more time exercising than people in the other two groups. According to the scale Dr. Emmons used to calculate well-being, the people in the gratitude group were a full 25 percent happier than the participants in the hassles or neutral groups.[6]

In subsequent studies Dr. Emmons also reported that people who regularly kept a gratitude journal and were in the habit of recognizing and expressing gratitude for their blessings reported feeling closer and more connected to people, had better relationships, were more likely to help others, felt less lonely, felt less depressed, slept better, and were more pleasant to be around.[7]

Another psychologist, Dr. Jeffrey Froh, summarized the practice of gratitude in this way:

As gratitude involves wanting what one has rather than having what one wants, instilling a sense of gratitude may help people appreciate the gifts of the moment and experience freedom from past regrets and future anxieties.[8]

Indeed, over the past decade there has been a growing body of scientific literature linking the practice of consistent or "chronic" gratitude with a host of positive outcomes for our lives. Said one researcher, "The practice of gratitude is incompatible with negative emotions and may actually diminish or deter such feelings as anger, bitterness, and greed."[9] It is little wonder, then, that both ancient and modern philosophers recognized the value of gratitude—from the Roman philosopher Cicero, who stated that gratitude is "not only the greatest of virtues, but the parent of all the others"[10] to David Steindl-Rast, a Benedictine monk who penned these beautiful words: "The root of joy is gratefulness. . . . It is not joy that makes us grateful; it is gratitude that makes us joyful."[11]

GOD'S CONSTITUTION OF GRATITUDE

I appreciate the academic contribution to our understanding of gratitude and its impact on our well-being. I also know that the scriptures and the words of prophets and apostles, both ancient and modern, teach us a great deal about gratitude and the need to cultivate a grateful heart. Through studying "the doctrine of gratitude" we can be instructed and motivated to develop a "gratitude attitude" in our lives. Remember Mormon's commentary regarding Alma's mission to the Zoramites:

> And now, as the preaching of the word had a great tendency to lead the people to do that which was just—yea, it had had more powerful effect upon the minds of the people than the sword, or anything else, which had happened unto them—therefore Alma thought it was expedient that they should try the virtue of the word of God.[12]

What, then, is the virtue of the word of God as it relates to gratitude? Given our time today, I would like to look at three scriptures (and a few supportive passages) that I believe form a central part of what I would like to call "God's Constitution of Gratitude."

Rendering Our Heartfelt Thanksgiving

My first scripture: Psalm 24:1–2:

The earth is the Lord's, and the fulness thereof; the world, and they that dwell therein.

For he hath founded it upon the seas, and established it upon the floods.

In a similar statement, the Psalmist also wrote, "The heavens are thine, the earth also is thine: as for the world and the fulness thereof, thou hast founded them."[13]

The earth and all of its creations—everything—belong to God. He has ownership and blesses us with His possessions—even the gift of life. Yet, I sometimes feel a sense of entitlement and find myself thinking about what I created, what I purchased, and what I own: property, car, food, clothing, and my health. But, in reality, brothers and sisters, I have created nothing; I own nothing. As the Psalmist proclaimed, the rightful owner is Heavenly Father—He who graciously bestows His creations (including the air I breathe) for me to use in the short season I am here in mortality. That kind of heavenly, divine benevolence deserves our highest gratitude and praise!

King Benjamin clearly understood this principle of God's ownership and our indebtedness to Him, as he so beautifully explained in the Book of Mormon:

And now, in the first place, he hath created you, and granted unto you your lives, for which ye are indebted unto him.

And secondly, he doth require that ye should do as he hath commanded you; for which if ye do, he doth immediately bless you; and therefore he hath paid you. And ye are still indebted unto him, and are, and will be, forever and ever; therefore, of what have ye to boast?

And now I ask, can ye say aught of yourselves? I answer you, Nay. Ye cannot say that ye are even as much as the dust of the earth; yet ye were created of the dust of the earth; but behold, it belongeth to him who created you.[14]

King Benjamin also said (and I'm paraphrasing) that if we were to muster up all of the thanks and praise we could possibly give, that would still be insufficient, given the multitude of blessings we receive from God.[15] King Benjamin was not saying, "Well, you can't possibly thank God for what He has given you, so why even try?" On the contrary, I believe he was saying that we ought to do our very best in thanking God and rendering our heartfelt thanksgiving to Him every day of our lives. In relation to this, I like what President Joseph F. Smith said:

The grateful man sees so much in the world to be thankful for, and with him the good outweighs the evil. Love overpowers jealousy, and light drives darkness out of his life. Pride destroys our gratitude and sets up selfishness in its place. How much happier we are in the presence of a grateful and loving soul, and how careful we should be to cultivate, through the medium of a prayerful life, a thankful attitude toward God and man![16]

Grateful People Are Happier People

My second scripture: Doctrine and Covenants 59:7, 21:

Thou shalt thank the Lord thy God in all things. . . .

And in nothing doth man offend God, or against none is his wrath kindled, save those who confess not his hand in all things, and obey not his commandments.

Does God need our thankful hearts and praise? Is Heavenly Father dependent upon our gratitude? Do our thankful prayers make God holier, wiser, or more omniscient? Absolutely not. Why, then, is it a commandment to be thankful in all things and acknowledge God's hand in our lives? I believe Joseph Smith gave us the answer to that question when he stated:

As God has designed our happiness—and the happiness of all His creatures, He never has—He never will institute an ordinance or give a commandment to His people that is not calculated in its nature to promote that happiness which He has designed.[17]

In short, we are commanded to thank God in all things because it promotes our happiness and well-being. Grateful people are happier people. If that were not the case, God would not command us to express our thanks to Him and to others. He loves us and desires our happiness, and He knows that expressions of gratitude to Him and to those around us will bring positive changes to our lives. As our Father, that pleases Him.

President Thomas S. Monson understands the connection between gratitude and happiness and often speaks about this topic. In a recent conference address he stated, "Sincerely giving thanks not only helps us recognize our blessings, but it also unlocks the doors of heaven and helps us feel God's love."[18] President Monson also said that "to express gratitude is gracious and honorable, to enact gratitude is generous and noble, but to live with gratitude ever in our hearts is to touch heaven."[19] I love President Monson's choice of words: Gratitude "unlocks the doors of heaven" and "to live with gratitude ever in our hearts is to touch heaven." As I have tried to live with a more grateful heart, I have felt the divine, experienced God's love, and been humbled.

I have also witnessed and felt gratitude's heavenly touch through other people, like an elderly Catholic nun my wife and I met in the city of Bethlehem. From 2007 to 2009 my wife and I had the privilege of working and teaching at the BYU Jerusalem Center. During that time we met a host of wonderful people (Christians, Muslims, and Jews) who influenced our lives in profound ways. On one occasion we were invited by one of the Jerusalem Center service couples—who oversaw the Church's humanitarian program in the Holy Land—to visit an orphanage in Bethlehem. The purpose of their visit was to determine needs and the appropriate assistance from the Church.

The orphanage was located in a residential neighborhood in Bethlehem near the Church of the Nativity. As we entered the building, the first sounds I heard were those of little children. We passed several rooms filled with small beds and noticed newborn infants lying in cribs and small children playing with one another.

I also noticed a shortage of adult staff compared with the number of children I could see.

Our meeting was with the director of the orphanage—one of the most impressive people I have met in my Middle East travels: a diminutive, elderly, Catholic nun from France. Though small in stature, she was large in heart and spirit. As we visited with her we learned about the history of the orphanage, the number of children cared for, and the challenges of feeding and clothing so many precious children. There was no doubt the orphanage had its challenges. I noticed, however, that as she described the needs of the children and the problem of the shortage of staff and materials, there was not one word of complaint. Her speech was often punctuated with "Thanks be to God; thanks be to God."

After the humanitarian couple had assessed needs, they asked this little nun if the orphanage could use supplies like powdered milk, newborn kits, and other necessities for older children. She excitedly replied, "Anything will help us; anything will help us." As arrangements were being made for shipping and delivery of the needed goods, she sat quietly in front of us with hands clasped, as though she were in the act of praying, and repeated the words "thank you, thank you, thank you." Her gratitude was real and heartfelt. Her expressions of thankfulness touched me deeply, and I often think of this experience when I want to relive a moment when I saw gratitude's divine nature. Her example of a grateful heart amplified the words of the Psalmist when he declared, "O give thanks unto the Lord; for he is good: for his mercy endureth for ever."[20]

Counting Your Blessings—Even in Adversity

My third scripture: 1 Thessalonians 5:16–18:

Rejoice evermore.

Pray without ceasing.

In every thing give thanks: for this is the will of God in Christ Jesus concerning you.

Do you wonder what God would like you to be doing every day? The Apostle Paul declared that it is to rejoice, to pray, and to give thanks in everything. Paul's writings are filled with admonitions to be grateful, to give thanks, and to live in thankfulness. His counsel encouraging us to be more thankful is especially inspiring when you stop to consider that he was a Church leader who was scourged (receiving thirty-nine lashes); beaten with rods; left for dead after being stoned by his countrymen; shipwrecked three times—spending one night and a day in the water; bitten by a deadly snake; betrayed by those he thought were his friends; and falsely imprisoned and who suffered weariness, hunger, thirst, and cold and was in peril of robbers.[21] And I've been depressed over losing two football games!

I believe Paul's statement that we should "in every thing give thanks" is his counsel to recognize our blessings and practice gratitude in the worst of times—even in adversity. Yet you and I know that finding and counting our blessings during challenging times can be difficult. As someone once said, "The hardest arithmetic to master is that which enables us to count our blessings."[22] The gratitude math can sometimes be difficult when life assaults us with unexpected hardships and trials. Life's challenges—some serious, some less so—are common to all of us. In those challenging times when there does not seem to be much to be grateful for, President Monson has wisely counseled us:

Our realization of what is most important in life goes hand in hand with gratitude for our blessings.

Said one well-known author: "Both abundance and lack [of abundance] exist simultaneously in our lives, as parallel realities. It is always our conscious choice which secret garden we will tend . . . when we choose not to focus on what is missing from our lives but are grateful for the abundance that's present—love, health, family, friends, work, the joys of nature, and personal pursuits that bring us [happiness]—the wasteland of illusion falls away and we experience heaven on earth."[23]

Studies have shown that focusing on the negative in times of adversity—using derogatory or critical words as we talk to ourselves or others—can darken our mood and, much like a virus, infect the moods of those we interact with. Consciously choosing to fill our minds with thoughts of our blessings and feeling appreciation for those blessings can change the way we feel and brighten our spirits during difficult times. Even spending a few minutes thinking about our blessings—even numbering them—as we walk from class to class can add a little sunshine and encouragement to our lives. It's so simple, yet so powerful.

INCREASING OUR GRATITUDE

What, then, are some of the ways we can recognize our blessings, increase our thankfulness, and practice gratitude? Briefly, I would to like to suggest five:

1. Try Keeping a Gratitude Journal

Think of three to five blessings you have experienced throughout the day or the week and record them in a gratitude journal. Look for blessings from the mundane to the magnificent. Before writing in his gratitude journal, President Henry B. Eyring pondered the following question: "Have I seen the hand of God reaching out to touch us or our children or our family today?"[24] As he faithfully kept his gratitude journal, President Eyring said:

Something began to happen. As I would cast my mind over the day, I would see evidence of what God had done for one of us that I had not recognized in the busy moments of the day. As that happened, and it happened often, I realized that trying to remember had allowed God to show me what He had done.[25]

Remember, looking for our blessings will help us focus on what we have rather than on what we do not have. As the Greek philosopher Epictetus reminded us, "He is a wise man who does not grieve for the things which he has not, but rejoices for those which he has."[26]

2. *Add More Thank-Yous to Your Vocabulary*

Saying "thank you" to someone brightens your day by affirming your positive feelings. It also lifts the spirits of those who are deserving of your thankfulness.

3. *Take Time to Write Thank-You Notes and Letters of Appreciation to People Who Have Blessed Your Life*

John Kralik, an attorney with a struggling law practice and personal family problems, determined to reverse the cycle of negative thinking through writing and sending one thank-you note each day of the year—365 thank-you notes in total. His note-writing endeavor taught him a valuable lesson: blessings can be easily overlooked unless we are consciously thinking about them each day.[27] To that end, note writing helps us identify, remember, and express our blessings.

4. *Live in the Present Moment and Try to Give Thanks for Small Blessings Encountered Every Day of Your Life*

As busy students, it is easy to get caught up in the tomorrow: next week's exam, next week's project, the paper due next Tuesday, the upcoming holidays. And while it's healthy to plan and prepare for future events, if you are too consumed with the tomorrows, there is a chance that you will miss something small and wonderful that is happening to you in the present moment. David Steindl-Rast posed this question: "Are we thankful or are we grateful? . . . Could it be that the mystic gratefulness in the depth of every human heart sings with 'a still, small voice,' and is easily drowned out by the noise we endure and the noise we make?"[28] Sometimes living in the future can produce just enough noise to miss the still, small voice of gratitude we could find in the present moment.

A short illustration: A few weeks ago I was waiting in the Chicago O'Hare Airport for a connecting flight to Salt Lake City with two of my colleagues: Blake Boatright and Vance Theodore. As we were seated near our gate, reading and relaxing before the last leg of our journey, I was interrupted by a rather enthusiastic black Labrador dog sniffing around my briefcase and other belongings I had on the floor. A police officer was standing nearby, and I immediately recognized the dog as a "sniffer" dog looking for drugs or the residue of explosive materials. While the dog moved rapidly from person to person, sniffing purses and carry-ons, it returned to my briefcase for a second check. After a few sniffs and what seemed like 100 wags of its tail, the dog and the police officer disappeared. A short time later, a second sniffer dog stopped by our gate to check things out as well.

Now, I could have dismissed the experience and continued to focus on my reading or think about needed preparations for the following week in school. Instead, my mind turned to the present moment, and I began to think about the two dogs and their training. They were there to make sure everything was in good order. They were there to ensure my safety and the safety of others who would be flying that day. After contemplating this, I quietly expressed thanks to Heavenly Father for trainers and dogs with wildly wagging tails who were there to bless my life. As mundane as that might sound to you, it was an enriching feeling—one that I have thought of frequently. Look for blessings in the now or the present moments of your life.

5. Thoughtful Prayer

Prayer awakens our grateful heart. Forgetfulness is an obstacle to being grateful while "awareness is a precondition" to having a grateful heart.[29] Our personal prayers provide us with sacred time to ponder our blessings and express gratitude to Heavenly Father. As we thank Him daily, our gratitude should be centered on God's greatest gift to us: the gift of His Beloved Son, who ransomed us through the shedding of His blood.

Brothers and sisters, gratitude is a heavenly, spiritual gift and a spiritual force in our lives. May we have hearts that can feel, ears that can hear, and eyes that can see our blessings and live in continual gratitude toward God and those around us is my prayer, in the name of Jesus Christ, amen.

NOTES

1. Melody Beattie, *The Language of Letting Go: Daily Meditations on Codependency* (Center City, Minnesota: Hazelden, 1990), 218.

2. Johnson Oatman Jr., "Count Your Blessings," *Hymns*, 2002, no. 241.

3. Quoted in Albert Bigelow Paine, *Mark Twain: A Biography: The Personal and Literary Life of Samuel Langhorne Clemens*, vol. 3 (New York: Harper and Brothers, 1912), 1334.

4. Robert A. Emmons, *Thanks! How Practicing Gratitude Can Make You Happier* (Boston: Houghton Mifflin, 2007), 2.

5. See Emmons, *Thanks!* 11.

6. See Emmons, *Thanks!* 27–30.

7. See Emmons, *Thanks!* 44.

8. Jeffrey J. Froh, Robert A. Emmons, Noel A. Card, Giacomo Bono, and Jennifer A. Wilson, "Gratitude and the Reduced Costs of Materialism in Adolescents," *Journal of Happiness Studies* 12, no. 2 (April 2011), 300.

9. Sonja Lyubomirsky, *The How of Happiness: A Scientific Approach to Getting the Life You Want* (New York: Penguin Press, 2008), 95.

10. Marcus Tullius Cicero, *Pro Plancio*, 54 B.C.; quoted in Joseph B. Wirthlin, "Live in Thanksgiving Daily," 31 October 2000, BYU devotional address.

11. David Steindl-Rast, *Gratefulness, the Heart of Prayer: An Approach to Life in Fullness* (Ramsey, New Jersey: Paulist Press, 1984), 204.

12. Alma 31:5.

13. Psalm 89:11.

14. Mosiah 2:23–25.

15. See Mosiah 2:20–21.

16. *GD*, 263.

17. *Teachings*, 256.

18. Thomas S. Monson, "The Divine Gift of Gratitude," *Ensign*, November 2010, 87.

19. Monson, "The Divine Gift," 90.

20. Psalm 106:1.

21. See 2 Corinthians 11:24–27.

22. Eric Hoffer, reflection 172 in *Reflections on the Human Condition* (New York: Harper and Row, 1973), 94.

23. Thomas S. Monson, "Finding Joy in the Journey," *Ensign*, November 2008, 86; quoting Sarah Ban Breathnach, *The Simple Abundance Journal of Gratitude* (New York: Warner Books, 1996), 83; quoted in John Cook, comp., *The Book of Positive Quotations*, 2nd ed. (Minneapolis: Fairview Press, 2007), 342.

24. Henry B. Eyring, "O Remember, Remember," *Ensign*, November 2007, 67.

25. Eyring, "O Remember," 67.

26. *The Discourses of Epictetus; with the Encheiridion and Fragments*, trans. George Long (London: George Bell and Sons, 1888), 429; quoted in Monson, "The Divine Gift," 88.

27. See John Kralik, *365 Thank-Yous: The Year a Simple Act of Daily Gratitude Changed My Life* (New York: Hyperion, 2010).

28. David Steindl-Rast, "Are You Thankful or Are You Grateful?"; gratefulness.org/readings/dsr_areyou.htm. The original essay commissioned by Beliefnet in November 2000 for Thanksgiving was titled "Life Is a Gift"; see page 3 of beliefnet.com/Wellness/2000/11/Life-Is-A-Gift.aspx?p=1.

29. Emmons, *Thanks!* 199.

Faith to Forgive Grievous Harms: Accepting the Atonement as Restitution

James R. Rasband

G ood morning. I must say I never imagined myself at this podium. But I have imagined myself on this playing floor—and *imagined* is the right word. I've wondered what it would have been like to be Danny Ainge, who, during my freshman year at BYU, went coast-to-coast in the closing seconds of a Sweet Sixteen game against Notre Dame and scored over Orlando Woolridge. I've dreamed what it would be like to drain a three from just inside half-court, like Jimmer Fredette did against Utah. Unfortunately, my actual skill set wasn't a match for such imagined heroics. I'm quite sure it's not a match for this podium either. Still, I consider it a great honor to have this opportunity to speak to you this morning.

I love this university. I love the cool, crisp air of a late fall football game and the soft, golden light that falls on Y Mountain and Rock Canyon just before sunset. I even love wandering the stacks in the Harold B. Lee Library. BYU has had a great impact on my life.

James R. Rasband was dean of the BYU Law School when this devotional address was given on 23 October 2012. © *Brigham Young University.*

My first experiences at BYU were in the late 1960s. Each summer my mother, my brother, and I came to BYU from our home in Pebble Beach, California, for spring or summer term so that my mom could work on completing her degree. We lived in Heritage Halls, or, to be more precise, we lived in what is now called "Classic Heritage" when it was almost new Heritage.

My mother ended up completing her English degree, and our home was forever enriched by what she learned at BYU. I mention my mom's education at BYU partly because important parts of my thinking on today's topic are derived from her thinking and writing on this topic.[1]

THE DOCTRINE OF FORGIVENESS

The title of my remarks is "Faith to Forgive Grievous Harms: Accepting the Atonement as Restitution." Now, to some, any talk from a lawyer that focuses on forgiveness may seem odd. Don't lawyers depend upon a lack of forgiveness to function? In lawyerspeak, is a talk on the necessity of forgiveness an admission against interest?

I am convinced that practicing law with civility and integrity is a noble endeavor and fully compatible with a forgiving heart, and I'll have a bit more to say about this later. Indeed, before you become too critical of lawyers, listen to the words of my good friend Jim Gordon: "It is true that some lawyers are dishonest, arrogant, greedy, venal, amoral, ruthless buckets of toxic slime. On the other hand, it is unfair to judge the *entire* profession by a few hundred thousand bad apples."[2] Such quips can be a bit tough for those of us who are attorneys, but how much worse can it get, given the number of us whose parents, when we decided to go to law school, made sure to scrape off their car the "Ask me about my children" bumper sticker?[3]

Turning to the concept of forgiveness, let me start with a familiar scripture. Matthew 18:21–22 reads:

Then came Peter to him, and said, Lord, how oft shall my brother sin against me, and I forgive him? till seven times?

Jesus saith unto him, I say not unto thee, Until seven times: but, Until seventy times seven.

Have you or a family member or a friend ever been terribly hurt by someone and found it difficult to forgive even once, let alone "until seventy times seven"? In such cases, do we say to ourselves, "The Lord can't really mean that I should forgive that sort of sin or abuse"?

Yet it seems clear that the Lord really does mean it. Our very salvation depends upon us being willing to forgive others. As Christ taught:

For if ye forgive men their trespasses, your heavenly Father will also forgive you:

But if ye forgive not men their trespasses, neither will your Father forgive your trespasses. [Matthew 6:14–15]

That our own forgiveness should be conditioned on forgiving others can be a hard doctrine, particularly if the sin against us is horribly wrong and out of all proportion to any harm we've ever committed. Even harder, the Lord has indicated in modern revelation that "he that forgiveth not his brother his trespasses standeth condemned before the Lord; for there remaineth in him the greater sin" (D&C 64:9). This is a very strong statement: if we refuse to forgive, there remaineth in us the greater sin. How can this be? As I hope to explain, our salvation is conditioned on forgiving others because when we refuse to forgive, what we are really saying is that we reject, or don't quite trust, the Atonement. And it is our acceptance of the Atonement that ultimately saves us.

Why is it that we sometimes have trouble accepting the Atonement as recompense for the harms we suffer at others' hands? My experience is that we can sometimes forget that the Atonement has two sides. Usually, when we think about the Atonement we focus on how mercy can satisfy the demands that justice would impose upon us.[4] We are typically quicker to accept the idea that when we sin and make mistakes the Atonement is available to pay our debts.

Forgiveness requires us to consider the other side of the Atonement—a side that we don't think about as often but that is equally critical. That side is the Atonement's power to satisfy our demands of justice against others, to fulfill our rights to restitution and being made whole. We often don't quite see how the Atonement satisfies our own demands for justice. Yet it does so. It heals us not only from the guilt we suffer when we sin, but it also heals us from the sins and hurts of others.

THE ANALOGY OF THE FORGIVING LANDLORD

To help explain the two sides of the Atonement, let me try a rather homely analogy. Like most analogies and metaphors, it is not perfect in all respects. I hope, though, that it can aid understanding.

Suppose I find myself in a home built for me by a very generous landlord. It is a nice home. He encourages me to maintain and improve the home and gives me a number of instructions for making the home a nice place to live.

Over the years I sometimes improve the home, but other times, through my negligence, I make it worse. One time I flood the home when I fail to set the faucets to drip during a freeze. Another time my kitchen catches fire because I fail to turn off a burner on the stove. A couple of times I lose my temper and put my fist through a wall.

In each instance the landlord forgives me and encourages me to pay a little closer attention to my home and to his instructions for making the home a joyful place to live. He does not charge me for the damage caused by my mistakes. Instead, sometimes he is patient while I figure out how to fix things on my own; sometimes he sends someone over to fix the problem; and sometimes I wake up and things are fixed in ways I don't quite understand.

This same landlord happens to have a son who is quite wayward. The son is always up to no good, and I don't particularly like or respect him. One night the landlord's son, as a prank, sets fire to the shed attached to the back of my house. The fire gets out of control, and the entire house burns down. I lose the home. I lose all of my possessions, including some particularly valuable possessions that I can't replace, such as photos and heirlooms.

I'm angry and distraught. I want the no-good son to pay. I want him to fix things and to make me whole. A part of me knows he can't really make it better. He may not have the resources to rebuild the house, and, even if he could rebuild the house, he can't retrieve the photos and heirlooms. And that makes me even angrier.

As I sit in anger, the landlord comes to visit me. He reminds me that he has promised to take care of me. He promises me that he is willing to rebuild my house. In fact, he says that he will do more than that: he will replace my house with a castle and then give me all that he himself has. He says that this might take a while, but he promises it will happen.

"What's the catch?" I say.

"Here are the conditions," he says. "First, you need to put your faith in me and trust that I really will build you that castle and restore all that you have lost. Second, you need to continue to work on implementing the instructions I gave you about keeping up your house. Finally, you need to forgive my arsonist son, just as I have forgiven you all these many years."

That sounds easy enough and seems like an obviously great deal, but why might it be hard for the tenant to accept the landlord's offer? Or, to move away from the analogy, why is it sometimes so hard for us to forgive others? Let me suggest some reasons:

First, we are probably angry. We want the arsonist to pay. But if we harbor this sort of anger, we may spend so much time pursuing the person who burned down our house that we don't get around to rebuilding our house. As someone once said: "Resentment is like taking poison and hoping the other person dies."[5]

It might also be hard to forgive because we can't quite believe that the landlord will fulfill his promise. He's never failed us when we've messed up the house before, but what about this time? Besides, it is usually easier for us to believe that the Lord will forgive our mistakes. This time it is someone else's mistake.

Trust can be particularly difficult if the rebuilding project will take time. We want things fixed now, not later. Trust may also be hard in the case of losses and hurts that do not seem easily fixable. Perhaps the landlord can rebuild the home, but can he really replace the photos and heirlooms? What if we lost a child in the fire? Can he really take away that pain?

My testimony is that the Atonement really can make us completely whole, even for those things that seem like they can't be fixed or repaired. As Isaiah foretold of the Savior: "The Lord hath anointed me to preach good tidings unto the meek; he hath sent me to bind up the brokenhearted, to proclaim liberty to the captives, . . . to comfort all that mourn; . . . to give unto them beauty for ashes, the oil of joy for mourning" (Isaiah 61:1–3).

I recognize that this doctrine—that the Atonement can heal us from the hurts of others—is well established.[6] Yet, in my experience, it remains difficult to trust and accept that the Atonement serves this purpose. My hope is that I can add to what has previously been said on this topic and help remove some barriers to forgiveness by offering some reasons why we should trust the Lord's promise.

THE ATONEMENT FULFILLS THE MOSAIC LAW'S RESTITUTION REQUIREMENT

I turn first to the Mosaic law and to an insight I owe to my mother.[7] Remember that Paul taught that the Mosaic law "was our schoolmaster to bring us unto Christ" (Galatians 3:24). Remember also Christ's statement to His disciples in the Sermon on the Mount:

> *Think not that I am come to destroy the law, or the prophets: I am not come to destroy, but to fulfil.*
>
> *For verily I say unto you, Till heaven and earth pass, one jot or one tittle shall in no wise pass from the law, till all be fulfilled.* [Matthew 5:17–18]

Think about Christ's statement for a minute. Christ was comforting His faithful disciples—those who loved and revered the law of Moses. He was making sure they knew that His plan was to fulfill all the terms of the Mosaic law. But what exactly were those terms that He would fulfill?

Our answer to this question typically focuses on the portion of the Mosaic law that addressed Israel's obligation to make sacrifices.[8] We tend to emphasize the Savior's admonition that "your sacrifices and your burnt offerings shall be done away" and that instead we should "offer for a sacrifice . . . a broken heart and a contrite spirit" (3 Nephi 9:19–20). Our usual focus on the law of sacrifice is again on ourselves—what sacrifices we need to offer up to access the power of the Atonement and heal our feelings of guilt and remorse.

But the law of sacrifice was just one component of the Mosaic law. The Mosaic law also included dietary laws and criminal laws—remember the *lex talionis* of an eye for an eye and a tooth for a tooth.[9] It also included family law and various civil laws that we today might recognize as tort or contract law.

Isn't it plausible that when the Savior said He came to fulfill the law, He was talking about more than just the law of sacrifice? Shouldn't we take Him at His word that "one jot or one tittle shall in no wise pass from the law, till all be fulfilled"? Although I am not an expert on the Mosaic law and surely do not understand exactly how Christ fulfilled the law in all its dimensions, let me suggest that the Atonement did, in fact, answer other demands of the Mosaic law.

Specifically, I want to focus on the civil law component of the Mosaic law and its requirement that restitution be made to persons harmed by the wrongful actions of another. I do so because the restitution requirement is so important to understanding the doctrine of forgiveness. Exodus 21 and 22 set forth several such restitution requirements. Consider two of many examples: If a person caused a fire to break out so that "the standing corn, or the field, be consumed therewith; he that kindled the fire" was required to "make restitution" (Exodus 22:6). Similarly, if someone caused his livestock to graze in the field or vineyard of another, he was obligated to "make restitution" out "of the best of his own field, and of the best of his own vineyard" (Exodus 22:5).

This concept of restitution remains a key part of our law today. Under tort law, which is just another word for personal injury law, courts can award damages to persons injured by the negligence of another; similarly, under contract law, damages may be awarded to those harmed by a breach of contract. In the criminal context, many states allow crime victims and their families to prepare victim impact statements that describe the way in which they have been harmed.

The basic point is that, just like current law, the Mosaic law was not designed only to punish the wrongdoer. The Mosaic law also existed to protect, compensate, and make whole those harmed by others, whether intentionally or negligently. If Christ came to fulfill all the terms of the law, this part of the Mosaic law should also be fulfilled by the Atonement.

If the Mosaic law schools us that Christ intended to make full restitution for the harms we suffer, it does not indicate how that could happen. Just as it is difficult to understand exactly how the Atonement satisfies the demands of justice for our sins, it is challenging to grasp how the Atonement works to make restitution to us for the sins of others. As is the case with most such "how" questions in the gospel, we must ultimately fall back on our faith and trust the Lord that His promises are true even if the mechanism is uncertain. But as an aid to our faith, let me suggest a couple of ways in which the Atonement can be understood as making restitution.

First, even for something as horrible as losing a child because of another's sin, the Atonement ensures significant restitution through the Resurrection. We are promised that "every thing shall be restored to its perfect frame" (Alma 11:44). In addition, just like the wealthy landlord in my analogy promised not only that he would build the tenant a castle but also give the tenant all that he had, in scripture after scripture the Lord promises us all that He has.

D&C 88:107 states: "And then shall the angels be crowned with the glory of his might, and the saints shall be filled with his glory, and receive their inheritance and be made equal with him."

D&C 84:37–38 provides: "He that receiveth me receiveth my Father; And he that receiveth my Father receiveth my Father's kingdom; therefore all that my Father hath shall be given unto him." If we can inherit all the Father has and if all will be restored to its perfect frame, is there a reason we should insist that the person who hurt us pay us back? Hasn't justice been satisfied?

FORGIVENESS: MAXIMIZING FAITH RATHER THAN MINIMIZING HARM

It is critical to understand that forgiving others is not just a practical virtue. It is a profound act of faith in the Atonement and the promise that the Savior's sacrifice repays not just our debts to others but also the debts of others to us.

In our live-and-let-live society, we may believe that being forgiving is just etiquette and good manners. It is not. We may think that forgiveness requires us to let mercy rob justice. It does not. Forgiveness does not require us to give up our right to restitution. It simply requires that we look to a different source. The nonjudgmental worldly phrases "don't worry about it" and "it's no big deal" are not illustrations of the doctrine of forgiveness. On the contrary, when a person sins against us, it can be a very big deal.[10] The point is that the Atonement is very big compensation that can take care of very big harms. Forgiveness doesn't mean minimizing the sin; it means maximizing our faith in the Atonement.

My greatest concern is that if we wrongly believe forgiveness requires us to minimize the harms we suffer, this mistaken belief will be a barrier to developing a forgiving heart. It is okay to recognize how grave a sin is and to demand our right to justice—if our recognition triggers gratitude for the Atonement. Indeed, the greater the sin against us—the greater the harm we suffer—the more we should value the Atonement. Consider Christ's parable of the two debtors from Luke 7:41–43:

> *There was a certain creditor which had two debtors: the one owed five hundred pence, and the other fifty.*

*And when they had nothing to pay, he frankly forgave them both. Tell
me therefore, which of them will love him most?*

*Simon answered and said, I suppose that he, to whom he forgave most.
And he said unto him, Thou hast rightly judged.*

If Simon is correct that the greater sinner will love the Lord
even more, doesn't the same reasoning suggest that our love for the
Savior will increase when He pays a particularly large debt owed to
us? There is little value in claiming that a wrong against us is slight.
Instead, if we give the wrong its full weight, we are better able to
give the Lord a full measure of gratitude for making us whole.[11] And
when we understand that the Lord promises us restitution, we can
recognize that our anger at our victimizer is ultimately unnecessary.
This in turn helps free us to love our enemy as the Savior commanded (see Matthew 5:43–44).

In sum, the principle of forgiveness does not require that we
give up our right to justice or that we give up our right to restitution. Christ answers the demands of the law for our sins and for the
sins of others. We just have to be willing to accept that He has the
power to do so.

FORGIVENESS AND THE LAWYER

Now, let me return briefly to the subject I raised at the beginning of my remarks. Specifically, some may still be wondering
whether focusing on the commandment of forgiveness is an admission against interest for a lawyer. To place the question squarely,
does the commandment that we forgive all men mean that litigation
and lawsuits are inherently wrong? I believe the answer to this question is no. But it is an important question that every lawyer must ask
herself and that every client should also confront. Indeed, it is often
a question with which those who have been grievously harmed must
wrestle.

One of the best explorations of this issue is contained in a
book by Elder Dallin H. Oaks entitled *The Lord's Way*. Elder Oaks
begins by rejecting what he describes as two "extreme" views: first,

that a Christian should "never use courts to resolve disputes," and second, that there are "no religious restraints on participating in litigation."[12]

As an aside, isn't it interesting how such tough questions often cannot be reduced to easy all-or-nothing answers? I hope it is not just the lawyer in me, but I have always found it simultaneously comforting and stressful that the restored gospel frequently requires us to wrestle with understanding principles in apparent tension. Thus, both faith and works are necessary for salvation; both faith and reason are the work of this university; both the body and the spirit constitute the soul of man; both personal inspiration and priesthood authority are important to understanding God's will. Whereas the world often suggests that the answer must be either/or, the restored gospel finds a way to say both/and. It seems that a core principle of the restored gospel is that we must learn by our experience to understand, obey, and navigate eternal truths that may appear to be in some tension. Perhaps, more accurately, we are expected to embrace both sides of such apparently opposing principles.

Although one might be able to categorize some lawsuits as clearly inbounds or out of bounds, Elder Oaks, unsurprisingly, largely eschews categorization and instead focuses on principles or preconditions that should govern whether to file a lawsuit. For example, he emphasizes that we must begin by forgiving our adversary and removing revenge as a motive.[13] We should then pursue settlement as a manifestation of the principle articulated by the Savior in Matthew 18:15: "If thy brother shall trespass against thee, go and tell him his fault between thee and him alone: if he shall hear thee, thou hast gained thy brother."[14] Elder Oaks also identifies another precondition—that a litigant should consider the impact a lawsuit will have on others. Again, this is simply a manifestation of the Savior's teaching of the Golden Rule: "All things whatsoever ye would that men should do to you, do ye even so to them" (Matthew 7:12).[15]

Today let me suggest one additional set of criteria by which the conduct of a lawyer should be judged. Those criteria come from section 121 of the Doctrine and Covenants and its teachings on exercising power in the priesthood. Now, I recognize that a license to practice law is quite different from holding the priesthood of God. Passing the bar doesn't give someone the authority to act in God's name, although critics may occasionally wonder if that's what some lawyers believe.

Still, if one stops and thinks about it, a legal education and a license to practice law are instruments of power. The power flows not just, or even primarily, from the state's exclusive license to give legal advice but also from the refined critical- and analytical-thinking skills and problem-solving skills that cause others to look to lawyers for help with their most vexing problems.

If, as lawyers, we have power, the question is how we should use it, or, for non-lawyers, how you should expect your lawyer to use his or her power. In that regard, let me paraphrase a few familiar verses from section 121:

The [power of a lawyer] *cannot be controlled nor handled only upon the principles of righteousness.*

That [a license to practice] *may be conferred upon us, it is true; but when we undertake to cover our sins, or to gratify our pride, our vain ambition, or to exercise control or dominion or compulsion upon the souls of the children of men, in any degree of unrighteousness, . . . Amen to . . . the authority of that* [lawyer]. . . .

No power or influence can or ought to be maintained by virtue of [a lawyer's status], *only by persuasion, by long-suffering, by gentleness and meekness, and by love unfeigned;*

By kindness, and pure knowledge, which shall greatly enlarge the soul without hypocrisy, and without guile. [D&C 121:36–37, 41–42]

Much more could be said on this topic, but today I simply want to emphasize that if lawyers use their power and authority consistent with the principles of section 121 and if clients, who may have been victimized, likewise adhere to these eternal yet challenging standards, litigation need not stand in opposition to the principle of forgiveness.

ACCEPTING BOTH SIDES OF THE ATONEMENT

As I finish, let me return to the heart of my message, which is the Savior's promise in Matthew that He will "forgive us our debts, as we forgive our debtors" (Matthew 6:12). These are two sides of the same coin. We can't have faith in only one side of the Atonement. To be efficacious—to have saving power—our faith in Christ and His Atonement must include both His power to pay for our sins and His power to pay for the sins of others.

Harking back to my landlord-tenant analogy, sometimes we burn the house down through our own carelessness—we play with fire. Sometimes the house burns down through no fault of our own—lightning strikes and there is nothing we can do about it. Sometimes our house burns down because of the sins of others—such as with the landlord's arsonist son in my analogy. The wonder of the Atonement is that it works for all three cases. But our own receipt of the Atonement is conditional on forgiving others. If we do that, accept Christ, and strive to keep His commandments, we will receive the castle and all else the Father has. In the name of Jesus Christ, amen.

NOTES

1. See Ester Rasband, *The Promise of the Atonement: Cure for Broken Dreams* (Springville, Utah: Cedar Fort, 2005).

2. James D. Gordon III, "How Not to Succeed in Law School," *Yale Law Journal* 100, no. 6 (April 1991): 1680; emphasis in original.

3. See Gordon, "How Not to Succeed in Law School," 1680: "Your grandparents will immediately scrape off their bumper sticker that says, 'ASK ME ABOUT MY GRANDCHILDREN.'"

4. See Alma 34:16.

5. The origin of this quote is uncertain, but it is sometimes attributed to St. Augustine of Hippo.

6. One of my favorite discussions is Elder Bruce C. Hafen's classic talk "Beauty for Ashes: The Atonement of Jesus Christ," *Ensign*, April 1990, 7–13.

7. My mother is the one who first focused me on the idea that the Mosaic law and its requirements regarding restitution was a schoolmaster to help those hurt by the sins of another to trust in the justice and fairness of the Atonement. She later published some of her thinking. See Rasband, *The Promise of the Atonement*, 3, 6–7, 9–12, 18–19.

8. See Leviticus 1–8.

9. See Exodus 21:23–25: "And if any mischief follow, then thou shalt give life for life, Eye for eye, tooth for tooth, hand for hand, foot for foot, Burning for burning, wound for wound, stripe for stripe."

10. See Rasband, *The Promise of the Atonement*, 26–27 (discussing this concept).

11. See Rasband, *The Promise of the Atonement*, 30–31 (discussing the parable of the two debtors).

12. Dallin H. Oaks, *The Lord's Way* (Salt Lake City: Deseret Book, 1991), 155–56.

13. See Oaks, *The Lord's Way*, 170–75, 181–82.

14. See Oaks, *The Lord's Way*, 175–80.

15. See Oaks, *The Lord's Way*, 181–85.

Free to Choose Liberty or Captivity

———◆———

Paul V. Johnson

We deal with one key aspect of the remarkable plan of salvation many times each day (in reality, many times each hour): agency, or the ability to choose for ourselves. As I was preparing these remarks, I tried to think of a comparison to convey the importance of agency in the plan of salvation. First I thought of a piece in a jigsaw puzzle. Have you ever put together a jigsaw puzzle and found out there was one missing piece? It can be frustrating, and the picture isn't totally complete without every piece of the puzzle. But I realized that this is not analogous to agency in the plan because the exercise of putting the puzzle together is basically the same whether or not you have all the pieces, and the finished project looks very similar to what was intended.

A more accurate comparison would be the crankshaft in an automobile engine. The crankshaft isn't just some emissions control gadget or even a power-steering pump or air-conditioning compressor. Without a crankshaft the engine will not start. It won't function at all.

Paul V. Johnson was a member of the First Quorum of the Seventy of The Church of Jesus Christ of Latter-day Saints when this devotional address was given on 6 November 2012. © *Intellectual Reserve, Inc.*

The purpose of the engine—to move a car—cannot be accomplished. There is no way around it. This is more like agency in the plan of salvation. Without it, the plan would not work.

Agency is essential to our progress and ability to become like our Father in Heaven and His Son, Jesus Christ. The Savior chose good over evil in every choice He made. Part of our earthly experience consists of being enticed by both good and evil and then learning how to choose good over evil. How could we become like the Savior if we did not have agency to make those choices? By using our agency to choose the right, we begin to put on the divine nature—to pattern our lives after His. We find peace, happiness, and freedom as we make right choices.

In the pre-earth life, Lucifer tried to destroy agency. The scriptures teach us that "Satan rebelled . . . and sought to destroy the agency of man, which I, the Lord God, had given him."[1] Our Heavenly Father did not allow him to destroy this precious gift of agency. In fact, his attempt to destroy it is one of the reasons he was cast out of heaven.[2] We also learn from the scriptures that "he became Satan, yea, even the devil, the father of all lies, to deceive and to blind men, and to lead them captive at his will, even as many as would not hearken unto my voice."[3]

This sounds a little like a contradiction. Satan tried to destroy agency. Our Heavenly Father wouldn't allow it and cast him out. Satan will now deceive and blind men, and he will lead them captive at his will. If he is leading people captive, doesn't that sound like he is destroying agency? The fact is, he couldn't destroy agency in the pre-earth life, and he can't do it now either. If he can't destroy agency, then how can he lead us captive? He does it by enticing us to sin. When we sin, we subject ourselves to him. We, in effect, give part of our agency to him. He can't take it from us, but we can relinquish it.

This concept is explained in the context of the early history here on earth: "Wherefore, it came to pass that the devil tempted Adam, and he partook of the forbidden fruit and transgressed the commandment, wherein he became subject to the will of the devil, because he yielded unto temptation."[4] When we yield to temptation, we become subject to the will of the devil. Again, even though he can't destroy or take away our agency by force, we can give it up.

Listen to some of the phrases from the scriptures illustrating this important idea:

- "Whosoever committeth sin is the servant of sin."[5]
- "To whom ye yield yourselves servants to obey, his servants ye are to whom ye obey."[6]
- "They chose evil works rather than good; therefore the spirit of the devil did enter into them, and take possession of their house . . . , and this because of their own iniquity, being led captive by the will of the devil."[7]

Lehi taught his sons very plainly:

Wherefore, men are free according to the flesh; and all things are given them which are expedient unto man. And they are free to choose liberty and eternal life, through the great Mediator of all men, or to choose captivity and death, according to the captivity and power of the devil; for he seeketh that all men might be miserable like unto himself.[8]

Lehi pleaded with his sons not to "choose eternal death, according to the will of the flesh and the evil which is therein, which giveth the spirit of the devil power to captivate."[9]

Joseph Smith observed:

Satan was generally blamed for the evils which we did, but if he was the cause of all our wickedness, men could not be condemned. The devil could not compel mankind to do evil; all was voluntary. Those who resisted the Spirit of God, would be liable to be led into temptation. . . . God would not exert any compulsory means, and the devil could not; and such ideas as were entertained [on these subjects] by many were absurd.[10]

Elder James E. Talmage wrote:

Satan exerts a mastery over the spirits that have been corrupted by his practises . . . ; he seeks to molest and hinder mankind in good efforts. . . . Yet in all these malignant doings, he can go no farther than the transgressions of the victim may enable him, or the wisdom of God may permit; and at any time he may be checked by the superior power.[11]

Satan's ultimate goal is to make each of us miserable like he is.[12] Since he can't impose this misery, he has to find a way to convince us to choose it. Does this even sound like a feasible business plan? "Convince people to choose to be miserable." It sounds more like *Mission Impossible:* "Your mission, should you choose to accept it, is to convince people to choose misery over joy, bondage over freedom." It just sounds ridiculous. And yet, by all observations, he has been fairly successful in the world at large. And to the degree we have chosen to commit sins, he has even been successful with each of us.

With such an implausible goal, how has he been able to convince so many to choose a path through life that leads to misery? How is he able to convince even good people who are generally choosing righteously in life to commit sins? We have to remember that for us to exercise our agency in a way to help us become more like the Savior, we must be enticed by good and evil. The evil has to be enticing or it would be no test—no challenge, no real choice—and thus we would not experience real growth. But by us choosing good in the face of an alternative that is truly enticing, our characters are shaped and we start to reap the rewards of freedom and peace. We learn more deeply that we trust in a God who cannot lie,[13] and our faith increases.

So what makes it possible for the adversary to make evil and sin seem enticing? How do you sell misery, bondage, and disappointment? Well, you have to lie. He is a liar. In fact, he is "the father of all lies."[14] The only way he can sell sin is to portray it as something it isn't. He has to convince people that evil is good, or, in other words, that sin is right, that momentary pleasure equates with long-term joy, and that sin leads to freedom and happiness instead of to bondage and misery. He also throws in the idea that good is evil and that righteousness is bondage. Satan is a master at marketing. He has been at it for a long time, but the foundation of his marketing scheme is always lies.

Let's look at a few examples from the scriptures.

Cain loved "Satan more than God."[15] He bought into Satan's lies and chose to sin. There is a very telling description of Cain's reaction after he killed Abel: "And Cain gloried in that which he had done, saying: I am free; surely the flocks of my brother falleth into my hands."[16] It is clear he had fallen for the adversary's portrayal that committing sin (although Satan doesn't call it that) will bring happiness and freedom. Cain's exclamation "I am free" has to be in the top-ten list of the most deluded statements in all of scripture. He found out very soon that he was anything but free and anything but happy because of his action. Yet how many people have felt the same thing—a burst of exhilaration or a sense of freedom when they have committed a sin—and think they've gotten away with it?

There was a time in the Book of Mormon when the Nephites had become very wicked. Samuel, a Lamanite, was sent to preach repentance to them. He explained to the people:

Ye have procrastinated the day of your salvation until it is everlastingly too late, and your destruction is made sure; yea, for ye have sought all the days of your lives for that which ye could not obtain; and ye have sought for happiness in doing iniquity, which thing is contrary to the nature of that righteousness which is in our great and Eternal Head.[17]

They had bought into the idea that they could find happiness in doing iniquity—the fundamental lie upon which Satan bases all of his enticements. Of course he doesn't label iniquity "iniquity." He portrays it as something good and natural. These Nephites had not learned the lesson Alma taught his son Corianton: that "wickedness never was happiness."[18] Corianton, for a time, had fallen for the lie that he could break the commandments and that doing so would lead to happiness.

The adversary doesn't stop after we have decided to commit one sin. He wants us in his power. He wants us to be subject to him. Some of the related terms in the scriptures include "cords,"[19] "bonds,"[20] "chains,"[21] "captive,"[22] "subjection,"[23] and even "seal."[24] The Book of Mormon teaches us about his tactics to bring people into bondage by degrees: "He leadeth them by the neck with a flaxen cord, until he bindeth them with his strong cords forever."[25] The imagery is instructive. It starts with a single cord and progresses until they are bound with strong cords. We also read, "Others he flattereth away, and telleth them there is no hell; and he saith unto them: I am no devil, for there is none—and thus he whispereth in their ears, until he grasps them with his awful chains."[26] He carefully leads people into bondage. It is not done in one big Faustian bargain. Just as we progress line upon line in righteousness, we move to bondage sin upon sin.

This is one reason parents and leaders are so concerned when a young person starts to make wrong choices. Once we get entangled in the adversary's cords, getting out is much more difficult than getting in.

This bondage can be powerful. In the Book of Mormon we read about a time when

Satan had great power, unto the stirring up of the people to do all manner of iniquity, and to the puffing them up with pride, tempting them to seek for power, and authority, and riches, and the vain things of the world. . . .

And thus . . . the people [were] *delivered up . . . to be carried about by the temptations of the devil whithersoever he desired to carry them, and to do whatsoever iniquity he desired they should. . . .*

. . . And all this iniquity had come upon the people because they did yield themselves unto the power of Satan.[27]

Later, as the civilization declined in Mormon's time, he lamented that his people were "led about by Satan, even as chaff is driven before the wind, or as a vessel is tossed about upon the waves, without sail or anchor, or without anything wherewith to steer her."[28] That imagery doesn't convey much freedom, does it? When we yield ourselves to the adversary, we become "things to be acted upon"[29] instead of being free to act for ourselves.

I don't know what the actual mechanism is for bringing about this bondage. I don't know exactly what happens in the soul, but I do know something happens, and it is very real.

There is a tendency to use bondage to sin as an excuse for sinful behavior. For example, someone who is abusive may say that they have always had a temper and can't help it if they yell at their family members. While it may be true that a person has a weakness, giving in to that weakness strengthens its hold on us. On the other hand, if we resist the temptation, the hold on us is weakened.[30]

One of Satan's most effective tools is to clothe bondage in the costume of liberty. Peter warned the early Saints about individuals among them who would try to pull them away from the path of righteousness. He described these wicked individuals as "having eyes full of adultery, and that cannot cease from sin. . . . They speak great swelling words of vanity, they allure through the lusts of the flesh. . . . Those that were clean . . . while they promise them liberty, they themselves are the servants of corruption: for of whom a man is overcome, of the same is he brought in bondage."[31]

These people tried to lure others to sin by promising them liberty even though they themselves were in the bondage of sin.

In the Book of Mormon we see that Korihor tried the same stunt, with a twist. He taught doctrines that brought people to the conclusion that sinning would bring them freedom and happiness, but he also focused on convincing people that the commandments and ordinances bound them down—that belief in God, Christ, and the prophets kept them in bondage.

Now that is a lie. The truth is that living the commandments makes us free. In fact, the irony in this situation is that Korihor was the one in bondage. He was not free. We don't know all of his sins, but one that bound him down was his lying. He always knew there was a God, but he repeatedly denied this fact and lied to others about it. When Korihor denied the existence of God to Alma, Alma told him, "I know that thou believest, but thou art possessed with a lying spirit, and ye have put off the Spirit of God that it may have no place in you; but the devil has power over you, and he doth carry you about, working devices that he may destroy the children of God."[32] Korihor had chosen to lie initially and then continued to lie repeatedly until Alma described him as possessed with a lying spirit.

Today there are many individuals promoting or condoning sin, and parts of our culture also carry these dangerous messages. For example, we see in the media a lot of modeling of sins with seemingly no negative consequences. We see meanness, law-breaking, disrespect, breaking of the law of chastity, immodesty, and profanity in an almost constant stream. Many times goodness and righteousness are portrayed as naïve and silly at best and evil at worst.

Each of us has sins that easily beset us and bind us down.[33] No one is exempt. You might struggle with something different than I face. Even Nephi grieved that he struggled with temptations: "And why should I yield to sin, because of my flesh? Yea, why should I give way to temptations, that the evil one have place in my heart to destroy my peace and afflict my soul?"[34]

Since each of us has sinned and thus has subjected ourselves to the will of the devil to some degree, we need to somehow be freed from the bondage of sin. The Atonement has power to break these bonds, these chains, this captivity. When the Savior began His public ministry, He referenced a prophecy about Himself and His mission: "The Spirit of the Lord is upon me, because he hath anointed me to preach the gospel to the poor; he hath sent me to heal the brokenhearted, to preach deliverance to the captives, and recovering of sight to the blind, to set at liberty them that are bruised."[35] Deliverance and liberty come through Him and His Atonement.

No matter what the nature of the sins in our lives—dishonesty, pride, hypocrisy, laziness, greed, challenges with the law of chastity, addictions, anger, Word of Wisdom problems—whatever sins we struggle with, we can be freed from any degree of bondage we may be in. Each of us has experienced this as we have repented in the past. We have felt true freedom as we have been forgiven and have jettisoned the behavior that has tormented us.

Sometimes these bonds are broken in a dramatic way. They seem to burst, and we are immediately freed. At other times the cords are loosed rather than burst.[36] It is almost as if a little at a time the cords that are wrapped around us are unraveled. But whether this happens all at once or gradually, the long-term effect is the same: we are free! And, either way, it is miraculous.

When we obey Satan, we give him power. When we obey God, He gives us power. This is not the message we get from the world, but it is the truth. Real power, the power to become like the Savior, is only found in obedience. Real freedom is found in obedience—in subjecting ourselves to God's will rather than to the will of the flesh or the will of the devil. Freedom through obedience: this sounds like a paradox, but those who have lived this way can testify it is true. Obedience brings power, freedom, joy, peace, and hope.

While obedience does protect us from spiritual bondage and the misery associated with sin, it doesn't bring us a life without challenges. There are things in this fallen world that can bring misery and suffering, such as sickness, death of loved ones, physical pain, and the actions of others. But misery from these sources will eventually be taken care of by the Atonement, and if we endure these challenges faithfully, they will not have eternal negative consequences for us. However, the misery resulting from sin can only be completely removed if we repent.

When we are righteous, Satan has no power over us. A prophecy about the Millennium teaches us that "because of the righteousness of his people, Satan has no power; wherefore, he cannot be loosed for the space of many years; for he hath no power over the hearts of the people, for they dwell in righteousness."[37] This scripture is speaking about the condition that will exist in the world when the people as a whole live in righteousness, but the principle can be true today for us individually. In a description of Captain Moroni, Mormon said, "If all men had been, and were, and ever would be, like unto Moroni, behold, the very powers of hell would have been shaken forever; yea, the devil would never have power over the hearts of the children of men."[38] Individually we can be free from any power the adversary would like to have over us by living righteously. He only gains power as we allow it by our choices.

If we have something in our life that has bothered us and bound us down to some degree, let's repent. Let's get rid of it and increase the freedom in our lives. If you'll pick something and work on it, I will too.

Agency—the ability to make choices—is a crucial and wonderful gift, and we rejoice that we are here on earth able to choose good over evil and to progress toward exaltation. As we use our agency to choose the right, reject evil, and love God, His grace is sufficient for us, and by that grace we will become perfected in Christ.[39] To this I testify in the name of Jesus Christ, amen.

NOTES

1. Moses 4:3.

2. See Moses 4:3.

3. Moses 4:4.

4. D&C 29:40.

5. John 8:34.

6. Romans 6:16.

7. Alma 40:13.

8. 2 Nephi 2:27.

9. 2 Nephi 2:29.

10. *HC* 4:358 (bracketed words in original); quoted in *Teachings of Presidents of the Church: Joseph Smith* (Salt Lake City: The Church of Jesus Christ of Latter-day Saints, 2007), 214.

11. James E. Talmage, *The Articles of Faith* (Salt Lake City: The Church of Jesus Christ of Latter-day Saints, 1924), 63.

12. See 2 Nephi 2:18, 27.

13. See Enos 1:6.

14. Moses 4:4.

15. Moses 5:28.

16. Moses 5:33.

17. Helaman 13:38.

18. Alma 41:10.

19. 2 Nephi 26:22.

20. Mosiah 27:29.

21. Alma 12:6.

22. 3 Nephi 18:15.

23. Mosiah 7:22.

24. Alma 34:35.

25. 2 Nephi 26:22.

26. 2 Nephi 28:22.

27. 3 Nephi 6:15, 17; 7:5.

28. Mormon 5:18.

29. 2 Nephi 2:14.

30. See James 4:7.

31. 2 Peter 2:14, 18–19.

32. Alma 30:42.

33. See Alma 7:15.

34. 2 Nephi 4:27.

35. Luke 4:18.

36. See Alma 5:9–10.

37. 1 Nephi 22:26.

38. Alma 48:17.

39. See Moroni 10:32.

Our Eternal Education

—————◆—————

Nancy Wentworth

It is a humbling experience to be asked to speak at a devotional, but I am happy to be with you today to share my testimony of the gospel.

I love being a teacher. I see myself as a teacher in every aspect of my life—in my work, with my family, and in my Church calling.

When I teach I like to ask questions to begin a discussion with my students. So standing in front of you as a speaker—as a lecturer—is uncomfortable for me. As I speak to you today I will ask you to think about what I am saying. You may not be able to answer me the way you would in a classroom, but you should be able to form answers in your mind—and in your heart. I hope this will help you feel the Spirit and use what I will talk about in your personal development.

Nancy Wentworth was chair of the BYU Department of Teacher Education when this devotional address was given on 27 November 2012. © Brigham Young University.

OUR ETERNAL EDUCATION

My first teaching assignment at BYU was a class for students in the secondary mathematics education major. The class was titled "Exploration of Teaching." On the first day of class I had a discussion with my students about how they viewed teaching and learning through the lens of several metaphors. Today I would like to share with you some of our discussion. I want to look at how each of these metaphors might help us understand the eternal education we have come here on earth to receive.

Our eternal education begins with an understanding of where we have come from, why we are here, and where we are going after this life. In many ways these are the same questions we address as educators. We want to know about our students: we want to know where they are from, what their background is, what their home life was like, what cultural experiences they've had—anything we can draw from to help us teach them in a language and with examples they will understand. We want to instill in them a vision of where they are going, encourage them to set goals for themselves, and help them to attain those goals.

Today I ask you to think about the purpose of your life here on earth. When asked why you are here, you might say, "To receive a body," "To learn how to keep the commandments," or "To become like Christ."

Elder Dallin H. Oaks wrote:

We are all children of a Heavenly Father who has sent us to earth with the invitation to prepare for eternal life. Every choice, every experience, every repentance and reformation, prepares us for what is to come. [*Life's Lessons Learned: Personal Reflections* (Salt Lake City: Deseret Book, 2011), 52]

President Thomas S. Monson has told us:

Clearly, one primary purpose of our existence upon the earth is to obtain a body of flesh and bones. We have also been given the gift of agency. In a thousand ways we are privileged to choose for ourselves. Here we learn from the hard taskmaster of experience. We discern between good and evil. We differentiate as to the bitter and the sweet. We discover that there are conse-quences attached to our actions. ["The Race of Life," *Ensign*, May 2012, 91–92]

Today I hope I can help you see how we use our gift of agency, how we learn from experience, and how we prepare for eternal life by becoming disciples of Christ.

That first day of class I asked my students to think with me about different ways to view education and about how those views might impact how they think about teaching and learning. I had the students get into groups, and I assigned each group a particular metaphor to use as a tool for thinking about education. One group discussed education as a race, another group was assigned to think about education as a garden, and the last group was asked to use family as their metaphor.

EDUCATION AS A RACE

When I asked my students to think about a race as a metaphor for education, they began the discussion with the notion of competi-tion. Competition—is that a positive or a negative thing in educa-tion? Some students mentioned that an athlete is willing to win at all costs. What about the idea of growth as an athlete? How does that happen? What is the role of the coach? What is the role of the athlete?

During the summer Olympics this year, a colleague said to me, "Why are we so glued to each event—even when we really don't know anything about that event or anyone competing in it?" Perhaps the reason is that we love to see people truly excel at something.

Some competitors were so sad to receive a silver medal. They wanted the gold. It was an all-or-nothing proposition for them. For some competitors success has been easy; they have continu-ally been told how good they are and that they are the best. Others were thrilled that they achieved their personal best time at the games. They were improving and getting better with each race or competition.

In the classroom there are some students who feel they can never be the best student in the class—the winner—so why should they continue to work? They might think, "If I can't be number one, then there is no point in trying at all."

As teachers we try to encourage growth in our students, not just winning. Is the student or athlete trying to improve his own learning and understanding or is he only trying to beat someone else? We want students to feel that their personal improvement is a victory and that working hard is the way to improve.

In our eternal education we should remember that we are not in competition with others. Elder Jeffrey R. Holland has spoken about how the success of others does not diminish our efforts. He stated:

> *Brothers and sisters, there are going to be times in our lives when someone else gets an unexpected blessing or receives some special recognition. May I plead with us not to be hurt—and certainly not to feel envious— when good fortune comes to another person? We are not diminished when someone else is added upon. We are not in a race against each other to see who is the wealthiest or the most talented or the most beautiful or even the most blessed. The race we are **really** in is the race against sin, and surely envy is one of the most universal of those.* ["The Laborers in the Vineyard," *Ensign*, May 2012, 31; emphasis in original]

From a spiritual perspective, are we in a race for eternal life? Elder Neil L. Andersen addressed this issue in his April 2012 conference talk:

> *Jesus's call "Come, follow me" (Luke 18:22) is not only for those prepared to compete in a spiritual Olympics. In fact, discipleship is not a competition at all but an invitation to all. Our journey of discipleship is not a dash around the track, nor is it fully comparable to a lengthy marathon. In truth, it is a lifelong migration toward a more celestial world. . . .*

Wherever you now find yourself on the road of discipleship, you are on the right road, the road toward eternal life. Together we can lift and strengthen one another in the great and important days ahead. ["What Thinks Christ of Me?" *Ensign*, May 2012, 112]

One more area of importance for me in the race metaphor is the role of the coach and the role of the athlete. The athletes at the Olympics were grateful to their coaches, who recognized their abilities, helped them know which race would best suit their natural talents, helped them improve, advised them about a strength that needed to be built, and encouraged them as they repeated a skill until their performance and their time improved.

I asked my education students if they had ever had a really good coach. If so, how did that coach help them improve? My students talked about how a coach helped them see what they needed to do to improve. A coach saw that to get off the blocks faster, a runner needed to strengthen a particular muscle. The coach gave the runner an assignment to spend time in the weight room to strengthen that muscle.

My students also talked about how they were the ones who needed to do the work. It is one thing to have a great coach who can see just what an athlete needs to do, but if the athlete does not follow the coach's guidance, then the muscle does not get stronger. And so it is in the classroom. The teacher can help the student know what he needs to do to improve his skill in reading or mathematics, but if the student does not do the work, then there is not much improvement.

How does this apply to our eternal education?

The scriptures are replete with stories of "coaches" who have advised and guided and taught others how they might better their performance as they strive to become disciples of Christ.

In Alma 39–42 we learn about the way Alma coached his son Corianton about the plan of salvation, about his current abilities and practices, and about what he needed to do to succeed in this life.

In chapter 39 Alma pointed out to Corianton the concerns he had with his performance:

Now my son, I would that ye should repent and forsake your sins, and go no more after the lusts of your eyes, but cross yourself in all these things; for except ye do this ye can in nowise inherit the kingdom of God. Oh, remember, and take it upon you, and cross yourself in these things. [Alma 39:9]

Alma then helped Corianton see what he needed to do next to improve:

And I command you to take it upon you to counsel with your elder brothers in your undertakings; for behold, thou art in thy youth, and ye stand in need to be nourished by your brothers. And give heed to their counsel. [Alma 39:10]

In verses 11 and 12 Alma reminded Corianton that he had sinned and that he needed to turn away from that activity.

In verse 13 Alma was very direct with Corianton when he told him:

Turn to the Lord with all your mind, might, and strength; that ye lead away the hearts of no more to do wickedly; but rather return unto them, and acknowledge your faults and that wrong which ye have done. [Alma 39:13]

Alma seems to have understood the role of a coach. He provided clear instructions to Corianton about what he needed to do, and he encouraged him to follow those instructions. Alma knew that he could not change Corianton, but he also knew that Corianton could change by following his direction. Corianton had to exercise his agency and do the work to change his behavior.

I wish I could hear from all of you now. Are you thinking about a person you have coached or someone who has coached you? Are you thinking about a time when you did the hard work a coach told you to do so that you could improve your skills? Has this idea helped you in your eternal education? Have you been instructed about what you need to do to become a disciple of Christ?

We can learn from the story of Alma and Corianton, whether we are thinking of ourselves as the coach or as the athlete. As a coach/teacher we need to be kind and loving and supportive of the person we are trying to help. As the athlete/student we are responsible for doing the work that will help us become eternal disciples of Christ. We need to be listening to those coaches in our lives who can help us develop spiritually. These people may be our bishops, home teachers, visiting teachers, family members, or friends. We need to listen to their counsel and then exercise our agency by doing the work they know will help us grow spiritually.

EDUCATION AS A GARDEN

How do we grow spiritually? What does that mean to us? Perhaps we can learn about that from the garden metaphor.

My students enjoyed discussing their views of education through the lens of the garden. They described the role of the teacher to be like that of the gardener who creates an environment in which children can learn, in which each student can grow into his or her full potential, whether that is an apple or a pumpkin—a scientist, an artist. It is the responsibility of the gardener to create an environment in which the seed can grow and in which students can thrive and develop.

I asked my students to think about what the role of the student is in this garden metaphor. We can learn a great deal about the role of the student when we read the parable of the sower in Matthew:

And he spake many things unto them in parables, saying, Behold, a sower went forth to sow;

And when he sowed, some seeds fell by the way side, and the fowls came and devoured them up:

Some fell upon stony places, where they had not much earth: and forthwith they sprung up, because they had no deepness of earth:

And when the sun was up, they were scorched; and because they had no root, they withered away.

And some fell among thorns; and the thorns sprung up, and choked them:

But other fell into good ground, and brought forth fruit, some an hundredfold, some sixtyfold, some thirtyfold. [Matthew 13:3–8]

When thinking about your eternal education to become a disciple of Christ, how have you prepared yourself to receive the gospel and to grow in your potential during this lifetime? Are you ignoring the gospel and not accepting the seeds, letting the fowls devour them? Are you the stony soil on which the gospel message falls but in which the roots of the gospel do not grow deep? Are you good ground in which the seeds of the gospel can take root and bring forth fruit?

Elder M. Russell Ballard said in his October 2012 conference address:

How do we take the seed of faith that has been nurtured in our minds and plant it deep in the fertile soil of our souls? How do we make the mighty change of heart that Alma says is essential for our eternal happiness and peace? ["Be Anxiously Engaged," *Ensign*, November 2012, 30]

These questions posed by Elder Ballard are important for our eternal education. What do we do to plant the seed of faith in our hearts so that we can become disciples of Christ? This is a key question in education. How do students truly learn? Is a lecture in a classroom the best way to help students gain knowledge? Can students do a few homework problems and feel confident that they know the material? Just listening to others who are experts in a field is not enough to truly know something—to have it planted in your heart.

As educators we want our students to experience learning in multiple ways. We want students to read, to practice skills, and to discuss with others how they understand what they are learning. We want them to have personal experiences with knowledge. Then understanding becomes embedded in them and makes their learning personal and real. If we are to become disciples of Christ, we need to have personal experiences with what that means. What personal experiences have you had that have helped you become like Christ?

Have you ever been asked to do something for someone when you really did not want to do it? If you did it anyway, did you feel good about it? Did you get that feeling that service is a good thing to do? One of the blessings of service is the feeling of becoming like Christ. Initially you might have served others because your mind knew that you should. You might have heard friends or family members talk about serving others, and you might have done service in a group with others. But then one day you experienced service that *you* decided was worth doing, and the seed was planted in your heart. It was planted deep in your heart, and it began to grow. From that time on it began to help you in your eternal education to become a disciple of Christ.

In Alma 41 and the story of Alma's instruction to Corianton we see that the true nature of our heart—that which is planted and growing in our heart—is the nature that will be restored to us in the Resurrection:

> *And it is requisite with the justice of God that men should be judged according to their works; and if their works were good in this life, and the desires of their hearts were good, that they should also, at the last day, be restored unto that which is good.*
>
> *And if their works are evil they shall be restored unto them for evil. Therefore, all things shall be restored to their proper order, every thing to its natural frame—mortality raised to immortality, corruption to incorruption—raised to endless happiness to inherit the kingdom of God, or to endless misery to inherit the kingdom of the devil, the one on one hand, the other on the other.* [Alma 41:3–4]

So our eternal education, that of becoming a disciple of Christ, requires that we plant the seed of the gospel in our hearts—and live it. The garden metaphor helps us understand that we can plant the seed of the gospel in our hearts through our personal experiences.

EDUCATION AS A FAMILY

The final metaphor that we discussed in my education class is that of education as a family. How does a family help us think about education in a classroom—and about our eternal education?

Elder Paul E. Koelliker stated:

> *The Father's plan designated the pattern of the family to help us learn, apply, and understand the power of love. . . .*
>
> *Because of the heaven-designed pattern of the family, we more fully understand how our Heavenly Father truly loves each of us equally and fully.* ["He Truly Loves Us," *Ensign*, May 2012, 18]

Children start life so dependent on their parents for everything: food, warmth, and safety. Parents teach their children, and sometimes that means correcting them. A truly loving parent is not demeaning when their children make mistakes. Instead, they help their children see what they need to do to make things right or to improve and to grow.

At school children learn many things beyond skills and knowledge. They learn to share, to work hard, to experience new things, to ask questions, and to explore new ideas. They learn to care about people other than themselves. Children in school may not always want to do their homework or practice a skill, but a teacher can help them see how this work will help them grow. Like loving parents, good teachers point out the small successes of their students so that their students will want to keep trying, to keep working, and to keep growing.

In a family in which children are taught the gospel, they learn to pray, to read the scriptures, and to go to church. They have experiences in which they feel the Spirit, and those experiences can help them recognize that feeling in the future. They *practice* being a disciple of Christ so that they can *become* a disciple of Christ. In the family is where they experience the gospel.

When I think of a family, I think of love and sacrifice. Parents love their children for many reasons, partly because they serve them every day. They sacrifice for them. They give their lives for them by giving their time and their resources to ensure their children's growth and success. Parents want the best for their children. I think that most parents would say their acts of love and service are not sacrifices—rather, giving their lives for their children is a joy.

There are many ways in which we learn to serve others and sacrifice for them. The Church provides opportunities for us to be of service. Last summer, when there was a great deal of wind damage in Davis County, bishops dismissed church after sacrament meeting so that members of the Church could cut up fallen trees and remove destroyed fences—truly serving each other. Similarly, Brigham Young sent Church members out from their meetings to help those struggling on the plains. During the 2012 general Relief Society meeting, President Henry B. Eyring spoke of the kind, loving Relief Society sisters who helped a family with preparing food, cleaning, and shopping when a tiny baby was born fifteen weeks early (see "The Caregiver," *Ensign*, November 2012, 121–22).

Are we learning to serve others from these examples? Do we see the needs of others even when Church leaders do not ask us to give service? How does the family metaphor help us answer these questions?

The family metaphor is critical to the way in which we live the gospel. We know we are all eternal brothers and sisters in an eternal family. We know we share a loving Heavenly Father and a common Savior, who is our Elder Brother. I hope that as we become more like Christ we will want the best for others in the same way we want the best for our earthly families. I hope that we can love and serve everyone around us because we see them as members of our eternal family. If we love and serve others as we do the members of our earthly family, then it is not such a sacrifice to love and serve them any more than it is a sacrifice to be a parent.

In Alma 43 we read about how Corianton had learned the lesson of the family metaphor. When Corianton came to understand all that his father, Alma, had taught him, he spent the rest of his life teaching others the gospel:

> *And now it came to pass that the sons of Alma did go forth among the people, to declare the word unto them. And Alma, also, himself, could not rest, and he also went forth.*
>
> *Now we shall say no more concerning their preaching, except that they preached the word, and the truth, according to the spirit of prophecy and revelation; and they preached after the holy order of God by which they were called.* [Alma 43:1–2]

Corianton and his brothers and his father lived the rest of their lives sharing the gospel with others. They showed their love for their eternal family through their service. Did Corianton do this as a sacrifice or because it gave him joy? I think it gave him joy because he understood that gaining his eternal education and becoming a disciple of Christ was not a race to be won but a lifelong journey. He began to coach others in how they should live the gospel. He had planted the seed of the gospel in his heart so that it could grow and rise with him in the Resurrection. He found joy in the loving service he gave to his eternal brothers and sisters by sharing the gospel with them.

"IN THE PATH OF DISCIPLESHIP"

It is my prayer today that you will think about what it means to gain an eternal education—an education in which you become a disciple of Christ.

I pray that you will remember the race metaphor—that you will know you are not in a race with others for eternal life and that you will listen to those who are like coaches and who teach you how to develop as a disciple of Christ.

I pray that you can place the seed of the gospel in your heart and that your experiences living the gospel will help that seed to grow.

I pray that you will prepare for eternal life by loving and serving all of mankind as part of your eternal family—not as a sacrifice but with joy in the service.

In the Priesthood session of general conference in October 2012, President Dieter F. Uchtdorf stated what it means to be a disciple of Christ. Let me close with his remarks:

Let us deepen our faith in our Lord, Jesus Christ. Let us take upon ourselves His name and commit each single day to walk anew in the path of discipleship. Let our works make our faith perfect. Through discipleship we may be perfected one step at a time by serving our family, our fellowmen, and God. ["The Joy of the Priesthood," *Ensign*, November 2012, 60]

In the name of Jesus Christ, amen.

"Did You Think to Pray?"

Bruce D. Porter

Some years ago I heard a story about a little boy in Primary class who was asked to say the opening prayer.

"Heavenly Father," said the boy, "I thank thee for the letter *A*. I thank thee for the letter *B*. I thank thee for the letter *C*."

The teacher realized this could be a very long prayer, but she restrained herself from stopping him.

He went on to give thanks for every letter of the alphabet through *Z*. Then he said, "And Heavenly Father, I thank thee for the number one. I thank thee for the number two." And so on he went.

His teacher nearly panicked. She didn't know how high the boy could count. She felt she had to stop him, but again something seemed to restrain her. The boy kept on praying until he reached the number twenty. And then he said, "And Heavenly Father, I thank thee for my Primary teacher, who is the only grown-up that ever let me *finish* my prayer."

Bruce D. Porter was a member of the First Quorum of the Seventy of The Church of Jesus Christ of Latter-day Saints when this devotional address was given on 4 December 2012. © *Intellectual Reserve, Inc.*

I have thought of that boy's prayer often. He helped me realize that I, too, am thankful for the alphabet, the numbers, and the shapes and the colors and for everything I learned in elementary school—things so easily taken for granted, the foundation stones of all learning. I feel grateful for every miraculous gift of God, for the wonders of His love, for the beauty of His creations, for all that is good and right and true flowing down from our Father in Heaven on high:

For the beauty of the earth,
For the beauty of the skies,
For the love which from our birth
Over and around us lies.
["For the Beauty of the Earth," *Hymns*, 2002, no. 92]

I am deeply thankful for the gift of prayer, which is surely among the greatest of gifts given by our Father in Heaven to His children on earth. Prayer is the ordained means by which men and women, and even little children, come to know God. It is our channel of communication with heaven. It is a priceless privilege.

My mother grew up in the small town of Liberty, Utah. When she was young, in the 1930s, her ward had an organist who could play only one hymn. The congregation sang other hymns a cappella, but at least once every Sunday they would sing, "Ere you left your room this morning, Did you think to pray?"

I especially love the third verse of the hymn:

When sore trials came upon you,
Did you think to pray?
When your soul was full of sorrow,
Balm of Gilead did you borrow
At the gates of day?
["Did You Think to Pray?" *Hymns*, 2002, no. 140]

I think of "the gates of day" as the opening to a realm of eternal daylight—gates of prayer that connect us with our heavenly home and the realm of glory where God and Christ dwell. When we pray, we borrow strength, love, and light at the very door of eternity.

Yet all too easily our prayers can become repetitive and perfunctory, a mere check on a checklist of duties and tasks in a given day. "I said my prayers" can be a phrase as routine and ordinary as "I did my homework" or "I bought the groceries." But prayer was never meant to be ordinary: it can be among the most exalted of privileges we enjoy in this mortal sphere.

Several years ago our oldest son shared with me a lesson he had learned about prayer. He was a very busy student at BYU. One evening he sat down to eat a quick dinner and, out of pure habit, said, "Please bless this food to nourish and strengthen my body." He opened his eyes and looked at his food: a Twinkie and a can of soda. He realized there was no way that food was going to nourish and strengthen his body.

He later explained to me that the experience taught him the meaning of the phrase "vain repetitions." When we repeat the same stock phrases over and over in prayer, but not with real intent—when our heart and mind are not in the prayer—then we are only engaging in vain repetition.

HEARTFELT PRAYER

Moroni's admonition about praying to know the truth of the Book of Mormon applies to all prayers: namely, that we "ask with a sincere heart, with real intent" (Moroni 10:4). True prayer is *heartfelt:* the words convey our deeply felt desires and are coupled with a commitment to act on the divine guidance we receive.

Heartfelt prayer comes from the depths of the soul. Our mind and heart are directed toward God with full and complete attention. When we pray from the heart, we are not just saying words or "going through the motions"; we are seeking to draw nearer to our Father in Heaven, to commune with Him in a personal and intimate manner. Heartfelt prayer is the furthest thing from a memorized recitation. We do not simply talk *at* God; rather, we talk *with* Him. This does not imply a face-to-face conversation as Moses experienced, but it does suggest communing with God by listening to the still, small voice of the Spirit. It means allowing time both during a prayer and after a prayer to hear spiritual promptings.

In Shakespeare's play *Hamlet*, Claudius, king of Denmark, kneels in prayer to seek forgiveness, but, upon rising, he knows that his entire prayer has been insincere and in vain. He says:

My words fly up, my thoughts remain below:
Words without thoughts never to heaven go.
[*Hamlet*, act 3, scene 3, lines 97–98]

The Lord desires that we speak with Him openly, honestly, and in plain, simple words. Any attempt at pretense in prayer is pointless, for the Lord knows our hearts perfectly; indeed, insincerity in prayer can become a subtle form of hypocrisy.

Huckleberry Finn in Mark Twain's great novel learned this when he tried to pray for forgiveness for having helped his black friend, Jim, escape from slavery:

*I about made up my mind to pray, and see if I couldn't try to quit being the kind of a boy I was and be better. So I kneeled down. But the words wouldn't come. Why wouldn't they? It warn't no use to try and hide it from Him. Nor from **me**, neither. I knowed very well why they wouldn't come. It was because my heart warn't right; it was because I warn't square; it was because I was playing double. . . . Deep down in me I knowed it was a lie, and He knowed it. You can't pray a lie.* [*The Adventures of Huckleberry Finn* (1884), chapter 31; emphasis in original]

If we examine our personal prayers carefully, we may discover that we often say things we do not really mean or even desire. We are not praying truthfully. The best corrective to this is to focus on the words and phrases we use in prayer and make sure we mean what we say. It also helps to set aside adequate time for prayer so as not to be rushed; to couple prayer with meditation; and to pray, if possible, in a place of quiet solitude.

The Lord's promise "Draw near unto me and I will draw near unto you" (D&C 88:63) captures the essence of heartfelt prayer. Heartfelt prayer is not just a list of things to give thanks for and things to ask for. It entails coming to know God. It means seeking understanding of divine truths, seeking to better understand the purposes of one's life and how to best please God; it means talking with the Lord about things that matter most, what Nephi called "the things of my soul" (2 Nephi 4:15). Such experiences in prayer are sacred and will be cherished throughout our lives.

When we truly pray from the heart, we open our innermost feelings to our Father in Heaven: we tell Him of our challenges, our feelings of inadequacy and weakness; we share our emotions and feelings about decisions that face us or trials and adversity we experience; we freely express our sorrows and joys. Now, God knows our innermost thoughts and feelings even better than we do, but as we learn to share them with Him, we make it possible for His Spirit to enter our souls and teach us more about our own selves and about the nature of God. By making ourselves totally honest, open, and submissive before God, our hearts become more receptive to His counsel and His will.

Prayer should always be reverent and respectful, but our Father in Heaven assuredly is less concerned about the outward form of our prayers than about the state of our heart. Kneeling in prayer is an expression of humility and reverence and is the manner we often assume when offering our most heartfelt prayers. Nevertheless, not all are able to kneel, and many cannot kneel for very long and still concentrate. The Lord will hear our prayers if they are said standing, sitting, or even lying on our back in a hospital bed—provided we genuinely pray from the heart. My mission president once said that some of his best prayers were said running between two foxholes during World War II.

What should we ask for when we pray? The Bible Dictionary offers this important insight:

Prayer is the act by which the will of the Father and the will of the child
are brought into correspondence with each other. The object of prayer is
***not** to change the will of God.* [Bible Dictionary, s.v. "prayer," 752–53;
emphasis added]

Prayer should never be a matter of trying to change God's mind,
to persuade Him of the rightness of our request, or to counsel Him
as to what is best. God's will is perfect. He knows all things and
sees the end from the beginning. He knows better than we do what
is best for us. Sometimes we fervently plead for the Lord to give us
certain things that He knows are not ultimately in our best interest
or in that of a loved one: for example, to receive a certain job offer in
a specific city or to prolong the life of a terminally ill or aged family
member. The first order of prayer should be to learn the will of God
and be given the strength to accept it. "Thy will be done" ought to
grace all prayers, as it does the Lord's Prayer.

RECEIVING ANSWERS TO PRAYER

Perhaps the most frequently asked question about prayer is this:
"When I am seeking an answer about a question or decision in my
life, how do I distinguish between the voice of the Spirit and my
own feelings and desires?" It is a good question, for the Spirit often
speaks to us in the form of feelings, but then we also have feelings
that come from within ourselves. How do we know the difference?

To begin with, revelation requires effort on our part. We cannot
expect answers without first preparing to receive revelation. When
Oliver Cowdery struggled with translating the plates, the Lord
counseled him to "study it out in your mind; then . . . ask me if it be
right" (D&C 9:8). We begin by learning all that we can about our
decision or problem, and then we prayerfully ponder and weigh what
course may be right, seeking counsel as appropriate from parents,
family members, and friends. Then, *after* we have made a decision,
we go to the Lord with the proposed answer or decision and seek
confirmation. Normally He will not give us revelation regarding

specific questions until we have taken this step and are prepared to ask if our decision be right.

Receiving answers to prayers also requires that both mind and heart be in tune. When Oliver Cowdery first began to translate the plates, the Lord told him this:

Behold, I will tell you in your mind and in your heart, by the Holy Ghost. . . .
Now, behold, this is the spirit of revelation. [D&C 8:2–3]

Notice that revelation comes both *in the heart* and *in the mind*. The feelings of the heart and the understanding of the mind come together to give us an answer. If we have a good feeling, but our minds are unsettled, we should continue to study and pray. If in our mind we have developed a plan of action that makes sense but does not feel right, we may not yet have the answer. Only when heart and mind are in accord can we be confident that we have reached the right conclusion.

The Prophet Joseph Smith taught the importance of our mind in the revelatory process when he said:

When you feel pure intelligence flowing into you, it may give you sudden strokes of ideas, so that by noticing it, you may find it fulfilled the same day or soon . . . ; and thus by learning the Spirit of God and understanding it, you may grow into the principle of revelation. [*Teachings*, 151]

It is important to understand that the feelings that come with personal revelation are not excited, agitated, or highly emotional. If we want a particular answer badly enough, we may stir up feelings of excitement or artificial enthusiasm within us and take that for an answer, but this is only a form of self-deception. The voice of the Lord comes as "a still, small voice," and we must silence our own prejudices to hear it. In this regard I believe that we can overanalyze the scriptural phrase "your bosom shall burn within you" (D&C

9:8). In my experience this simply means a feeling of inner peace. Elder Dallin H. Oaks taught the following:

> *What does a "burning in the bosom" mean? Does it need to be a feeling of caloric heat, like the burning produced by combustion? If that is the meaning, I have never had a burning in the bosom. Surely, the word "burning" in this scripture signifies a feeling of comfort and serenity.* ["Teaching and Learning by the Spirit," *Ensign*, March 1997, 13]

Another way to describe the feeling associated with revelation is a sense of correctness or rightness. The answer will feel right, rather than leaving one with a sense of uneasiness or wrongness.

One great obstacle to receiving answers from God is fear, for fear is the opposite of faith. I have heard President Boyd K. Packer teach many times, "Brethren, do not take counsel from your fears." If you are fearful about leaving Provo or the state of Utah, it will be difficult for the Lord to give you an answer to take a job elsewhere. If you are afraid of getting married, you will somehow never find the answers needed to get there. If we fear to act on the inspiration we receive, it will become more difficult in the future to receive answers. If we learn to move forward in faith as the Spirit guides, we will make progress in life and grow in the principle of revelation. Remember Paul's great counsel to Timothy: "God hath not given us the spirit of fear" (2 Timothy 1:7).

A PRAYER IN PARIS

Now, brothers and sisters, sometimes circumstances will arise in our lives when we face an urgent need for divine guidance and have neither the time to study it out nor any possible way of learning more about what course we should take. In such circumstances the Lord will surely guide us if we are open to the promptings and impressions of the Spirit.

In the summer of 1976 I spent two months in the Soviet Union with 150 other American students studying Russian. When the program ended late in July, we were given a week free to travel at our own expense anywhere in Europe before catching a charter flight from Paris back to the United States. I spent that week on a shoestring budget visiting friends and converts in the Düsseldorf Germany Mission, where I had earlier served.

Unfortunately, after booking a second-class train ticket from Düsseldorf to Paris, I realized I was down to the equivalent of only $38 in cash. I had no traveler's checks or credit cards. As the train sped toward Paris, I began to worry about how I would find a place to spend the night with so little money.

Arriving at the main train station in Paris, I got off the train with my luggage and looked around. I didn't know anyone in France, and I didn't speak the language. The sun was just setting, and I knew it would soon be dark. Suddenly I felt very lonely and somewhat anxious. I offered a simple, heartfelt prayer to the Lord: "Heavenly Father, please help me find a safe place to spend the night."

An impression came to me as plain and clear as any I have ever felt: *Walk two blocks forward and turn left, and there will be a hotel where you can spend the night.* With a deep feeling of peace I walked the two blocks forward and turned left. About a hundred feet in front of me was a small sign: Hotel. I knew this was where the Lord had led me to spend the night. Entering the hotel lobby, I stepped forward to the front desk where a man was sitting. "One single room, please," I said. The man hardly looked up.

"I'm sorry," he said, "Every room is booked. We have no vacancies." He proceeded to ignore me.

I asked, "Are you sure that you have no rooms? Perhaps there's been a change or a cancellation?"

He looked up at me and said firmly, "Young man, we have no rooms. It is the peak of the tourist season, and we have been booked solid for weeks. Every hotel around has been booked for weeks. You will not find a room anywhere in Paris."

What could I do? I began to leave the hotel, but as I reached the door onto the street, I thought, I *can't* just leave. The Lord led me here. I went back to the desk and said, "Sir, could you *please* at least look in your book and verify for sure that you have no rooms available this evening?"

Somewhat miffed, the clerk stood up, almost slammed his reservation book on the desk, and began flipping the pages quickly. "You see," he said, "there is nothing. We have no rooms, we have no rooms, we have no . . ."

Suddenly he stopped and stared at the page in puzzlement for a long time. Then he became very businesslike and said, "Well, it appears after all that we do have one single room vacant. That will be $35."

I do not remember much of that night, only that I felt safe and very blessed. The next morning I learned that the bus to Charles de Gaulle Airport stopped right in front of the hotel. To my great relief the fare was only $3. I arrived at the airport in time to catch my flight to JFK Airport, where, with only a few small coins left in my pocket, I was met by my beloved fiancée, Susan.

I have reflected on that experience many times. I was no one really—one of tens of thousands of students traveling through Europe that summer. The Lord could have said, "You got yourself into this, you can get yourself out." I suppose I might have slept in the train station or just wandered the streets all night. But, instead, as a loving Father, He led me to a place of refuge when I sought it in humble prayer.

I testify that He will bless and be merciful to you, too, as you seek Him in prayer. I know that God the Eternal Father lives. I know that His Son is our Redeemer. I was eighteen years old when I first received a pure witness by the power of the Holy Ghost that Jesus Christ is a living being, a real person, my friend and support in every time of need. In the intervening years I have come to know that the fruits of the Spirit are joy beyond expression and a deep inner peace that passes all understanding.

May His joy and peace be with each one of you at this sacred season of the year. I offer this prayer and bear this testimony in the name of Jesus Christ, amen.

The Lord's Hand in Our Lives

Cecil O. and Sharon G. Samuelson

SGS: We are so grateful for the blessing of being with you this morning as we begin winter semester. We like the new beginnings, new routines, and new opportunities that are part of this time of year. We are glad all of you are with us. We are also happy for those who have chosen to begin their missionary service with the recent announcement made by President Monson.

COS: During general conference this past October, we were very interested in the many references, both direct and indirect, that assured us of the continued influence of heaven in our lives. We believe this is true for us individually, for us as a Church, and also for us as the BYU community. Lest any be confused or misled, I am not suggesting that our agency is compromised or limited. In fact, our agency or responsibility to make proper choices is a fundamental and inescapable doctrine of our Heavenly Father's plan. Likewise, it is also essential we understand that in our mortal probation we are

Cecil O. Samuelson was president of Brigham Young University when he and his wife, Sharon G. Samuelson, gave this devotional on 8 January 2013. © *Intellectual Reserve, Inc.*

entitled to have the interventions of "the hand of the Lord" in our lives when we live so as to merit such blessings.

Usually, at least in our experience, the touch of the Lord's hand is soft and subtle—so soft and subtle that we may not recognize it. Happily, in necessary situations our experience can be as that of Ezekiel when he said, "The hand of the Lord was strong upon me" (Ezekiel 3:14).

SGS: What is increasingly clear to us is that as we reflect on what has transpired in our lifetimes and in yours, we have been influenced more than we previously imagined by the blessings and guidance available to us in answer to our prayers. How this happens occurs in multiple ways. We believe in the scriptural assurances of the ministering of angels. We also know that the Holy Ghost has a tremendous influence in our lives when we live so that such help is appropriate. We also understand better as we get older that often the help we need is provided by our loving Heavenly Father and His Son, our Savior, through other people who have been prompted to help, guide, and rescue us in times of need or consequential decision making.

COS: As President Henry B. Eyring recounted the special events that led him to surrender his tenured faculty appointment at Stanford University and took him to preside at Ricks College (see "Where Is the Pavilion?" *Ensign*, November 2012, 72–75), we have reflected on our own experiences. In some ways what has happened to us is very different and in other ways is exactly the same as has unfolded for others. A common characteristic in our case seems to be that we recognize the hand of the Lord much better in retrospect than while interventions are actually taking place. Another is that the Lord's hand often is so gentle that what happens seems to be usual in the normal course of current events but later turns out to be of very great import. Likewise, when we have not been careful to acknowledge or recognize the reality of our blessings, we have been tempted to conclude that a special outcome was only the result of our own careful thinking, efforts, or strategy. We now confess that we fully believe that rarely, if ever, do good things happen to us without the influence of the hand of heaven.

SGS: Please forgive a few personal examples. We just recently celebrated our forty-eighth wedding anniversary. When my husband was still in medical school more than forty years ago, we thought we had been married a fairly long time. Now, as we look back, our entire married life doesn't really seem very long at all. Given the time limitations of our devotional today, we will mention just a few experiences that we have had together when the hand of the Lord played a prominent role in our lives. Again, we did not necessarily think about how this was happening at the time, but, in retrospect, what transpired clearly was not just by chance or coincidence. Likewise, we want to emphasize that customized, special blessings that have come to us are not predictive of what might or will happen with you. Similarly, you will have individualized blessings and interventions that have not been afforded to us or to other people. While Jesus Christ has promised that those who are faithful, keep the commandments, and make and observe their sacred covenants will receive all that the "Father hath" (D&C 84:38), the timing is unique for each person and does not always happen in this life.

COS: You might begin by telling our special friends just how we got together. Since I was away on my mission at the beginning of what turned out to be an "arranged marriage," you can share a few of the details, and then I may need to tell my side of the story.

SGS: While I was attending the University of Utah, I acquired a part-time secretarial position in the Department of Educational Psychology. I enjoyed it very much, and it was so convenient to be right on campus, since my previous job had been off campus and transportation had proven difficult. One of the professors I worked for was Dr. Cecil O. Samuelson Sr. He was very nice and pleasant, as were the other professors, but he was especially so. Eventually he mentioned to me that he had a son serving a mission and hoped that I "might be available" when he returned home. I am sure I gave an appropriate response. What I do recall thinking, however, is that dating someone your parents believe would be the perfect match for you usually ends in an embarrassing situation. Am I right? On the other hand, I felt that if his son were at all like his dad, it might be a possibility.

When his son and namesake returned from his mission, I met him when he came to the office so he and his father could drive home together. It did not take me long to change my mind, and I hoped his dad was giving him encouragement to ask me out on a date. I regret to say that it did not occur as quickly as I desired. Nevertheless, I broke off a relationship with another fellow and waited patiently. It is obvious from the fact that we are standing here together that with a little time and encouragement from his dad, we dated and eventually married—one parent-arranged marriage that was successful.

COS: My father was a wise but also crafty man. Since I did not have my own car for a few months after my mission, I would meet my father at his office at the university to ride home with him. Somehow he always managed to have just a few more things to do, and so I was left to visit with and get to know his secretary better. We didn't date for a few months, but once we began, it didn't take long for us to know that it was a sure thing. We were sealed in the Salt Lake Temple the day before Thanksgiving in 1964 by my former mission president.

SGS: By then I was teaching school, and we were able to get by financially. Since we both came from rather large families, we knew we wanted to have several children. However, our first wasn't born until after we had been married for more than three years. Initially we were not terribly concerned and were content to be getting farther along with my husband's medical education and saving money from my full-time teaching career.

COS: I can still remember how excited we were when we learned we were expecting. As I recall, the pregnancy was rather uneventful— meaning I never had a single day of morning sickness!

SGS: And I suppose you don't want me to tell anyone that you studied for your pathology final while sitting with me in labor at the hospital. I certainly wouldn't want them to know you hoped I would be as quiet as possible while experiencing a contraction.

COS: I think I passed the medical school test, but we were over the top to be the parents of the cutest little baby boy. We enjoyed very much being new parents and had the usual challenges of that blessing most parents experience, including a night in the hospital with his severe croup. Like everyone's children, he was very precocious. He just turned forty-five last month, and we no longer describe him as cute, but he has a wonderful wife and three adorable daughters who challenge him just enough to convince his parents that there is indeed justice in the world for all the pranks, demands, and surprises he authored during his adolescence.

SGS: Still, it was my dream and my blessing to be a mother, and in that I have never felt otherwise. I think we expected to have our other children come along in due course without too much further delay, but that was not to be. Finally, after more than five years and several surgeries, our second "cutest baby boy" was born. We were again thrilled and felt blessed but didn't perceive the special circumstances that allowed for that pregnancy. We were told by our doctors that if we desired more children, we should not delay unduly because my condition could make further pregnancies unlikely over time.

We should add that our older son, now five, was disappointed, because while he had joined us in prayers for the new baby, his own prayer was for a baby brother *and* a baby sister. Now he only had the baby brother. We told him not to worry and that if there were a baby sister for him, she would eventually come. He was skeptical but seemed to be resolved.

COS: Since obstetrics was not my field in medicine, we were perhaps naïve in our understanding about the hand of heaven in our lives at that time. Just a few months later we learned that we were in the early stages of another pregnancy, and we were very happy. Then one evening Sharon began to experience severe and acute abdominal pain. Again—although not my expertise in medicine—we knew we were in trouble, and so we went to the emergency room at the hospital where I worked. She was examined and a couple of laboratory tests were performed. The attending physician was a very good man who was experienced in such matters but who did not know my wife well. He felt the situation was not serious and that perhaps Sharon was just having an anxiety attack. Now, those who know her well know that she does get very anxious at football, basketball, soccer, and volleyball games, but this wasn't a game, and we knew our physician friend was in error.

SGS: As we left the emergency room, I was still very uncomfortable, and we were both quite unsettled. We were praying for guidance and comfort, and it became clear that we needed a second opinion. Consequently, we headed for another hospital in our community and finally were able to reach my personal obstetrician, who had been on a Church assignment earlier when we had first decided the problem was serious.

COS: At the second hospital we were quickly met by Sharon's doctor, who knew her well. He determined her anxiety and pain were due to an acute surgical emergency. She was rushed to the operating room and was there found to be bleeding profusely internally. The cause of the problem was an ectopic or tubal pregnancy, which required immediate surgery to stop the bleeding. She had lost a great deal of blood, but her life was saved. Unfortunately, her doctor and we thought it meant that she would never be able to have another pregnancy because of this incident and the previous necessary surgery she had undergone. We did rejoice that her life was spared and that we already had two little boys in our family.

SGS: I healed rather quickly and soon returned home to the active life of a young mother with two lively children and a husband who had a major Church calling as well as a busy professional life teaching, researching, caring for patients, and fulfilling administrative duties. We didn't really mourn but did feel rather constant disappointment that the large family we had expected and frankly took for granted was not to be.

As a young girl growing up, I had four younger brothers but no sisters. While I had girl cousins and girlfriends, I always wished for a younger sister. As I grew up, I knew that was not likely, but I looked forward to being the mother of daughters. Now that possibility seemed to have evaporated too.

COS: Few, if any, outside of immediate family knew of this small but significant grief Sharon carried in her heart. Our boys were healthy and our life was full. About four years quickly passed, and we felt ourselves resolved and settled. We built our home with the plan that it would accommodate the four of us well, and we really were grateful for our general good fortune and happy lives. Then, one weekend in early February 1977, our lives changed.

SGS: The married student stake in which my husband was serving as second counselor in the stake presidency was being reorganized. Elder Marvin J. Ashton of the Quorum of the Twelve was releasing the stake presidency and calling a new one. When he interviewed my husband, Elder Ashton asked if there were any difficulties or disappointments in our family life, and Cec said the only thing he could think of was the set of experiences we have just shared that seemed to determine we would always be a small family. Elder Ashton told my husband not to worry and that things "would work out the way they should." He then went on to call my husband to be the new stake president.

COS: After the Sunday meetings and other formal activities were concluded, a member of the stake high council approached us and asked to be excused from the regular meetings for the next few days because he was returning to Guatemala, where he had served his mission, to look into the possibility of adopting a child. Without any previous discussion or consideration, at least on my part, we wished him well, excused him from his duties for the period he would be gone, and then, almost offhandedly, mentioned that perhaps this was something we should look into as well.

SGS: Within just a few days we received an unexpected call explaining that a set of twins to be born near the end of the month would be available for adoption. The birth mother, a maid with an older child, had been abandoned by the birth father, and she hoped that somehow her twins, a boy and a girl, could have a better life than what was likely for them in their Guatemalan village. We think one dimension of the concern of this pregnant Indian mother was that having twins was not considered good fortune. The practice in their area at that time was to choose the potentially strongest infant of the two and let that baby be nursed fully. The weaker baby would then be neglected because most nursing mothers did not have sufficient milk for two babies. Thus the outlook for the smaller or weaker baby was dismal.

COS: When we mentioned that my wife had four brothers, we should have also noted that the two immediately younger than Sharon were twins and were quite a handful for her parents and also for their elder sister. Thus our immediate reaction was that we couldn't consider adopting these twins. But after a few days of careful thought and serious prayers, we had our answer that these little ones should be ours. We made the necessary arrangements and provided powdered infant formula to the wonderful people caring for the twins. Then I and our friend made our way to Guatemala to bring the babies home.

We are confident that the hand of the Lord was on those good people, because our twins were healthy when I arrived, although our daughter was still very tiny. Our eldest son's prayer for "a brother *and* a sister" was answered.

SGS: We have told parts of this experience before at BYU and elsewhere. Suffice it to say, with a number of other miracles—some of which we did recognize as they occurred—we had our baby girl and baby boy home in Utah in just a couple of months after their birth. Next month they will be thirty-six, and each is happily married with children of their own.

Now, having doubled the number of our children almost over-night and having the little sister for our older boys, the daughter for me, and a third son for all of us, we felt our quiver was finally full. Surely we had been richly blessed, and we acknowledged our gratitude for these very happy circumstances, although we learned that this many little people, particularly twin infants, was not necessarily a picnic much of the time.

COS: I should confess that during all this time when I would sit on the stand in Church, it was left to Sharon to struggle with the kids. When asked by a well-meaning member of our ward whether or not I ever helped with the children in Church, my wife would answer, "Oh, yes! Whenever they misbehave, he scowls at them from the stand." But there is yet another interesting—at least to us—part of our story. Another four years passed, and then my dear wife returned from a doctor's appointment to announce that she was pregnant. What a surprise! My older sister Carol has always described our fifth child, Sara, as the "miracle child" because her birth occurred against very long medical odds.

SGS: Now no one can ever say that my husband has not given a medical devotional! We share these experiences only to show the hand of the Lord in our lives and to remind ourselves and others that seeming disappointments and disasters are often the keys that open the doors to greater blessings and opportunities than might have ever been hoped for or even conceived.

For those of you wondering why similar blessings are not now yours, we can only remind you of Jesus' promises and blessings that will yet be yours but that are not possible without significant trials and disappointments beforehand.

COS: The scriptures are replete with accounts of the hand of the Lord influencing the lives of the Father's children. You will have your favorites, and we have ours. A useful exercise that we recommend is to go through the scriptures and count the many references to the reality of the Lord's hand in the lives of His people. The promise made by the Lord to Abraham is one promise He makes to all of us: "Behold, I will lead thee by my hand" (Abraham 1:18).

Before we close, we must mention one other very significant and major event in our lives that has been lifting and even transforming for us. It also involves "children"—and lots of them! But unlike those we have mentioned, we are not formally sealed to them like we are to the five who have grown up in our home.

We speak of the great privilege of our assignment to BYU. Because we are now getting just a little bit older, we hope we can be excused for considering all of the students who have been at BYU during our tenure or are currently here to be "our children." Now, we know you are all grown-ups, but we do feel the pride and pain of parenthood as we see you grow, struggle, achieve, and excel. While not officially codified in the BYU Aims and Mission Statement, you and the thousands like you are great blessings in our lives. We feel the same about our colleagues in the administration and in various staff assignments and of course your teachers and faculty members.

SGS: Candidly, coming to BYU, especially in our current positions, was never part of any of our plans or even wildest considerations. I must confess that when my husband told me of this assignment after he was invited to President Hinckley's office, I thought he was kidding. And then, when I saw he was serious, I thought President Hinckley must have been kidding! Now, after a few years, we seriously wonder what we might have done that brought us to enjoy the good fortune of experiencing all that is BYU. We do know that the hand of the Lord is on this very special university. We know that God lives and loves us and will guide, correct, and direct us if we are willing to have Him do so.

COS: Perhaps I will save for another occasion a litany of sacred experiences I could share that confirms deeply in my heart and mind the truthfulness of what Sister Samuelson has said about the involvement of heaven in the work of BYU. I am a witness and know that this is true and occurs with great regularity. BYU is a very important part of the great cause of the restored gospel of Jesus Christ found in The Church of Jesus Christ of Latter-day Saints. We are led by prophet leaders and are greatly blessed to serve under the direction of President Thomas S. Monson, whom we love and sustain. Please know of our faith in you, our faith in BYU, and especially our faith in the tender hand of the Lord. In the name of Jesus Christ, amen.

What Is Truth?

———◆———

Dieter F. Uchtdorf

My beloved brothers and sisters, my dear young friends, I am grateful for the privilege to be with you today. It always lifts my spirits to be surrounded by the young adults of the Church, and you inspire me to declare, "Let Zion in her beauty rise." As you are living all around the world, you represent in a beautiful way the future and strength of the Church. Because of your righteous desires and your commitment to follow the Savior, the future of this Church looks bright.

I bring you the love and blessing of President Thomas S. Monson. The First Presidency prays for you often. We always ask the Lord to bless, keep, and guide you.

THE BLIND MEN AND THE ELEPHANT

Well over one hundred years ago, an American poet put to rhyme an ancient parable. The first verse of the poem speaks about

Dieter F. Uchtdorf was second counselor in the First Presidency of The Church of Jesus Christ of Latter-day Saints when this CES devotional address was given on 13 January 2013. © Intellectual Reserve, Inc.

six men of Indostan
To learning much inclined,
Who went to see the Elephant
(Though all of them were blind),
That each by observation
Might satisfy his mind.

In the poem each of the six travelers takes hold of a different part of the elephant and then describes to the others what he has discovered.

One of the men finds the elephant's leg and describes it as being round and rough like a tree. Another feels the tusk and describes the elephant as a spear. A third grabs the tail and insists that an elephant is like a rope. A fourth discovers the trunk and insists that the elephant is like a large snake.

Each is describing truth.

And because his truth comes from personal experience, each insists that he knows what he knows.

The poem concludes:

And so these men of Indostan
Disputed loud and long,
Each in his own opinion
Exceeding stiff and strong,
Though each was partly in the right,
And all were in the wrong![1]

We look at this story from a distance and smile. After all, we know what an elephant looks like. We have read about them and watched them on film, and many of us have even seen one with our own eyes. We believe we know the truth of what an elephant is. That someone could make a judgment based on one aspect of truth and apply it to the whole seems absurd or even unbelievable. On the other hand, can't we recognize ourselves in these six blind men? Have we ever been guilty of the same pattern of thought?

I suppose the reason this story has remained so popular in so many cultures and over so many years is because of its universal application. The Apostle Paul said that in this world the light is dim and we see only part of the truth as though we are looking "through a glass, darkly."² And yet it seems to be part of our nature as human beings to make assumptions about people, politics, and piety based on our incomplete and often misleading experience.

I am reminded of a story about a couple who had been married for sixty years. They had rarely argued during that time, and their days together passed in happiness and contentment. They shared everything and had no secrets between them—except one. The wife had a box that she kept at the top of a sideboard, and she told her husband when they were married that he should never look inside.

As the decades passed, the moment came that her husband took the box down and asked if he could finally know what it contained. The wife consented, and he opened it to discover two doilies and $25,000. When he asked his wife what this meant, she responded, "When we were married, my mother told me that whenever I was angry with you or whenever you said or did something I didn't like, I should knit a small doily and then talk things through with you."

The husband was moved to tears by this sweet story. He marveled that during sixty years of marriage he had only disturbed his wife enough for her to knit two doilies. Feeling extremely good about himself, he took his wife's hand and said, "That explains the doilies, but what about the $25,000?"

His wife smiled sweetly and said, "That's the money I got from selling all the doilies I've knitted over the years."

Not only does this story teach an interesting way to deal with disagreements in marriage, but it also illustrates the folly of jumping to conclusions based on limited information.

So often the "truths" we tell ourselves are merely fragments of the truth, and sometimes they're not really the truth at all.

Today I would like to speak of truth. As I do, I invite you to ponder a few important questions.

The first question is "What is truth?"

The second, "Is it really possible to know the truth?"

And third, "How should we react to things that contradict truths which we have learned previously?"

WHAT IS TRUTH?

What is truth? During the closing hours of His life, the Savior was brought before Pontius Pilate. The elders of the Jews had accused Jesus of sedition and treason against Rome and insisted that He be put to death.

When Pilate came face to face with the Man of Galilee, he asked, "Are you a king?"

Jesus replied, "For this cause came I into the world, that I should bear witness unto the truth. Every one that is of the truth heareth my voice."[3]

I don't know what kind of man Pilate was, nor do I know what he was thinking. However, I suspect that he was well educated and had seen much of the known world.

I sense a certain weary cynicism in Pilate's reply. I hear in his words the voice of a man who may once have been an idealist but now—after a great deal of life experience—seems a little hardened, even tired.

I don't believe Pilate was encouraging a dialogue when he responded with three simple words: "What is truth?"[4]

To amplify, I wonder if what he really was asking was "How can anyone possibly know the truth?"

And that is a question for all time and for all people.

CAN ANYONE KNOW THE TRUTH?

Now, can anyone know the truth? Some of the greatest minds that have ever lived on this earth have attempted to answer that question. The elusive nature of truth has been a favorite theme of history's great poets and storytellers. Shakespeare seemed especially intrigued with it. The next time you read one of Shakespeare's tragedies, notice how often the plot turns on a misunderstanding of an important truth.

Now, never in the history of the world have we had easier access to more information—some of it true, some of it false, and much of it partially true.

Consequently, never in the history of the world has it been more important to learn how to correctly discern between truth and error. Part of our problem in the quest for truth is that human wisdom has disappointed us so often. We have so many examples of things that mankind once "knew" were true but have since been proven false.

For example, in spite of one-time overwhelming consensus, the earth isn't flat. The stars don't revolve around the earth. Eating a tomato will not cause instant death. And, of course, man actually can fly—even break the sound barrier.

The scriptures are filled with stories of men and women who misinterpreted "truth."

In the Old Testament, Balaam could not resist "the wages of unrighteousness"[5] offered him by the Moabites. So he convinced himself to believe a new truth and helped the Moabites get the Israelites to curse themselves through immorality and disobedience.[6]

The apostate Korihor, after leading many away from the truth, confessed that the devil had deceived him to the point where he actually believed that what he was saying was the truth.[7]

In the Book of Mormon, both the Nephites as well as the Lamanites created their own "truths" about each other. The Nephites' "truth" about the Lamanites was that they "were a wild, and ferocious, and a blood-thirsty people,"[8] never able to accept the gospel. The Lamanites' "truth" about the Nephites was that Nephi had stolen his brother's birthright and that Nephi's descendants were liars who continued to rob the Lamanites of what was rightfully theirs.[9] These "truths" fed their hatred for one another until it finally consumed them all.

Needless to say, there are many examples in the Book of Mormon that contradict both of these stereotypes. Nevertheless, the Nephites and Lamanites believed these "truths" that shaped the destiny of this once-mighty and beautiful people.

HUMAN NATURE AND TRUTH

In some way we are all susceptible to such strange thinking.

The "truths" we cling to shape the quality of our societies as well as our individual characters. All too often these "truths" are based on incomplete and inaccurate evidence, and at times they serve very selfish motives.

Part of the reason for poor judgment comes from the tendency of mankind to blur the line between belief and truth. We too often confuse belief with truth, thinking that because something makes sense or is convenient, it must be true. Conversely, we sometimes don't believe truth or reject it—because it would require us to change or admit that we were wrong. Often, truth is rejected because it doesn't appear to be consistent with previous experiences.

When the opinions or "truths" of others contradict our own, instead of considering the possibility that there could be information that might be helpful and augment or complement what we know, we often jump to conclusions or make assumptions that the other person is misinformed, mentally challenged, or even intentionally trying to deceive.

Unfortunately, this tendency can spread to all areas of our lives— from sports to family relationships and from religion to politics.

IGNAZ SEMMELWEIS

A tragic example of this tendency is the story of Ignaz Semmelweis, a Hungarian physician who practiced medicine during the mid-nineteenth century. Early in his career, Dr. Semmelweis learned that 10 percent of the women who came to his clinic died of childbed fever, while the death rate at a nearby clinic was less than 4 percent. He was determined to find out why.

After investigating the two clinics, Dr. Semmelweis concluded that the only significant difference was that his was a teaching clinic where corpses were examined. He observed doctors who went directly from performing autopsies to delivering babies. He concluded that somehow the corpses had contaminated their hands and caused the deadly fevers.

When he began to recommend that doctors scrub their hands with a chlorinated lime solution, he was met with indifference and even scorn. His conclusions contradicted the "truths" of other doctors. Some of his colleagues even believed that it was absurd to think that a doctor's hand could be impure or cause sickness.

But Semmelweis insisted, and he made it a policy for doctors in his clinic to wash their hands before delivering babies. As a consequence, the death rate promptly dropped by 90 percent. Semmelweis felt vindicated and was certain that this practice would now be adopted throughout the medical community. But he was wrong. Even his dramatic results were not enough to change the minds of many doctors of the day.

IS IT POSSIBLE TO KNOW THE TRUTH?

The thing about truth is that it exists beyond belief. It is true even if nobody believes it.

We can say west is north and north is west all day long and even believe it with all our heart, but if, for example, we want to fly from Quito, Ecuador, to New York City in the United States, there is only one direction that will lead us there, and that is north—west just won't do.

Of course, this is just a simple aviation analogy. However, there is indeed such a thing as absolute truth—unassailable, unchangeable truth.

This truth is different from belief. It is different from hope. Absolute truth is not dependent upon public opinion or popularity. Polls cannot sway it. Not even the inexhaustible authority of celebrity endorsement can change it.

So how can we find truth?

I believe that our Father in Heaven is pleased with His children when they use their talents and mental faculties to earnestly discover truth. Over the centuries many wise men and women—through logic, reason, scientific inquiry, and, yes, through inspiration—have discovered truth. These discoveries have enriched mankind, improved our lives, and inspired joy, wonder, and awe.

Even so, the things we once thought we knew are continually being enhanced, modified, or even contradicted by enterprising scholars who seek to understand truth.

As we all know, it is difficult enough to sort out the truth from our own experiences. To make matters worse, we have an adversary, "the devil, [who] as a roaring lion, walketh about, seeking whom he may devour."[10]

Satan is the great deceiver, "the accuser of [the] brethren,"[11] the father of all lies,[12] who continually seeks to deceive that he might overthrow us.[13]

The adversary has many cunning strategies for keeping mortals from the truth. He offers the belief that truth is relative; appealing to our sense of tolerance and fairness, he keeps the real truth hidden by claiming that one person's "truth" is as valid as any other.

Some he entices to believe that there is an absolute truth out there somewhere but that it is impossible for anyone to know it.

For those who already embrace the truth, his primary strategy is to spread the seeds of doubt. For example, he has caused many members of the Church to stumble when they discover information about the Church that seems to contradict what they had learned previously.

If you experience such a moment, remember that in this age of information there are many who create doubt about anything and everything, at any time and every place.

You will find even those who still claim that they have evidence that the earth is flat, that the moon is a hologram, and that certain movie stars are really aliens from another planet. And it is always good to keep in mind that just because something is printed on paper, appears on the Internet, is frequently repeated, or has a powerful group of followers doesn't make it true.

Sometimes untrue claims or information are presented in such a way that they appear quite credible. However, when you are confronted with information that is in conflict with the revealed word of God, remember that the blind men in the parable of the elephant would never be able to accurately describe the full truth.

We simply don't know all things—we can't see everything. What may seem contradictory now may be perfectly understandable as we search for and receive more trustworthy information. Because we see through a glass darkly, we have to trust the Lord, who sees all things clearly.

Yes, our world is full of confusion. But eventually all of our questions will be answered. All of our doubts will be replaced by certainty. And that is because there is one source of truth that is complete, correct, and incorruptible. That source is our infinitely wise and all-knowing Heavenly Father. He knows truth as it was, as it is, and as it yet will be.[14] "He comprehendeth all things, . . . and he is above all things, . . . and all things are by him, and of him."[15]

Our loving Heavenly Father offers His truth to us, His mortal children.

Now, what is this truth?

It is His gospel. It is the gospel of Jesus Christ. Jesus Christ is "the way, the truth, and the life."[16]

If we will only have enough courage and faith to walk in His path, it will lead us to peace of heart and mind, to lasting meaning in life, to happiness in this world, and to joy in the world to come. The Savior is "not far from every one of us."[17] We have His promise that if we seek Him diligently, we will find Him.[18]

OUR OBLIGATION TO SEEK FOR TRUTH

But how can we know that this "truth" is different from any other? How can we trust this "truth"?

The invitation to trust the Lord does not relieve us from the responsibility to know for ourselves. This is more than an opportunity; it is an obligation—and it is one of the reasons we were sent to this earth.

Latter-day Saints are not asked to blindly accept everything they hear. We are encouraged to think and discover truth for ourselves. We are expected to ponder, to search, to evaluate, and thereby to come to a personal knowledge of the truth.

Brigham Young said:

I am . . . afraid that this people have so much confidence in their leaders that they will not inquire for themselves of God whether they are led by him. I am fearful they settle down in a state of blind self-security. . . . Let every man and woman know, by the whispering of the Spirit of God to themselves, whether their leaders are walking in the path the Lord dictates.[19]

We seek for truth wherever we may find it. The Prophet Joseph Smith taught that

Mormonism is truth. . . . The first and fundamental principle of our holy religion is, that we believe that we have a right to embrace all, and every item of truth, without limitation or . . . being . . . prohibited by the creeds or superstitious notions of men.[20]

Yes, we do have the fulness of the everlasting gospel, but that does not mean that we know everything. In fact, one principle of the restored gospel is our belief that God "will yet reveal many great and important things."[21]

The Restoration of the gospel of Jesus Christ came about because of a young man with a humble heart and a keen mind seeking for truth. Joseph studied and then acted accordingly. He discovered that if a man lacks wisdom, he can ask of God and the truth really will be given unto him.[22]

The great miracle of the Restoration was not just that it corrected false ideas and corrupt doctrines—though it certainly did that—but that it flung open the curtains of heaven and initiated a steady downpour of new light and knowledge that has continued to this day.

So we continually seek truth from all good books and other wholesome sources. "If there is anything virtuous, lovely, or of good report or praiseworthy, we seek after these things."[23] In this manner we can resist the deceit of the evil one. In this manner we learn the truth "precept upon precept; line upon line."[24] And we will learn that intelligence cleaves unto intelligence, and wisdom receives wisdom, and truth embraces truth.[25]

My young friends, as you accept the responsibility to seek after truth with an open mind and a humble heart, you will become more tolerant of others, more open to listen, more prepared to understand, more inclined to build up instead of tearing down, and more willing to go where the Lord wants you to go.

THE HOLY GHOST—OUR GUIDE TO ALL TRUTH

Just think about it. You actually have a powerful companion and trustworthy guide in this ongoing search for truth. Who is it? It is the Holy Ghost. Our Heavenly Father knew how difficult it would be for us to sift through all the competing noise and discover truth during our mortality. He knew we would see only a portion of the truth, and He knew that Satan would try to deceive us. So He gave us the heavenly gift of the Holy Ghost to illuminate our minds, teach us, and testify to us of the truth.

The Holy Ghost is a revelator. He is the Comforter, who teaches us "the truth of all things; [who] knoweth all things, and hath all power according to wisdom, mercy, truth, justice, and judgment."[26]

The Holy Ghost is a certain and safe guide to assist all mortals who seek God as they navigate the often troubling waters of confusion and contradiction.

The *Witness* of truth from the Holy Ghost is available to all, everywhere, all around the globe. All who seek to know the truth, who study it out in their minds,[27] and who "ask with a sincere heart, with real intent, having faith in Christ, [will know] the truth . . . by the power of the Holy Ghost."[28]

And there is the additional, unspeakable *Gift* of the Holy Ghost available to all who qualify themselves through baptism and by living worthy of His constant companionship.

Yes, your loving Father in Heaven would never leave you alone in this mortality to wander in the dark. You need not be deceived. You can overcome the darkness of this world and discover divine truth.

Some, however, do not seek for truth so much as they strive for contention. They do not sincerely seek to learn; rather, they desire to dispute, to show off their supposed learning and thus cause contention. They ignore or reject the counsel of the Apostle Paul to Timothy: "Foolish and unlearned questions avoid, knowing that they do [generate contention]."[29]

As disciples of Jesus Christ, we know that such contention is completely inconsistent with the Spirit upon whom we depend in our search for truth. As the Savior warned the Nephites, "For verily . . . I say unto you, he that hath the spirit of contention is not of me, but is of the devil, who is the father of contention."[30]

If you follow the Spirit, your personal search for the truth inevitably leads you to the Lord and Savior, even Jesus Christ, for He is "the way, the truth, and the life."[31] This may not be the most convenient way; it will probably also be the road less traveled, and it will be the path with mountains to climb, swift rivers to cross, but it will be His way—the Savior's redeeming way.

I add my witness as an Apostle of the Lord, that Jesus is the Christ, the Son of the living God. I know this with all my heart and mind. I know this by the witness and power of the Holy Ghost.

I ask you to spare no efforts in your search to know this truth for yourself—because this truth will make you free.[32]

My dear young friends, you are the hope of Israel. We love you. The Lord knows you; He loves you. The Lord has great confidence in you. He knows your successes, and He is mindful of your challenges and questions in life.

It is my prayer that you will seek the truth earnestly and unceasingly, that you will yearn to drink from the fount of all truth, whose waters are pure and sweet, "a well of water springing up into everlasting life."[33]

I bless you with confidence in the Lord and a deep-rooted desire to rightfully discern truth from error—now and throughout your life. This is my prayer and my blessing, in the sacred name of Jesus Christ, amen.

NOTES

1. John Godfrey Saxe, *The Poems of John Godfrey Saxe* (Boston: James R. Osgood, 1873), 135–36, books.google.com.

2. 1 Corinthians 13:12.

3. John 18:37.

4. See John 18:33–38.

5. 2 Peter 2:15.

6. For Balaam's story, see Numbers 22–24; see also Numbers 31:16; Revelation 2:14.

7. See Alma 30:52–53.

8. Mosiah 10:12.

9. See Mosiah 10:12; Alma 20:13.

10. 1 Peter 5:8.

11. Revelation 12:10.

12. See John 8:44.

13. See D&C 50:3.

14. See D&C 93:24.

15. D&C 88:41.

16. John 14:6.

17. Acts 17:27.

18. See Deuteronomy 4:29; Proverbs 8:17; Acts 17:27; D&C 88:63.

19. *DBY,* 135.

20. *Teachings of Presidents of the Church: Joseph Smith* (Salt Lake City: The Church of Jesus Christ of Latter-day Saints, 2007), 264.

21. Articles of Faith 1:9.

22. See James 1:5.

23. Articles of Faith 1:13.

24. Isaiah 28:10.

25. See D&C 88:40.

26. Moses 6:61.

27. See D&C 9:8.

28. Moroni 10:4.

29. 2 Timothy 2:23.

30. 3 Nephi 11:29.

31. John 14:6.
32. See John 8:32.
33. John 4:14.

Prophetic Priorities and Dedicated Disciples

Elaine S. Dalton

I wish to begin today by expressing to you my witness that God
is our Eternal Father, that He lives, that we are His children,
and that He loves us. His great love was manifest when He sent His
Only Begotten Son, Jesus Christ, to the earth to atone for our sins
and to teach and exemplify for each of us the things we should do
in order to qualify and be worthy to return back into God's presence. I bear you my testimony that Jesus Christ is the Son of God.
He is our Savior and He is our Redeemer. He lives and He loves us
and He knows each of us individually by our names. I love Him, and
I know each of you do too. I also wish to bear my testimony that
President Thomas S. Monson is God's prophet on the earth today.
I know this through my personal experience in incorporating his
counsel into my life and also because of the powerful witness that
comes into my heart from the Holy Ghost each time I am in his
presence or hear him speak. Today I express my commitment to him
and my resolve and desire to assist him in his heavy responsibilities.

*Elaine S. Dalton was the Young Women general president of The Church of Jesus
Christ of Latter-day Saints when this devotional address was given on 15 January
2013. © Intellectual Reserve, Inc.*

I desire to serve as he does, with all my heart, might, mind, and strength.

Today we stand at the beginning of a brand-new year—part of an epic journey here in mortality. As we approach this clean, fresh page of our lives, unmarred and unspoiled, we have before us a new opportunity to rally the best within us. Everything that has gone before has prepared you for this moment in time. And I might hasten to testify to you that this is indeed a magnificent moment. It is yours. And set before you is the opportunity of a lifetime to become a force for good in the world. As a modern-day prophet of God foretold, "Make no mistake about it—this is a marked generation." He further said:

> There has never been more expected of the faithful in such a short period of time than there is of us. . . .
> Each day the forces of evil and the forces of good enlist new recruits. Each day we personally make many decisions showing the cause we support. The final outcome is certain—the forces of righteousness will win. But what remains to be seen is **where** each of us personally, now and in the future, will stand in this battle—and **how tall** we will stand. Will we be true to our last days and fulfill our foreordained missions?[1]

When the gospel was restored to the earth through the instrumentality of a young teenage boy named Joseph Smith, Oliver Cowdery recorded these words: "These were days never to be forgotten."[2] He then went on to describe—in some of the most beautiful language I have ever read—his experiences with the Prophet Joseph Smith as they translated the sacred records that are the Book of Mormon. I feel a deep sense of gratitude today for those young men—for their faithfulness, for their obedience and commitment, and for the purity of their lives. They were exceptional! And because they went forward undaunted to do what the Lord had revealed and commanded them to do in answer to their sincere prayers and questions, today we have another testament of Jesus Christ: the Book of Mormon—a true and precious record that was written for me and for you to help us become the leaders we have been reserved and prepared to become in these latter days. These are your days, and I am confident that you will also make them "days never to be forgotten."

To those who listen carefully, the Lord regularly prompts us to act. Never before has there been more opportunity than now. I believe the Lord is calling to each of us to become dedicated disciples. President Dieter F. Uchtdorf said that in order to become a dedicated disciple, "it is not enough merely to speak of Jesus Christ or proclaim that we are His disciples. It is not enough to surround ourselves with symbols of our religion. Discipleship is not a spectator sport."[3]

The movie *Chariots of Fire* is the moving story of Eric Liddell, the gold medal winner in the 400-meter track event in the 1924 Paris Olympics. Liddell was not only a gifted athlete who held to his convictions, but he lived out his faith to the very end as a Christian missionary in China. He was such an incredible athlete that his goal was to get to the 1924 Olympics in France and run in his best race—the 100-meter race. He trained hard to get in top shape, and his country of Scotland was sure that he would win a gold medal for them. There was just one problem. The heat to decide who would make the Olympics was on a Sunday, and Liddell would not run on Sunday. Due to this conflict he chose not to run in the 100-meter race. Instead he qualified for the 200- and 400-meter races because those heats were not held on Sunday, but no one expected him to come close to winning. Just prior to the start of the 400-meter race, he was given a piece of paper on which was written words from 1 Samuel 2:30: "Them that honour me, I will honour." Liddell ran with that piece of paper in his hand and held onto this promise tightly. And, to everyone's surprise, he won the gold medal and broke a world record.[4] Listen to what his character in the film *Chariots of Fire* said after winning a previous race:

You came to see a race today. To see someone win. It happened to be me. But I want you to do more than just watch a race. I want you to take part

in it. I want to compare faith to running in a race. It's hard. It requires
concentration of will, energy of soul. You experience elation when the win-
ner breaks the tape—especially if you've got a bet on it. But how long does
that last? You go home. Maybe your dinner's burnt. Maybe you haven't got
a job. So who am I to say, "Believe, have faith," in the face of life's realities?
I would like to give you something more permanent, but I can only point
the way. I have no formula for winning the race. Everyone runs in her
own way, or his own way. And where does the power come from to see the
race to its end? From within.[5]

We must do more than just watch the race: we must take part
in it. Believe! Have faith! Discipleship is not a spectator sport. "And
where does the power come from to see the race to its end? From
within." I think the Lord is saying, "Let's move forward. Let's build
the kingdom. Hasten my work." Those who have been prepared
and reserved for this moment in time are here on the earth. You are
here! The Lord knows what lies ahead, and this is just the beginning
of your life's race and the many mighty miracles that will occur as
He hastens His work! The Lord has said, "I will hasten my work in
its time."[6] And now is the time! To hasten means to be quick to do
something, to move forward quickly, to accelerate, to hurry and not
delay. Several years ago President Boyd K. Packer said, "My young
friends in the Church, I bear witness that this is the day of hastening, and as I speak to you about opportunity and obligation, I stress
the word 'obligation.'"[7]

In the Pearl of Great Price we have a record of Abraham written
by his own hand. He described the decadent society in which he was
living and his difficulty in standing alone, because even his parents
had departed from the ways of the Lord. He recorded that it got so
bad that it was necessary for him to flee his home because his father
had offered him up to the priest as a human sacrifice to their gods.
He recorded:

And, finding there was greater happiness and peace and rest for me,
I sought for the blessings of the fathers, and the right whereunto I should

be ordained to administer the same; having been myself a follower of righteousness, desiring also to be one who possessed great knowledge, and to be a greater follower of righteousness.[8]

The desire of his heart was to be a follower of righteousness—which is, simply, a disciple. And the Lord, through His prophet, is calling you to determine to be an even "greater follower of righteousness." A disciple of Christ is a follower of Jesus who lives as He taught and exemplified. As we learn in Doctrine and Covenants 41:5, "He that receiveth my law and doeth it, the same is my disciple; and he that saith he receiveth it and doeth it not, the same is not my disciple."

Thus, as dedicated disciples we must act and make prophetic priorities our priorities. In order to do this we will need to be riveted on the words of the current prophets, seers, and revelators. Some of those prophetic priorities include (1) missionary work, (2) teaching and learning for youth, and (3) temple and family history work.

MISSIONARY WORK

A few months ago we listened in general conference as President Thomas S. Monson announced the lowering of the age at which both young men and young women may serve missions. From my perspective on the stand in the LDS Conference Center, I watched as young men gasped, young women raised from their seats and started texting their bishops, and mothers started crying—already missing their sons and daughters. Since then, the response has been overwhelming as both young men and young women have responded to the feelings in their hearts and started their preparations to serve missions. I loved the tweets, the chatter on the Internet, and the pictures you posted about what this would mean in your personal lives.

Now, if missionary work is one of the prophetic priorities, shouldn't it be one of our priorities in the coming year? Many here today are contemplating serving a mission. Many of you have already served missions. For the young men, this is a priesthood responsibility for which you should be and are preparing. For young women, this is a wonderful opportunity, but not an obligation. But do we need a formal call to serve a mission? After you return from your mission, has your identity as one of the Lord's missionaries changed? Can we, as dedicated disciples, follow a prophet of God and help to hasten the Lord's work by continuing to do our part to flood the earth with righteousness?

Clayton M. Christensen, a Harvard business professor and well-known expert on innovation and growth, decided to call himself on a mission and to simply become an "everyday missionary"[9] by talking about the things he believes and about the gospel to anyone with whom he comes in contact and with anyone who will listen. He is not ashamed of the gospel of Jesus Christ. He is a dedicated disciple. As we follow a prophet of God, could each of us determine to become an everyday missionary?

TEACHING AND LEARNING FOR YOUTH

Prior to the last general conference, a First Presidency letter was sent to priesthood leaders announcing new teaching and learning resources for youth to be implemented starting this month. The focus of this new resource is to build faith, testimony, and conversion in the Savior. This will hasten personal spiritual progress. This new way of learning will give all who participate an added edge because they will know how to learn by study and also by faith. What you and I will observe in the coming days will be a wave of articulate advocates of the gospel of Jesus Christ—filled with the Spirit and deeply converted—going forth into all the world. This new way to learn will prepare youth for missionary work, for marriage, and for parenthood. This is not just for youth but for *you!* Get on lds.org and become familiar with and practice these same principles. Apply the doctrine in your daily decisions and work to become a dedicated disciple of our Savior.

TEMPLE AND FAMILY HISTORY WORK

Another prophetic priority was announced by the First Presidency in a letter dated October 8, 2012, that encouraged youth and adults to do their own family history work and to take their own family names to the temple. You may recall in the October 2011 general conference, prior to this letter, that Elder David A. Bednar invited the youth (including each of you) to become engaged in family history and temple work for their own ancestors.[10] Following that invitation, Elder Richard G. Scott urged again for each of us to be worthy to enter the temples and do the work of turning "the hearts of the children to the fathers."[11]

Also, one year ago a revised *For the Strength of Youth* booklet was issued to help not just youth but you—all of us—understand the standards of the gospel. Living these standards enables each of us to be worthy to enter the temple and to do this work. A new limited-use recommend has also been made available, making it possible for anyone who is worthy to go to the temple and do baptisms for the dead. The hand of the Lord has brought all these things together in a most miraculous way.

It is so vitally important that each of us determine now to make the necessary adjustments and changes in our lives to be worthy always of a temple recommend. As you take your own family names to the temple, the Lord will amplify your ability to learn and to focus on the things that matter most. You will come forth from the temple armed with power, and His "angels [will be] round about you, to bear you up."[12] Always with prophetic priorities come prophetic promises. Elder Bednar promised to those who would seek out their ancestors and do their work that "your testimony of and conversion to the Savior will become deep and abiding. . . . You will be protected against the intensifying influence of the adversary [and,] as you participate in and love this holy work, you will be safeguarded in your youth and throughout your lives."[13] What would happen if each of us simply got on the Internet and found a few family names to take to the temple?

During the past several years I have been on the front row, so to speak, as I have watched these things unfold and come together. I have been an eyewitness to the arm of the Lord being revealed. None of these things has randomly happened. His hand is in this work, and He is hastening our preparation if we will listen and act. I testify that we are led by a prophet of God and that the Lord is inspiring every announcement, every letter, and every talk. It is an amazing time. And it is a time when we, like Abraham, must determine to act and not be acted upon.

These events make it clear that the Lord is indeed hastening His work, and they send a very powerful message that God loves and trusts you, the rising generation. President Monson said, when speaking of you, "I think the youth today are stronger than they have ever been before in the history of the Church."[14] I agree. You are amazing! You are not ordinary, and these are not ordinary times in which we live. You have been reserved and prepared to be on the earth at this time, and though the circumstances in which we live present many challenges, you can do it! You are, as the Savior stated, "children of the prophets . . . and . . . of the covenant."[15] You are of the noble birthright of our Father Abraham. You are exceptional, and you are doing difficult but correct things in the midst of great opposition. Your actions and decisions now will bless future generations. Indeed, you are a pivotal generation.

COUNSEL FOR DEDICATED DISCIPLES

As you witness these prophetic priorities unfolding and as you participate in many of them, I would like to give you some counsel similar to the counsel Paul gave to his young friend Timothy. Paul said, "Let no man despise thy youth; but be thou an example of the believers, in word, in conversation, in charity, in spirit, in faith, in purity."[16]

First, don't let anyone tell you that you are too young. Paul told Timothy, "Let no man despise thy youth." Many times you will hear, "Well, come back when you have a little more experience." Or, "Wait to decide that until you are a little older." Or, "Delay marriage until you have a little more financial security and schooling." But buying into that worldly philosophy denies the knowledge you already have that you are not ordinary and that you have come here to go forward with faith and with the power of your youth and your unique perspective. Don't let old paradigms become your parameters.

I am personally keenly aware that many of the blessings I am enjoying now in this life stem from decisions I made when I was between the ages of eighteen and thirty. This amazing man sitting with me here on the stand happens to be the best decision I made while here at BYU. To this day he still thinks he saw me first, but the fact is that I spotted him on campus, went to the administration building, found out his schedule, and just happened to be near some of his classes occasionally. I believe you might call that "stalking" today! But I called it flirting then. And I clearly remember sitting in a devotional similar to this having prayed about making the decision to marry or not marry this man. I was worried. I felt so young. That day the speaker spoke about how to make decisions. I can still vividly recall feeling that I was the only one in the entire devotional that morning, and I left with the formula for how to receive personal revelation—to know all things that I should or should not do. That formula is one that all of you are familiar with in sections 8 and 9 of the Doctrine and Covenants—but that day it was news to me. And, as you can see, I applied the formula, and the rest is history!

I don't think either Steve or I realized or visualized what the future would hold then. We felt so young. We were so young! This Christmas I gave my husband a family portrait. As he opened it, it was one of those magic moments when heaven and earth come together. We looked at our eternal family and we sat in the living room and cried as we counted our blessings and as we thought about all those critical decisions along the path of life—made when we were young, following the guidance of the Spirit. So I invite you to read Doctrine and Covenants sections 8 and 9, learn the pattern, follow the Spirit, and don't let anyone tell you that you are too young. "Let no man despise thy youth."

The Lord loves and trusts the youth. He always has. He gave Joseph Smith the responsibility to open this dispensation, to translate the Book of Mormon, to hold the keys of the priesthood and the sealing power, and to receive prophetic witness and guidance.

He was just fourteen. Through a prophet of God the Lord called Mormon when he was just ten to continue in his habit of being quick to observe and to prepare to keep the record when the time came. That record guides you and me today: the Book of Mormon. To Mary and Joseph, God entrusted His Only Begotten Son to be raised in virtue and holiness. They were young. Moroni led an army to defend family, religion, and God when he was about your age. And to Samuel was entrusted a kingdom because the Lord looked on his heart, not on his age. To 2,060 young men was given the responsibility to defend their parents' covenants. And the list goes on and on and on. So don't let anyone or anything convince you that you are too young. You must seize the day because these are your days, and if the adversary can get you to postpone or delay your progress or to freeze you in fear or to get you to wait because he has convinced you that you are too young, he wins. Your youth is your strategic advantage.

Second, "neglect not the gift that is in thee."[17] The gift that you received at baptism is one of your greatest assets. When hands were laid on your head and you were told to "receive the Holy Ghost," it was not a passive pronouncement. Rather, those words implied that you would do all in your power to be worthy of that constant companionship. The guidance of the Holy Ghost is critical to you for your successful mission here on the earth. Is it any wonder then that the great deceiver has manipulated media, the Internet, pop stars, women's fashion—anything he can—to cause you to neglect "the gift that is in thee." We must value virtue, which is defined as chastity and moral purity.[18] Virtue is solidified as we form patterns of thought and behavior based on high moral standards. We have all been eyewitnesses to the consequences of a disregard for virtue in our society and in families. You have heard me talk about it before, but virtue is absolutely necessary because, as Mormon taught Moroni, it is "most dear and precious above all."[19] Why? Because the Holy Ghost simply does not dwell in "unholy temples"[20]—"which temple ye are."[21]

We must qualify to have the companionship of the Holy Ghost. This is difficult in a very noisy and polluted world, so that is precisely why the Lord gave us the sacrament so that we could each partake of the sacrament and become unspotted from the world. What blessings are available to us and what power we may have to be able to renew our covenants on a weekly basis and receive the promise that we will "always have his Spirit to be with [us]!"[22] Because you are members of the Church, you have an edge in the world—an added advantage that puts you ahead of the crowd. You have the right to the constant companionship of the Holy Ghost, and the roles of this third member of the Godhead are to teach, testify, warn, comfort, lead, guide, and purify, to name a few. Elder Bruce R. McConkie once said, "There is no price too high, . . . no struggle too severe, no sacrifice too great, if out of it all we receive and enjoy the gift of the Holy Ghost."[23]

I am sure when we learned that we would be able to have the constant companionship of the Holy Ghost while here in mortality, we shouted for joy and confidently embraced our Father's plan because we knew that we would never be alone and that knowing what is right and wrong would be and is always possible. And we also knew that through the guidance of the Holy Ghost we would be magnified and, because of the Savior and His infinite Atonement, we could do hard things. We knew we would be enabled and strengthened to do whatever we must do and to endure whatever we must endure to be victorious in fulfilling our divine missions. I believe we knew and understood perfectly that mortality would not be easy, but, if we proved faithful, we would be able to return once again to our heavenly home proven, pure, and sealed in eternal families.

Third, as the words of the hymn suggest, be "more fit for the kingdom."[24] I heard about one young man who set a New Year's goal to do one push-up on January 1st and then each day add one more push-up to his fitness routine. He envisioned that at the end of the year he would pound his chest and with his buff body and his strong arms complete his goal by doing 365 push-ups. He lasted until January 12th. So, set little, attainable goals. Establish and rely on the power of habit. Your spiritual fitness routine will look different than mine. But make it a routine.

My husband has a routine he does every single morning. First, he prays. Then it is off to the stationary bike, the elliptical trainer, and then the treadmill. I call him a "greenhouse runner" because he does all this inside. Nonetheless, on the bike he reads from the Book of Mormon, on the elliptical he studies a conference talk, and on the treadmill he memorizes things like scriptures, the family proclamation, "The Living Christ," and even the Young Women theme! I am in awe at his discipline—he doesn't have to decide daily what to do. He is relying on the power of habit. And those habits have ripple effects in the rest of his life and in the lives of our entire family. He is a disciplined, dedicated, discerning disciple.

Now, last, "cast not away [thy] confidence."[25] Don't get distracted, discouraged, or disqualified. The word *confidence* is composed of two Latin words: *con*, meaning "with," and *fideo*, meaning "faith." So you see, *confidence* means "with faith." Faith is a powerful power that can move mountains and call down miracles. You have exercised your faith up to this point, so keep on. Even if things do not go according to your plan, even if you think you are being delayed because of the actions or nonactions of others, press forward. Continue to draw close to the Lord. Cherish virtue. Stand firm and stand tall. You have been reserved to be here now on account of your exceeding faith in the premortal existence in our Heavenly Father's plan.[26] Your life also has a plan, and, as you trust in the Lord, you will see that plan unfold in miraculous ways.

I believe that a great miracle is taking place right before our eyes. In these magnificent latter days you will see the "army [of the Lord] become very great."[27] You will see the gospel preached in every nation. You will emerge from the temple accompanied by angels and "endowed with power from on high."[28] This will enable you to navigate in increasingly turbulent times with a peaceful walk.[29]

Young women, you will be the ones who will provide the example of virtuous womanhood and motherhood. You will continue to be virtuous, lovely, praiseworthy, and of good report. You will also be the ones who will provide the example of family life in a time when families are under attack, being redefined, and disintegrating. You will understand your roles and your responsibilities and thus will see no need to lobby for rights.

Young men, you will be the ones who will know that priesthood power—the power to act for God on the earth—is to be accessed only through purity. And you will use that priesthood power to bless generations.

For each of you, the very purity and virtue of your lives will attract the gaze of all the world in these latter days, and, because of you, many will say, "Come, let us go up to the mountain of the Lord's house, and we will learn His ways and we will walk in His paths."[30] You will be the ones who will help establish Zion because you understand that Zion is the pure in heart.

In the Musée d'Orsay in Paris, France, hangs a painting I love by Eugène Burnand. It depicts two of the Lord's disciples—Peter and John—running in the light of a new day toward the Savior and the empty tomb.[31] A print of this painting hangs in our home as well as in the homes of each of our children. It is a tangible representation of our vision as a family—to be dedicated disciples who will always be found running toward the Savior.

We are being invited to take part in the greatest race there has ever been. Make prophetic priorities your priorities. Dedicate yourself to discipleship. Don't let anyone tell you that you are too young. Seek the Holy Ghost. Become more fit for the kingdom and go forward with confidence.

I want you to know that you are magnificent. You are making more progress than you think you are. Your trials, your challenges, and your triumphs are forging your character and destiny. Your virtue and purity is tangible. And today, as I gaze into your eyes and faces, I truly believe that one virtuous young woman or young man led by the Spirit can change the world!

Truly these are days never to be forgotten. As you run your personal best, as you run your personal race, may you never forget that "they that wait upon the Lord shall renew their strength; they shall mount up with wings as eagles; they shall run, and not be weary; and they shall walk, and not faint."[32] In the name of Jesus Christ, amen.

NOTES

1. Ezra Taft Benson, "In His Steps," *Ensign*, September 1988, 2; emphasis in original; see also Ezra Taft Benson, "In His Steps," BYU fireside address, 4 March 1979.

2. JS—H 1:71, note.

3. Dieter F. Uchtdorf, "The Way of the Disciple," *Ensign*, May 2009, 76–77.

4. See Kristin Charles, "An Olympic Story: The Gold Medal Life of Eric Liddell," http://ministry-to-children.com/an-olympic-story-the-gold-medal-life-of-eric-liddell.

5. Ian Charleson as Eric Liddell, *Chariots of Fire* (1981).

6. D&C 88:73.

7. Boyd K. Packer, *CR*, April 1962, 118.

8. Abraham 1:2.

9. Clayton M. Christensen, *The Power of Everyday Missionaries: The What and How of Sharing the Gospel* (Salt Lake City: Deseret Book, 2012).

10. See David A. Bednar, "The Hearts of the Children Shall Turn," *Ensign*, November 2011, 24–27.

11. D&C 27:9; see also Richard G. Scott, "The Joy of Redeeming the Dead," *Ensign*, November 2012, 93–95.

12. D&C 84:88.

13. Bednar, "Hearts of the Children," 27.

14. William R. Walker quoting Thomas S. Monson in Sarah Jane Weaver, "Roundtable: 'Hastening the Work,'" *Church News*, 30 December 2012, 5.

15. 3 Nephi 20:25.

16. 1 Timothy 4:12.

17. 1 Timothy 4:14.

18. See D&C 121:45; see footnote 45b on the word *virtue*.

19. Moroni 9:9.

20. Mosiah 2:37.

21. 1 Corinthians 3:17.

22. D&C 20:77.

23. Bruce R. McConkie, *A New Witness for the Articles of Faith* (Salt Lake City: Deseret Book, 1985), 253; quoted in David M. McConkie, "Learning to Hear and Understand the Spirit," *Ensign*, February 2011, 41.

24. "More Holiness Give Me," *Hymns*, 2002, no. 131.

25. Hebrews 10:35.

26. See Alma 13.

27. D&C 105:31.

28. D&C 38:32, see also D&C 109:13.

29. See Moroni 7:4.

30. See Isaiah 2:3.

31. Eugène Burnand, *The Disciples Peter and John Running to the Sepulchre on the Morning of the Resurrection* (ca. 1898).

32. Isaiah 40:31.

Created in the "Image and Likeness of God": Apprentices in the Master's Workshop

David Rolph Seely

I am honored to be here today to address you. I have been blessed with goodly parents, a noble and accomplished wife, and valiant children. I am especially honored to be here with my colleagues and with you, the students of Brigham Young University. Many devotional talks through the years have shaped my life.

Brother Hugh Nibley, one of the great teachers at Brigham Young University, used to say our lives are like going to a Broadway play. Arriving late, we miss the opening—and, leaving early, we miss the ending. To complicate matters, instead of being spectators when we arrive at the play, someone pushes us onstage and we hear a voice saying, "Do something intelligent." Brother Nibley's point was that in order to "do something intelligent" with our lives onstage, we need to know the beginning and the ending of the play—and we only get that information through revelation.

David Rolph Seely was a BYU professor of ancient scripture when this devotional address was given on 29 January 2013. © *Brigham Young University.*

IN THE BEGINNING

In the spirit of Brother Nibley's parable, let us sketch out, based on the scriptures, the beginning, the middle, and the end of the play in order to help us "do something intelligent."

In the beginning, the crown of Heavenly Father's creative work was the creation of the man and the woman: "So God created man in his own image, in the image of God created he him; male and female created he them" (Genesis 1:27). This statement teaches us of our divine origins and that from the beginning "the measure of [our] creation" is to be like God (D&C 88:19; see also D&C 49:17).

Biblical scholars explain the two Hebrew terms behind the words *image* and *likeness* as references to being created in the form of God as well as to having His divine attributes.[1] President Dieter F. Uchtdorf summarized what we have learned from modern revelation when he taught, "We are created in the image of our heavenly parents; we are God's spirit children."[2] Whereas in ancient Near Eastern temples it was common to have the image of the god in that god's temple, in the Garden of Eden the image of God is found in the man and the woman. The biblical story further explains Adam and Eve's purpose. As bearers of the divine image, Adam and Eve were to be representatives of God in His creation—to "multiply, and replenish the earth"—and they were to care for the earth and the creatures therein (Genesis 1:28).

The effects of the Fall made it possible for Adam and Eve to experience mortality with agency—through which they could be tested and tried in order to become like their Creator. Armed with the knowledge of good and evil, Adam and Eve were able to exercise faith and obedience in discerning between good and evil and in choosing the good. According to Mosiah 3:19, we too must discern and choose either "the natural man," which "is an enemy to God," or yield "to the enticings of the Holy Spirit" to become "a saint through the atonement of Christ."

Mosiah 3:19 is one of my favorite scriptures. In the summer of 1968 I was sitting with my Grandmother Payne at the Manti

Pageant. I was fourteen, and it was the day that she would ruin my life. We had arrived early, so we had time to visit.

Grandma Payne was always interested in our lives, and she asked me, "David Rolph, what are you planning to do with your life?"

Being a child of the sixties, I thought long and hard before revealing my well-thought-out plans to a grown-up—a member of the Establishment. But I took the risk, and I carefully began to explain how I planned to leave our warlike, corrupt, and materialistic society and retire to the woods to study the outdoors and to learn to play the guitar and to write poetry. I concluded my short sermon, declaring somewhat innocently, "I am going to be the natural man."

She smiled at me, almost incredulously, and said, "Boy, are you in trouble! Don't you know that the Book of Mormon teaches that the natural man is an enemy to God?"

I have never forgotten that day. It changed my life. I always read this passage with a smile—and I learned that it is risky to tell your plans to an adult.

Throughout history the Lord has commanded His children to be like Him. In the Old Testament He commanded, "Ye shall be holy: for I the Lord your God am holy" (Leviticus 19:2). In the meridian of time Jehovah, the God of the Old Testament, came to earth to live among us to show us the way and to accomplish the Atonement and make it possible for us to return to our Heavenly Father. Jesus repeated the commandment to be like God, in whose image and likeness we were created: "Be ye therefore perfect, even as your Father which is in heaven is perfect" (Matthew 5:48; see also 3 Nephi 12:48).

In the final scene of our play, the Savior returns in His glory to judge us, to see if we have "filled the measure of [our] creation" (D&C 88:19). Elder Dallin H. Oaks has taught, "The Final Judgment is not just an evaluation of a sum total of good and evil acts—what we have *done*. It is an acknowledgment of the final effect of our acts and thoughts—what we have *become*."[3]

Let us now turn to another scripture. In Moses 1, God dramatically introduced Himself to Moses by showing him the splendor and glory of His creations. And then He said, "And I have a work for thee, Moses, my son; and thou art in the similitude of mine Only Begotten" (Moses 1:6). Here the Lord teaches Moses (and us) that he is His son and reminds him of his divine potential, being created in the similitude of the Son. He later reveals to Moses the ultimate purpose of creation: "For behold, this is my work and my glory—to bring to pass the immortality and eternal life of man" (Moses 1:39).

These passages remind us that creation as described in the Bible is not just an event but is a process that continues to this day. This was eloquently stated in a BYU devotional years ago by one of my good friends, Professor George S. Tate:

Wasn't the Creation completed a very long time ago? Yes, in a sense it was. . . . But in another sense, creation is ongoing, since its aim has not been fulfilled. If it is God's "work and [his] glory" to "bring to pass the immortality and eternal life of man" (see Moses 1:39), creation is not complete until we have fulfilled the measure of our creation.[4]

The scriptures record God's continued creation of His children through covenant, and covenant is very important. I am reminded this morning of a Jewish midrash on Exodus 19, which recounts how the children of Israel were gathered at the foot of Mount Sinai, prepared to receive the law. The midrash describes how God impressed upon the children of Israel the weight of the covenant they were about to enter into. He uprooted Mount Sinai and lifted it in the air, where it hovered like a barrel over the children of Israel. And then God emphasized the crushing weight of the mountain and said, "If you accept the Torah, all is well; if not, here will be your grave."[5] As I walked in the building this morning, I looked up, and I want to tell you that, to me, this has felt like the weight of Mount Sinai.

The Lord uses covenant in the process of the spiritual creation of His children. Adam and Eve were required to be born again through water, the Spirit, and blood (see Moses 6:58–60). Ancient Israel is collectively described as "the work of mine hands" created at Mount

Sinai (Isaiah 29:23; see also Isaiah 43:21) and, throughout her history, as being shaped and formed as the clay in the hand of the potter (see Isaiah 45:9; Jeremiah 18:1–10). And Jesus taught that we must be born again "of water and of the Spirit" (John 3:5). Our lives, then, are about creation. They are about what it is we are becoming.

THE MASTER AND HIS APPRENTICES

Several years ago I began a discussion with the Lord that has proven to be a pivotal point in my life. One day, in a moment of serious self-reflection—which we commonly call a midlife crisis (and which for some of us began the day after our missions and continues to the present)—I sat down to determine if I had done anything significant with my life. I asked myself and the Lord this simple question: "What is my masterpiece? What is the culmination of all of my years of training and hard work?" As a young person I longed to be an artist or a musician, but after years of study and practice I concluded that my talents lay elsewhere. But still I continue to think of producing in my life a "masterpiece."

The Lord responded to my question with three thoughts.

First, He said to me that my task was to fulfill the measure of my creation—to be in the image and likeness of God, to be holy and perfect like Him. I walked over and looked into my spiritual mirror, and the result was not encouraging.

He then told me that my greatest work was to be my wife, Jo Ann, and my children.

And then the Lord said to me, "But you are not a master, so why do you think you can produce a masterpiece? You are just an apprentice in my workshop."

Having always been a lover of great art (my son and I have walked every hall of the Louvre—it took us three days), I am familiar with the roles of the apprentices that worked in the shops of the master artists and craftsmen. Especially during the Renaissance the great artists had workshops in which they employed apprentices to help them produce their masterpieces. Leonardo da Vinci served as an apprentice in the studio of Verrocchio, Michelangelo in the studio of Ghirlandaio, and Raphael in the studio of Perugino. The apprentices sought engagement in the workshops to do three things.

First, they came to get to know the master, his values, and his personality and to see up close how he produced his masterpieces.

Second, they came to learn from the master by doing. They began by doing the mundane jobs: sweeping the shop and preparing the pigments and the panels. As they progressed in skill, they were given more responsible tasks: painting backgrounds or minor figures, thus participating in the creation of great masterpieces.

Third, the apprentices came because they aspired to become like their masters. They hoped that by knowing the master and working by his side, they could one day become masters themselves.[6]

Remember the Lord's conversation with Moses: "And I have a work for thee, Moses, my son; and thou art in the similitude of mine Only Begotten" (Moses 1:6). In Heavenly Father's workshop, we, like Moses, are both God's masterpieces in process—"in the similitude of mine Only Begotten"—as well as His children, His sons and daughters, whom He has engaged in His workshop as apprentices, saying, "I have a work for you."

RECEIVING GOD'S IMAGE AND LIKENESS

I believe the metaphor of the master and his apprentices can help us better understand how we can become God's masterpieces—His children in the "image and likeness of God."[7] Just like an apprentice in a workshop, our first step is to get to know the Master. The Prophet Joseph Smith taught, "It is the first principle of the gospel to know for a certainty the character of God"[8] and to have "a *correct* idea of his . . . perfections, and attributes."[9] We know that we can come to know the Lord by studying the scriptures, through prayer, and by associating with others who know Him.

In order to help us to know the Master, Heavenly Father sent His Only Begotten Son to earth to reveal to us the Father: "The Son can do nothing of himself, but what he seeth the Father do" (John 5:19). Thus Jesus Christ came to earth as Heavenly Father's masterpiece in His image as well as in the image of a man, and through His Atonement Jesus Christ became the Master of the workshop. The Savior's life teaches us that His primary attribute is love. He loves His Father and He loves us, and He expects us, as His creations and as His apprentices, to love one another: "By this shall all men know that ye are my disciples, if ye have love one to another" (John 13:35).

Through reading the accounts of the life of the Savior we can learn what He is like, what He values, and how He treated others. The Apostle Peter gave us an example of the power of knowing the Savior. Recall with me the account in Matthew when the Savior, who was walking upon the stormy sea, invited Peter to walk on the water with Him. When Peter left the boat and began to go to Jesus, the text records:

> But when he saw the wind boisterous, he was afraid; and beginning to sink, he cried, saying, Lord, save me.
> And immediately Jesus stretched forth his hand, and caught him, and said unto him, O thou of little faith, wherefore didst thou doubt? [Matthew 14:30–31]

Later, after the death and resurrection of the Savior, Peter found himself the head of the Church. Fearless in the face of persecution, Peter was teaching at the temple with John when a lame beggar asked for alms. Peter, following the example of the Savior, stretched out his hand and said:

> Silver and gold have I none; but such as I have give I thee: In the name of Jesus Christ of Nazareth rise up and walk.
> And he took him [following the example of the Savior on the Sea of Galilee] by the right hand, and lifted him up. [Acts 3:6–7]

The second step is learning in the workshop by doing. Latter-day Saints are familiar with the gospel of doing: we do good works, we do our home teaching and visiting teaching, and we even call temple worship "temple work." The scriptures are replete with commandments of doing or not doing. The Savior simply said, "Come, follow me" (Luke 18:22; see also Matthew 4:19). By imitating the life of Jesus we learn obedience, compassion, love, and how to treat our fellows as if they were the Master: "Inasmuch as ye have done it unto one of the least of these my brethren, ye have done it unto me" (Matthew 25:40).

As we become skilled apprentices, we come to realize that the Master has given us a breathtaking responsibility in the workshop. In the beginning, Adam and Eve were commanded to "multiply, and replenish the earth" (Genesis 1:28), and they were given the gift of procreation—to create the bodies for the spirit children of our heavenly parents, in the image of God. This sacred gift of procreation is one of the greatest gifts imaginable and gives us the power to work as co-creators with God.

Elder Jeffrey R. Holland described this role as follows:

You will never be more like God at any other time in this life than when you are expressing that particular power. Of all the titles he has chosen for himself, Father is the one he declares, and Creation is his watchword—especially human creation, creation in his image.[10]

Genesis 5:3 records, "And Adam . . . begat a son in his own likeness, after his image." Here is where the fun begins, as Heavenly Father has given us the privilege of creating these children in our image as well. When we first held our babies, we would greet each new spirit with wonder, and then we would begin to note the distribution of the genes from our families. The results can be both spectacular and comical. As we raise our children in the image and likeness of God, we are shocked as they assume our image and likeness as well. One morning, a few days after I finished a grueling two years working on my dissertation, we were lying on our bed when our darling two-and-a-half-year-old son raced into the room and began jumping on the bed, gleefully shouting, "I am sure glad that darned dissertation is done!" But he didn't say "darned"!

Several years later our family was living in New York City for the summer, and we were attending a scholarly workshop together with lots of other aspiring scholars. Many of my colleagues were Christian, and one week we decided to perform an ecumenical gesture by attending the Riverside Church with my Christian colleagues. We got up in the morning and announced to our children that we were going to the Riverside Church, and our little boy said, "Wow, I really don't want to put on my crunchy clothes today, and I really don't want to go to that church." First I pleaded. Then I just grabbed his arm and dragged him out the door. As we got to the Riverside Church and went through the entrance, we looked in and realized that people had not brought their children to this meeting. The two thousand people in the church were sitting there quietly, waiting for the beginning of the meeting, and my five-year-old son shouted out, "But Daddy, this isn't even the true church!" So much for the ecumenical gesture of the Seelys that week.

One of the most exhilarating jobs in the workshop is to work with Heavenly Father's children in the creation of families. And it is here that our family has experienced the grandest of adventures. But helping to create Heavenly Father's children in His image and likeness is not confined to parenthood. Throughout our lives we become co-creators with the Master in our relationships with all of those around us: our families, friends, mission companions, roommates, colleagues, teachers, and students, as well as those we visit teach and home teach.

Let me share with you several important things that I have learned in the workshop as we have worked as co-creators with the Master. I have learned that the image and likeness of God is not to be found in outward appearances—it is to be found in our hearts. In our modern culture, especially in the media, there is overwhelming attention and concern given to "image," which is almost always a reference to outward appearances. A powerful story in the scriptures addresses this issue. When the prophet Samuel was sent to find the Lord's anointed among the sons of Jesse in Bethlehem, he examined the seven eldest sons of Jesse, expecting to find among them the next king of Israel. He was disappointed to find that none of them was the one the Lord had chosen, and he finally had Jesse send for his youngest son, David. The Lord then taught us a lesson that should pierce our souls: "For the Lord seeth not as man seeth; for man looketh on the outward appearance, but the Lord looketh on the heart" (1 Samuel 16:7). The Lord wants us to learn to see ourselves and others as He sees us: not looking on outward appearances but looking on the heart. In our search for friends, associates, and, most important, our future spouses, we need to learn to see each other "not as man seeth" but as "the Lord looketh on the heart."

Another thing I have learned in the workshop is that being created in the image and likeness of God does not mean that we are all the same. As spirit children of Heavenly Father, we come to earth with our individuality. Heavenly Father tells us that He has blessed us with different spiritual gifts:

For all have not every gift given unto them; for there are many gifts, and to every man is given a gift by the Spirit of God.

To some is given one, and to some is given another, that all may be profited thereby. [D&C 46:11–12; see also 1 Corinthians 12]

President James E. Faust taught:

We do not lose our identity in becoming members of this church. . . . We say to all who have joined the Church, keep all that is noble, good, and uplifting in your culture and personal identity.[11]

As we look through the scriptures, we see the way the Lord has made use of many different individuals: in the Old Testament there was a Moses and an Aaron, a Ruth and an Esther; in the New Testament a Peter and a Paul, a Mary and a Martha; and in our day a Joseph Smith and a Brigham Young, a Gordon B. Hinckley and a Thomas S. Monson.

In the workshop we come to appreciate that the Lord's master-pieces are created through a great price. Abraham demonstrated the ultimate faith in God when he took his son Isaac to sacrifice him on Mount Moriah. The Lord exclaimed, "Now I know that thou fearest God, seeing thou hast not withheld thy son, thine only son from me" (Genesis 22:12). On that day Abraham showed us the image of God the Father when he, like his Heavenly Father, demonstrated his willingness to sacrifice his beloved son, and Isaac showed us the image of God the Son as he willingly submitted to the will of his father.

We are surrounded by many who have taught us by example the principles of faith, obedience, and sacrifice. In the *Lectures on Faith* we are taught, "The faith necessary unto the enjoyment of life and salvation never could be obtained without the sacrifice of all earthly things."[12]

My grandfather J. Leo Seely received a mission call in 1914 to serve the Lord in Ireland. He left his wife and little children for two years. The depth of his sacrifice has become clear to us as we have read their letters. Upon his return he grabbed my grandmother in an embrace, and his little daughter Ina, who hadn't seen her father for years, raced out to chastise this unfamiliar man, shouting, "You naughty man, leave my mother alone!"

Because of the power of this man's example and that of my noble grandmother, my father served a mission, and then over fifty of his grandchildren and now his great-grandchildren have gone forth to serve the Lord in missions all over the world. Great-great-grandfather William Bramall crossed the plains seven times and served five missions to England. Great-grandparents German E. and Mary Rachel Ellsworth presided over the Northern States Mission for seventeen years. And Great-Grandmother Sumsion began a great tradition of sister missionary service followed by her daughter, her granddaughters, and now her great-granddaughters. As we watch our children—and as you watch your friends and families—open mission calls, we see the image of God in a person who is willing to follow in the footsteps of the Savior to sacrifice for the salvation of His children. They have the faith and the courage to go wherever the Lord calls them.

Esau is another unheralded example of one who showed us how to shape our lives in the image of God. When his brother, Jacob, tricked him out of the birthright, Esau was enraged to the point of seeking to kill his brother. After many years of avoiding each other, there was a dramatic moment when Jacob encountered his brother. Jacob, fearing for his life, prepared gifts for Esau. When the moment of the encounter came and Jacob met his brother, Esau unexpectedly forgave him. Looking into Esau's forgiving face, Jacob exclaimed, "For therefore I have seen thy face, as though I had seen the face of God" (Genesis 33:10).

The image of God is forgiveness. As Brother Nibley always used to remind us, "The two things you can do in life are to repent and forgive."[13]

The third step of our apprenticeship is the most important and perhaps the most difficult. Ultimately we are commanded to "be holy" and to "be perfect" like the Master. As we live the gospel and fill our lives with knowing and doing, something miraculous happens to us: we begin to become like the Savior and like our Father in Heaven. But we cannot complete the process of becoming like God on our own. Only the Master can make a masterpiece, and only He can make us in His own image.

Let me tell you about something I love. There is a fragment of a Dead Sea scroll from Cave 4 at Qumran that I had the privilege to work on several years ago. It is a piece of a hymn called *Barkhi Nafshi*—"Bless, O My Soul." One cold winter day I was in the workroom at the Shrine of the Book in Jerusalem examining this fragment. It had not yet been mounted in a protective frame, and a gust of wind came through the window and blew the fragile fragment onto the floor. Horrified, I quickly got a large piece of paper and knelt down to scoop it up. As I stood to put it back onto the table, I was overcome with emotion—holding in my hands this precious piece of the past, a piece of leather that contained the hymn of praise from a Jewish author two thousand years ago. In this fragment of text the ancient hymnist expressed the mystery of acquiring the attributes of God: "Bless, O my soul, the Lord. . . . He has been gracious to the needy, and he has opened their eyes to see his ways, and their ears to hear his teaching. And he has circumcised the foreskins of their heart" (4Q434 1.i.1–4).[14] Paraphrasing from Deuteronomy (10:16–17; 30:6), another sacred text that I love, the ancient author of this poem acknowledges that it is only God who can, through His grace, open our eyes and ears and change our hearts.

This doctrine is taught throughout the scriptures. The Lord says in Ezekiel, "A new heart also will I give you, and a new spirit will I put within you" (Ezekiel 36:26). And Paul describes the death of "our old man" and the birth of the new that we experience at baptism (Romans 6:6; see verses 1–6).

Occasionally things go wrong in the workshop, and we, as the Master's masterpieces in progress, become distorted or deformed. Sometimes the problem is sin—giving in to the enticings of the natural man. Sometimes it is discouragement, disappointment, sickness, or death. The Master of the workshop came to earth and, as explained by Alma, experienced mortal "infirmities, that his bowels may be filled with mercy, according to the flesh, that he may know according to the flesh how to succor his people according to their infirmities" (Alma 7:12). He has the power to cleanse us, to heal us, and to restore us to His image and likeness, for the Atonement "bring[s] about the bowels of mercy" that "can satisfy the demands of justice, and encircles them in the arms of safety" (Alma 34:15–16).

I testify that the power of the Atonement is real and that His "grace is sufficient for all" (Ether 12:27). As we call upon our Father in Heaven in repentance, through the power of the Savior's Atonement we can find forgiveness. Through the Holy Ghost He can send encouragement and comfort. We as apprentices in the workshop should remember that, as my daughter says, "often the Holy Ghost needs helpers." We can help the Master by reaching out to those around us, offering forgiveness, encouragement, and comfort.

CONCLUSION

At this very moment in our lives we are in the process of creation—of choosing between the natural man and becoming, through the power of the grace of our Savior, individuals in the image and likeness of God. As apprentices in His workshop, the Lord has called us to work with Him in producing His masterpieces—His children in His own image. We do so as families, as mothers and fathers, as sons and daughters, as brothers and sisters in the gospel, as missionaries, as teachers and students and through service to our fellowman. There is great joy in the workshop as we see the miraculous growth and the changes of heart that occur through the power of the Atonement. The eternal and enduring masterpieces that we produce in our lives are not works of art or music or scholarly books or articles—they are the people around us. As we help the Master with His masterpieces, we are engaged in His work and His glory: "the immortality and eternal life of man."

I find joy in being an apprentice in the Savior's workshop, and I aspire to be like Him. As we work in the Lord's kingdom, serving His children, we can become like Him.

I love the Lord Jesus Christ. I testify that He lives and He loves us, and I pray "that when he shall appear we shall be like him, for we shall see him as he is" (Moroni 7:48). In the name of our Master, Jesus Christ, amen.

NOTES

1. "The 'image' is problematic in its own right. For in most of its occurrences, [ṣelem] 'image' is a concrete noun. And as such, it refers to a representation of form, figure, or physical appearance (see §7.2.1). Thus if the human race is created in the 'image of God', there is an unavoidable logical implication: God must also be material, physical, corporeal, and, to a certain degree, humanoid (see also §7.1.4)" (W. Randall Garr, *In His Own Image and Likeness: Humanity, Divinity, and Monotheism*, vol. 15 of *Culture and History of the Ancient Near East*, ed. Baruch Halpern, Manfred H. E. Weippert, Theo P. J.

van den Hout, and Irene J. Winter [Leiden and Boston: Brill, 2003], 5–6).

John H. Walton notes that in ancient Near Eastern cultures the "image of god" can also refer to the idealized representation of the attributes of the deity. For example, "When the Assyrian king Esarhaddon is referred to as 'the perfect likeness of the god,' it is his qualities and his attributes that are meant. . . . In the Israelite context as portrayed in the Hebrew Bible, people are in the image of God in that they embody his qualities and do his work" (*Ancient Near Eastern Thought and the Old Testament: Introducing the Conceptual World of the Hebrew Bible* [Grand Rapids, Michigan: Baker Academic, 2006], 212).

2. Dieter F. Uchtdorf, "The Love of God," *Ensign*, November 2009, 22.

3. Dallin H. Oaks, "The Challenge to Become," *Ensign*, November 2000, 32; emphasis in original.

4. George S. Tate, "Obedience, Creation, and Freedom," BYU devotional address, 25 July 1995.

5. "'They took their places at the foot of the mountain' (19:17): . . . This teaches that God suspended the mountain [Sinai] over them, like a barrel, and told them, 'If you accept the Torah, all is well; if not, here will be your grave'" (Babylonian Talmud, *Shabbat*, 88a). Quoted from Avivah Gottlieb Zornberg, *The Particulars of Rapture: Reflections on Exodus* (New York: Doubleday, 2001), 270.

6. The three steps of "knowing, doing, and being" as elements of Mormonism have been elegantly explored by my friend Arthur R. Bassett in "Knowing, Doing, and Being: Vital Dimensions in the Mormon Religious Experience," *Sunstone*, December 1979, 64–67; May 1985, 59–63; June 1999, 70–77.

7. *HC* 6:305.

8. *HC* 6:305.

9. *Lectures on Faith* (1985), 38 (3:4); emphasis in original.

10. Jeffrey R. Holland, "Of Souls, Symbols, and Sacraments," BYU devotional address, 12 January 1988; emphasis in original.

11. James E. Faust, "Heirs to the Kingdom of God," *Ensign*, May 1995, 62.

12. *Lectures on Faith* (1985), 69 (6:7).

13. See Hugh Nibley, transcript (at 24:50) from the film *The Faith of an Observer: Conversations with Hugh Nibley* (1985): "We're just sort of dabbling around, playing around, being tested for our moral qualities, and, above all, the two things that we can be good at, and no two other things can we do: We can forgive and we can repent"; http://maxwellinstitute.byu.edu/publications/multimedia.php?id=5.

14. Moshe Weinfeld and David Seely, *"Barkhi Nafshi,"* in *Qumran Cave 4.XX: Poetical and Liturgical Texts, Part 2*, vol. 29 of *Discoveries in the Judaean Desert*, ed. Esther Chazon et al. (Oxford: Clarendon Press, 1999), 271.

Live Your Life with Purpose

Janie Penfield

Good morning. I am humbled to be with you today. I am grateful for family, friends, and colleagues who are in the audience and watching at home to support me. I have prayed diligently over the past months that something I say today will benefit each of us, and I do that now as well.

I am an adventure seeker, especially in the outdoors. I love to hike, bike, swim, and ski. Through my many adventures I have learned that each one must be planned with clear purposes or objectives—to summit a peak, to complete a course, or to enjoy the views. I have found that planning with purpose is the best way to ensure that each adventure is successful.

For example, I love to Nordic ski. As with all skiing, there is a trail map that allows you to chart a successful course through the woods and terrain. My favorite place to ski is at Sundance's Nordic Center. The trails lead you through evergreen and aspen trees and include views of Mount Timpanogos and frozen Stewart

Janie Penfield was a BYU associate athletic director when this devotional address was given on 5 February 2013. © *Brigham Young University.*

Falls. There are several trails to choose from; some are out of the way and less traveled than others. All the trails are surrounded by ungroomed or wooded ground with unknown obstacles beneath the meringue-like layer of snow. Leaving the trail could be troublesome or even perilous.

Each ski trek begins with the question Where to? followed by Which route? Each trail takes us to a different spot with different options for adventure and scenery—a steep climb, a flat meadow, or an incredible view. Before we begin to ski we must determine the purpose of our trek so we know which trails to take. Then we must ski on course or we will not reach our destination.

DETERMINE YOUR PURPOSE

We are here on earth in a type of adventure. We left our Heavenly Father to obtain bodies, to be tested, to make covenants, to gain knowledge and experience, and to hopefully return to live with Him. But we do not always remember these purposes. Many who do not have the gospel have forgotten these purposes because of the veil. We often get weighed down by the daily monotony of school, church, family, and work and forget about our aspirations— aspirations that our Heavenly Father wants us to have. We often even get distracted and waylaid by "good" things.

Elder Dallin H. Oaks taught:

> *As we consider various choices, we should remember that it is not enough that something is good. Other choices are better, and still others are best. Even though a particular choice is more costly, its far greater value may make it the best choice of all.* ["Good, Better, Best," *Ensign*, November 2007, 104–5]

He goes on to say that "we have to forego some good things in order to choose others that are better or best because they develop faith in the Lord Jesus Christ and strengthen our families" ("Good, Better, Best," 107). There are many good things that we can do, but we must stay true to our purpose and live the life of a disciple. We can get married or, better/best, we can get married in the temple. We can pray for the missionaries or, better/best, we can invite our friends and family to visit with them in our homes.

Individually we may become discouraged because of the distance between us and the mortal life we've aspired to. We may not be married, have children, or have the degree or success that we thought would give us the life we'd planned. Fame, fortune, fashion, and fun will play a part in our eventual destination. But we have the power to control what role, if any, these play in keeping us on or taking us off the path of discipleship. Our collection of choices will determine our final destination.

President Thomas S. Monson said:

Eternal life in the kingdom of our Father is [our] *goal. Such a goal is not achieved in one glorious attempt but rather is the result of a lifetime of righteousness, an accumulation of wise choices, even a constancy of purpose.* ["Decisions Determine Destiny," BYU devotional address, 6 November 2005]

So what can we do to ensure that we build a lifetime of righteousness and accumulate wise choices? We can live our life with purpose—the purpose to gain eternal life and be counted as a disciple of Jesus Christ.

Keeping our destination or the purpose of our life in mind influences our decisions. We are choosing friends, majors, careers, social activities, priorities, and many more things. But the most important decision that we must map out is the course to our destination if we are ever to get there. Where are we skiing to? If we make a conscious decision to be on the Lord's side and to seek the highest degree of glory in the celestial kingdom, then many of our decisions in daily life fall into place. Knowing that we will *not* go toward so many other destinations provides us with significant direction. We can make our judgments and decisions based on the decided purpose of our life. Does this friend bring me closer to or further from the Spirit? Does this major or career allow me to be the disciple of

Christ I aspire to be? Does this activity keep me close to the Lord? Committing to achieve the greatest possible outcome from mortality frees us from much of the push and pull of the world.

In the last general conference President Dieter F. Uchtdorf said, "The foundational principles of the gospel of Jesus Christ can affect our life's direction for good, if only we will apply them" ("Of Regrets and Resolutions," *Ensign*, November 2012, 21). If we want to enjoy eternal life we must apply the principles President Uchtdorf is referring to and become disciples of Christ. As he says, "The pursuit of holiness and happiness . . . is the path to our best and happiest self" ("Of Regrets," 23). We must plan our lives with the purpose of becoming a disciple of Jesus Christ. President Uchtdorf says we can do this by following the Savior, striving to be like Him, listening to and obeying the Spirit's promptings, and devoting ourselves to the pursuit of holiness and happiness (see "Of Regrets," 23). Becoming a disciple also includes being baptized, making and keeping temple covenants, and building the kingdom of God.

It can sometimes be difficult to remember our predetermined course. The scriptures and the prophets counsel us to remember the things of the Spirit—our Savior and the Atonement, our covenants, and the commandments. Remembering helps us keep proper perspective and focus on our purpose. We must choose to remember. We must remember what we want and why we want it. President Henry B. Erying taught us that "the key to the remembering that brings and maintains testimony is receiving the Holy Ghost as a companion" ("O Remember, Remember," *Ensign*, November 2007, 68). If we live worthy of the Holy Ghost we will remember our purpose. The Savior taught, "But the Comforter, which is the Holy Ghost, whom the Father will send in my name, he shall teach you all things, and bring all things to your remembrance" (John 14:26).

DETERMINE YOUR COURSE

Once we are fixed on our purpose, we must determine our course to fulfill that purpose. We have to make a plan for how we will reach our destination.

Last January there were twelve of us geared up in Wyoming with our skis on, ready to go. Granite Hot Springs was over ten miles in front of us. We knew we needed to stay on the road and keep going in spite of the serious negative temperatures, the hills, and the lack of sunshine. We also planned to take time to enjoy the scenery around us. We had planned to do an out-and-back route of over twenty miles in a day, and we needed to start early, stay together, keep fueled, keep moving, and stay the course. We did, and we finished the out-and-back trek exhausted!

Just as my friends and I were as we skied on our adventure in Wyoming, we must be fixed on our course and our purpose. We must continue to press forward despite adverse conditions. We must not be deterred by challenges—big and small—all the while taking in the beauty and wonders mortality affords us.

The map to navigate life on earth has been provided to us through the restoration of the gospel. The standard works, modern-day prophets, and inspired leaders help us navigate through the challenges of mortality. Lehi's dream is a broad sketch of mortality. The latter-day prophets fill in the challenges and specific guidance for our day, helping us keep hold of the iron rod. We must determine our course to ensure that our daily choices have a chance of leading us to eternal life—we will not arrive there by chance. In Doctrine and Covenants 132:22 we read, "For strait is the gate, and narrow the way that leadeth unto the exaltation and continuation of the lives." We need to be on the path when we reach the gate. Having the goal of eternal life, we know where we can look for direction to stay on the narrow way and to find the strait gate.

The scriptures and the teachings of the prophets have provided us with a course for our life on earth. The path of discipleship is the path that runs within reach of the iron rod. We move each hand and each foot in front of the other, progressing as we make decisions to prioritize the work of the Lord, the keeping of our covenants, and our constant efforts to emulate the Savior. What is on the narrow way? Temple marriage, missionary service, paying a full tithe, keeping the Sabbath day holy, fulfilling callings, being charitable—and the list goes on.

Staying on the strait and narrow path requires us to make consistent "best" choices. As a skier, in order to return to the trailhead you have to take the right trails, turn at the right times, and have the skill to descend the mountain safely. As many inexperienced Nordic skiers have noted, the hills look easy to navigate until you strap on boots that only bind in the front and skis that are slightly wider than Popsicle sticks. We must chart our course carefully. Where will we turn, go straight, or climb? The trail map and master teachers will give us all of the information we need.

We learn from Elder L. Lionel Kendrick that the guidance we need is in the scriptures. He said:

Those revelations received by prophets are given to us in the form of scripture or by the voice of the living prophets. Thus, the scriptures become a road map, a set of divine directions to assist us on our journey through mortality and our return trip home. ["Search the Scriptures," *Ensign,* May 1993, 13]

Just as Lehi and his family looked to the Liahona for direction through the wilderness to the promised land, we should let the scriptures and the teachings of the prophets serve as our map as we make our way through the wilderness of mortality.

President Dieter F. Uchtdorf said:

We all search for happiness, and we all try to find our own "happily ever after." The truth is, God knows how to get there! He has created a map for you; He knows the way. . . . The map is available to all. It gives explicit directions of what to do and where to go to everyone who is striving to come unto Christ. ["Your Happily Ever After," *Ensign,* May 2010, 126–27]

All you have to do is trust your Heavenly Father—trust Him enough to follow His plan, keep your covenants, and keep His commandments.

President Uchtdorf continued:

Nevertheless, not all will follow the map. They may look at it. They may think it is reasonable, perhaps even true. But they do not follow the divine directions. Many believe that any road will take them to a "happily ever after." ["Your Happily Ever After," 127]

As members of the Church, we know that not all roads or trails lead to the eternal life we seek. "Happily ever after" will only be ours if we choose to follow the Savior and be His disciples.

We are constantly making decisions, and if your life is like mine, most of those decisions are made while in "survival mode." This is decision making in the moment, instead of planning out a course and moving forward when the time is right. This is not the best way to make decisions, for when I live in survival mode, I too often fail to accomplish the things I prioritized in my mind—that phone call to a friend, lunch with my brother, an evening at the temple, a workout, and even what I'm going to do on vacation. It is also while I am in survival mode that I see opportunities pass me by—a weakening friendship with a kindred spirit, waning family relationships, a decrease in desire to do the things to stay close to the Spirit, decreased fitness level, and even a missed opportunity to kayak the Napoli Coast in Hawaii! (How did I let that happen?)

Perhaps you are like me. Perhaps you, too, let the chaos of life, your studies, your calling, your job, or your fun crowd out the opportunities the Spirit has to speak to you. Perhaps your prayers have become hurried or your scripture study is more reading than study. Perhaps you have reshuffled your priorities and have put staying close to the Spirit off to the side simply as a result of *not* prioritizing it. President Uchtdorf said, "Discipleship is the pursuit of holiness and happiness. It is the path to our best and happiest self" ("Of Regrets," 23). So it follows that pursuing and prioritizing discipleship will lead us to the best life we can build for ourselves on earth, but we have to seek it by choosing to be a disciple of Christ. We have to choose it by being forgiving, charitable, grateful, and anxiously engaged in serving others. We have to make discipleship our course.

How do we know what we can do to be a disciple? How do we know what we can do to fulfill our purpose on earth and build the kingdom of God? We have to ask Him—through prayer. The scriptures have taught us that the Lord will give us answers to our prayers: "Behold, I will tell you in your mind and in your heart, by the Holy Ghost, which shall come upon you and which shall dwell in your heart" (D&C 8:2). We will hear by the whisperings of the Spirit what we can do to be more like Christ. We will be quietly drawn to opportunities that will allow us to serve on His behalf. We will find ourselves using our talents to build the kingdom of God if we follow the guidance in our heart.

In the last general conference Elder Craig C. Christensen taught:

> *Through the gift of the Holy Ghost, we receive added capacity and spiritual gifts, increased revelation and protection, steady guidance and direction, and the promised blessings of sanctification and exaltation in the celestial kingdom. All of these blessings are given as a result of our personal desire to receive them and come as we align our lives with the will of God and seek His constant direction.* ["An Unspeakable Gift from God," *Ensign*, November 2012, 14]

When Alma gives counsel to his son Helaman, he too tells him to stay aligned with our Heavenly Father and seek His guidance: "O, remember, my son, and learn wisdom in thy youth; yea, learn in thy youth to keep the commandments of God" (Alma 37:35). What great counsel—from both Elder Christensen and Alma. Alma continued to call on Helaman to "counsel with the Lord in all thy doings, and he will direct thee for good" (Alma 37:37). We know how to get the direction of the Spirit. Now we have to do it.

How can we allocate our time, talents, and resources to align with our purpose and stay on course? We can do it through goals. I have a lot of goals that aren't the New Year's type of goals. I have the goal of being married in the temple, having and raising children in the gospel, and witnessing them serve missions and raise a righteous posterity. I have the goal of serving a mission myself. I have the goal of being worthy of eternal life with my Father in Heaven and with my family. I have the goal of making my earthly and my heavenly parents proud because I have heeded their counsel and made the gospel of Jesus Christ an integral part of my life. I have the goal of being happy here on earth and in the eternities.

Your goals may be similar to mine. These are our individual course markings. They are the significant choices in our lives that allow us to recognize that we are in alignment with our Father in Heaven. He has given us the personal guidance and direction we need to accomplish our goals.

The companionship of the Holy Ghost provides us with unlimited personal revelation, direction, comfort, strength, and guidance from God. Humility and faith in the Lord Jesus Christ are essential to being worthy of personal revelation and answers to our prayers. All answers do not come when we ask for them. They often come as Alma describes our faith growing: over time as we ponder, study, and seek direction from the Lord (see Alma 32). President Boyd K. Packer tells us that "[we] must learn to seek the power and direction that is available to [us], and then follow that course no matter what" ("How to Survive in Enemy Territory," *Ensign*, October 2012, 29).

We then learn in Doctrine and Covenants 45:57: "For they that are wise and have received the truth, and have taken the Holy Spirit for their guide, and have not been deceived—verily I say unto you, they shall not be hewn down and cast into the fire, but shall abide the day." We must choose to be wise and take the Holy Spirit for our guide. We can benefit from the direction of the Holy Ghost in everything we do. He will guide me—helping me avoid cliffs while skiing, potholes while biking, and terrible snafus at work—if I seek His direction and am aligned with Him and His will.

Prayer is our communication piece with our Heavenly Father, and the Holy Ghost is His communication piece with us. We must keep the line open by seeking out the Father in prayer and by living worthy of the Holy Ghost's companionship. President Packer also taught:

[We] *can always have a direct line of communication with* [our] *Father in Heaven. Do not allow the adversary to convince you that no one is listening on the other end. Your prayers are always heard. You are never alone!* ["How to Survive," 29]

STAYING ON COURSE

Over the last few years I have participated in several road bike rides with wonderful friends. To get in the full mileage—sixty, eighty, or one hundred miles—the courses are marked on the streets with colored arrows and spray paint. There are signs at intersections, and there are usually other riders to follow. However, on more than three different occasions we have ended up off course. On one ride my friends and I mistakenly followed other riders off course— they were riding a different route than we were. On another ride we found the rest stop from the "less traveled" side, as we had apparently missed a turn or two. And on yet another ride we knew we were close to the finish line because of the traffic and noise, but we couldn't find the roads that led us to it. We couldn't find any markings. On each of these road rides my friends and I did get back on course and finish the race, and we learned several lessons—each of which are transferable to our lives.

If we are to reach our intended destination, we must pay attention to the big and the small course markings. In life these markings are not spray-painted arrows and signs; instead they are advancements, covenants, and the companionship of the Spirit. If we are not committed to our course and purpose, we will move with the push and pull of the world, away from the path that leads us to return to our Father in Heaven. We must be committed, and we must do all that we can to stay the course. We must look to the prophets to learn how to read the course's legend to ensure that we stay firmly planted on the strait and narrow path, holding onto the iron rod with both hands.

I don't know exactly when my friends and I went off course on these three occasions, but I can clearly remember when we realized it. Our surroundings weren't familiar or expected, we didn't have the biking companions we'd had before, and when we looked for course markings, we could not find them. There are too many things that could have distracted us and allowed us to get off course, even when we were within blocks of the finish line. What distracted us is far less important than how we got off course. It happened so subtly that we didn't notice until we were off the course—not right next to it or parallel to it, but off.

So it is with the strait and narrow path. At one point in our lives we have two feet firmly planted on it. With a change of roommates or friends, a new girl- or boyfriend, a new city, a new schedule, or even a new job, we can slowly start moving to the path's edge until we realize that we are doing things we never imagined doing: we haven't prayed for days or weeks, we pass on spiritual things, our scriptures are covered in layers of dust, or so many other things happen that indicate we haven't been feeding our testimony the nourishment it needs. Most of the time we cannot pinpoint what changed in our life, but we know our testimony isn't as firm as it once was. Maybe we can't even remember why we keep the commandments.

But there are many things we can do to ensure that we stay on course—on the strait and narrow path. Like my friends and I learned on our road-riding races, we must keep a lookout for the course markings or warning signs. The prophets and the scriptures give us significant counsel on how to stay on course and live our lives with the right purpose. Elder Quentin L. Cook taught, "Immersion in the scriptures is essential for spiritual nourishment" ("Can Ye Feel So Now?" *Ensign*, November 2012, 7). We need to make sure we are constantly feeding ourselves spiritually from the scriptures. Do you immerse yourself in the scriptures?

Mother Teresa and Alma both reminded us of the power of small acts in our lives such as prayer, scripture study, and charity. Mother Teresa said, "Be faithful in small things because it is in them that your strength lies" (*In the Heart of the World: Thoughts, Stories and Prayers* [Novato, California: New World Library, 1997], 15). Alma taught:

> By small and simple things are great things brought to pass; and small means in many instances doth confound the wise.
>
> . . . And by very small means the Lord doth confound the wise and bringeth about the salvation of many souls. [Alma 37:6–7]

There are no small things, because combined, they are our strength and they will bring about our salvation!

There are a few other seemingly "small" things that will have a great impact on our ability to stay true to our purpose. One of these seemingly small things is our friends. Who do we choose to associate with? Who do we choose to date? To marry? To seek advice from and counsel with? To play and study with? President Thomas S. Monson said, "Choose your friends with caution" ("Decisions Determine Destiny"). We must cautiously choose who we allow to have a great impact on our lives. We do many "small" things with our friends. Brother Scott Robley on the Mormon Channel said that true friends treat you like a campsite—they leave you better than they found you (see Mormon Channel, *For the Youth*, "Mapping Your Way," part 2, episode 25, at 21:40; www.mormonchannel.org/for-the-youth/25). We all have companions in our time on earth. They may be siblings, friends, spouses, missionary companions, and even strangers who observe us or briefly interact with us. Are you the true friend you should be to those you are with, and are they the friends they should be for you? Do your friends make it easier for you to live the gospel or not? Do they help you draw closer to the Spirit, even in small degrees? Do they leave you better than they found you, and you them?

If we do not bolster and feed our faith, we will not have the strength to keep covenants or commandments and stay on course. Maintaining our testimony and staying on course will require righteousness and regular repentance. It will require great faith. We must be spiritually strong. We must live worthy of the Holy Ghost's companionship. Elder D. Todd Christofferson said, "Faith comes by the witness of the Holy Spirit to our souls, Spirit to spirit, as we hear or read the word of God. And faith matures as we continue to feast upon the word" ("The Blessing of Scripture," *Ensign*, May 2010, 35). We must delve into the scriptures to know what to do in times of trial, how to help others, and how to answer our questions. The answers are in them. We learn about the Master Teacher and His ways in the scriptures. By studying the scriptures we develop our faith and learn about the Savior, His teachings, the commandments, our Father, and the plan of salvation. Studying the scriptures will keep us on course.

President Thomas S. Monson has given us exceptional counsel for how to stay on course:

Obey the laws of God. They are given to us by a loving Heavenly Father. When they are obeyed, our lives will be more fulfilling, less complicated. Our challenges and problems will be easier to bear. We will receive the Lord's promised blessings. . . .

. . . Make every decision you contemplate pass this test: "What does it do to me? What does it do for me?" And let your code of conduct emphasize not "What will others think?" but rather "What will I think of myself?" Be influenced by that still, small voice. . . . Open your hearts, even your very souls, to the sound of that special voice which testifies of truth. ["Believe, Obey, and Endure," *Ensign*, May 2012, 128, 129]

We need to open our hearts to that special voice, as President Monson said. The Holy Ghost is the only companion of constancy. All of the others will leave us—even if only temporarily—to run errands, go to class, or go to work for the day. The Holy Ghost will be a constant presence in our lives if we will live worthily. We control the level of influence He has in our lives. Do we listen to or ignore Him? Do we act or relax? Do we provide an environment that will allow the Holy Ghost to remain with us? Do we remove the "worldly habits, customs, and traditions" from our lives (Robert D. Hales, "Being a More Christian Christian," *Ensign*, November 2012, 90)?

As the hymn by Penelope Moody Allen says:

Let the Holy Spirit guide;
Let him teach us what is true.
He will testify of Christ,
Light our minds with heaven's view.

Let the Holy Spirit guard;
Let his whisper govern choice.
He will lead us safely home
If we listen to his voice.

Let the Spirit heal our hearts
Thru his quiet, gentle pow'r.
May we purify our lives
To receive him hour by hour.
["Let the Holy Spirit Guide," *Hymns*, 2002, no. 143]

While the challenges of each day do not fade with each sunset, I know that if we can do as the prophets have counseled us, we will be able to continue moving forward on the strait and narrow path. I also know that this path will lead us to eternal life—a life worth every amount of effort required to get there. If we will firmly establish the purpose of our life and stay the course that leads us to it, we will live in the house the Lord has prepared for us "among the mansions of [our] Father" (Ether 12:32).

Let Heavenly Father guide and direct you. Live your life with purpose.

I know the gospel of Jesus Christ is true. I know He is our Savior. I know Thomas S. Monson is a prophet of God, and I know our Father in Heaven loves us and leads us through the Holy Ghost. Of this I testify, in the name of Jesus Christ, amen.

Living a Reverent Life

Donald L. Hallstrom

B eing on the Brigham Young University campus with you extraordinary students, our remarkable administration (including my colleague and friend President Cecil O. Samuelson), and the outstanding faculty is always a thrill. Whenever I am here, nostalgically I recall entering BYU as a freshman (now forty-five years ago) and then meeting Diane here four years later. How else could a boy from Hawaii and a girl from southern Alberta, Canada, meet, fall in love, and marry? We both graduated in 1973, and she did it six months pregnant! Facilitating the introductions needed to begin eternal relationships is an important role of this university.

One of the things we deeply enjoy during these devotionals is the performance—the worshipful performance—of a highly accomplished choral group or choir. Today is no exception. It always causes me to think of the story I heard about someone who observed the signboard in front of a church that is not of our faith. Announcing the coming week's sermon, the sign said, "What Is Hell Really

Donald L. Hallstrom was a member of the Presidency of the Seventy of The Church of Jesus Christ of Latter-day Saints when this devotional address was given on 12 February 2013. © *Intellectual Reserve, Inc.*

Like?" Along the bottom of the sign, as if in response, it said, "Come Hear Our Choir!" I believe we could put a sign in front of the Marriott Center on devotional days with the bold but accurate words "What Is Heaven Really Like? Come Hear Our Choir!"

Diane and I have been privileged to observe the influence of BYU around the world. During our worldwide travels and while residing in international locations, we have personally witnessed the impact of performing groups, study abroad students, faculty lecturers, and outreach programs in building relationships of trust for the university and for the Church. Additionally and significantly, graduates of this institution are powerful tools of the Lord, actively and effectively being used to further His kingdom throughout the world.

The good accomplished by this university is extraordinary. Each of us should want to be an active participant in that good. In the "Preface to the doctrines, covenants, and commandments given in this dispensation" (heading of D&C 1), speaking of "the only true and living church upon the face of the whole earth," the Lord states that He is "well pleased, speaking unto the church collectively and not individually" (D&C 1:30). I am confident the Lord is well pleased with BYU—"collectively." Let each of us "individually" be a positive contributor to the Lord's joy in this institution.

We meet here today in the name of Jesus Christ. We meet under the direction of His holy Apostles, who have given me this assignment to be with you. It is not important that I am the one here. I am simply an ambassador, an envoy. My desire is to appropriately represent the Lord and His Apostles and for the true teacher in this meeting to be the Holy Spirit.

When we gather in a meeting of the Church like this one, we all have an important duty. Most may assume that I have the greatest responsibility: to give a talk that is informative and interesting. I fully accept my role and have prayerfully prepared; however, I share the success of this meeting with each of you. Some may leave inspired, others not. It is really our choice. Each of us has access to the inspiration and revelation that can come to us directly from the Spirit, unfiltered by a speaker. All have different needs and circumstances, and the Spirit can effectively communicate with each of us. Consequently, different messages may be heard today. That is as it should be.

The Doctrine and Covenants states (and this was given by way of commandment) "that when ye are assembled together ye shall instruct and edify each other, that ye may know how to act . . . upon the points of my law" (D&C 43:8). In the next verse it says, "And thus ye shall . . . be sanctified by that which ye have received, and ye shall bind yourselves to act in all holiness before me" (D&C 43:9). We share the responsibility to instruct and be edified, but the duty to act is ours individually. And that is the key! When we participate with the intention to act (meaning to improve), the Spirit has full access to our hearts and minds. "And it shall come to pass, that inasmuch as they . . . exercise faith in me"—remember, faith is a principle of action and of power—"I will pour out my Spirit upon them in the day that they assemble themselves together" (D&C 44:2). That is my hope for this meeting.

I speak of a subject today that may appear to be an unusual one for this setting. I speak of reverence. Upon hearing that word, many may quickly reflect that reverence is merely the act of keeping our children and ourselves quiet when we attend meetings of the Church. I suggest that is not reverence—it is simply one of the ways we demonstrate our reverence. Reverence is to revere, to have a profound love and respect for Deity. In referring to God the Father, latter-day scripture reads: "Before whose throne all things bow in humble reverence, and give him glory forever and ever" (D&C 76:93).

With the Pharisees and Sadducees gathered together, one of them, a lawyer, asked Jesus Christ:

> *Master, which is the great commandment in the law?*
> *Jesus said unto him, Thou shalt love the Lord thy God with all thy heart, and with all thy soul, and with all thy mind.*
> *This is the first and great commandment.* [Matthew 22:36–38]

While serving as president of the Church, David O. McKay stated:

> *Inseparable from the acceptance of the existence of God is an attitude of reverence, to which I wish now to call attention most earnestly to the entire Church. The greatest manifestation of spirituality is reverence; indeed, reverence is spirituality. Reverence is profound respect mingled with love. It is "a complex emotion made up of mingled feelings of the soul."* [Thomas] Carlyle [the Scottish philosopher] *says it is "the highest of human feelings." I have said . . . that if reverence is the highest, then irreverence is the lowest state in which a man can live in the world.* [*CR*, October 1956, 6; quoting Charles Edward Jefferson, *The Character of Jesus* (New York: Thomas Y. Crowell, 1908), 312, and Thomas Carlyle, "On Boswell's Life of Johnson" (1832)]

In April 2001 general conference, President James E. Faust said:

> *I fear that through prosperity many of us have been preoccupied with what Daniel called "gods of silver, and gold, of brass, iron, wood, and stone, which see not, nor hear, nor know"* [Daniel 5:23]. *These, of course, are idols.*
>
> *In reverence for the sacred, overarching and undergirding all else is a love and respect for Deity. During most of the world's history, mankind has labored much in idolatry, either worshiping false gods or becoming preoccupied with acquiring the material opulence of this world.* ["Them That Honour Me I Will Honour," *Ensign*, May 2001, 45]

Today I do not wish to only address lofty doctrines and principles, although they are essential in providing a clear vision. I want to be practical. I hope to discuss ways in which each of us can elevate our actions, not just our thinking. Indeed, my aspiration is for each of us to want to live a more *reverent life*—a life reflective of our love for God the Eternal Father and Jesus Christ, His Son and our Savior.

Do not confuse reverence with being quiet. Of course there are times and places when reverence is shown by not speaking or by using hushed tones. Also, in the correct setting and circumstance, being boisterous and reverent are not conflicting. Real reverence is simply not doing anything disrespectful, demeaning, or degrading to the Godhead. It has to do with how we think, how we act, and how we speak. It relates to our integrity and the way we treat one another. The level at which we keep the covenants made in the holy ordinances is a powerful indication of our reverence.

Spencer W. Kimball, while he was Church president, counseled:

> *We must remember that reverence is not a somber, temporary behavior that we adopt on Sunday. True reverence involves happiness, as well as love, respect, gratitude, and godly fear. It is a virtue that should be part of our way of life. In fact, Latter-day Saints should be the most reverent people in all the earth.* [*We Should Be a Reverent People* (Salt Lake City: The Church of Jesus Christ of Latter-day Saints, 1976), 2]

Those who seek a reverent life have continual and vital opportunities to worship Deity and elevate their reverence. These include public worship, family worship, and personal worship.

PUBLIC WORSHIP

Public worship is when we assemble as children of God, as brothers and sisters, as a community of Saints. These meetings are sometimes large like stake or even general conference or are sometimes small like a quorum or Relief Society meeting or a Sunday School class. Our devotional assembly today is a form of public worship. In each of these meetings we pray, we teach, we testify, and we edify—all with the purpose of increasing our understanding of our Father in Heaven, Jesus the Christ, and the Holy Spirit. We then have the responsibility to translate that ever-increasing knowledge into wisdom—to continually lessen the gap between what we know and how we live.

Temple worship is a sacred form of public worship because it directly involves ordinances and covenants that connect us with Deity. How connected are you to the temple and your covenants? Are you regularly using this holy form of public worship to strengthen your knowledge and your wisdom? As I have sought to live a reverent life, my prayers have focused more on a desire to live true to my covenants.

The most important of public worship meetings outside the temple is sacrament meeting. In addition to the worshipful activities that are part of most Church meetings, this service centers on the living ordinance of the sacrament. As we begin and end the meeting and, specifically, in preparation to partake of the holy sacrament, we sing and we pray. Are we full participants? Are our minds and our hearts there or are they somewhere else? Are our smartphones off or do we text and tweet (or, for us older people, email) during the ordinance or during any part of the service? When the speakers speak, especially if they are less polished orators, do we arrogantly disconnect, thinking, "I've heard it all before"?

If we are guilty of any of these mistakes, what we are doing is reducing—perhaps eliminating—the ability of the Spirit to communicate with us. And then we wonder why we are not edified by sacrament services and other Church meetings.

Public worship is a magnificent opportunity to develop reverence.

FAMILY WORSHIP

Public worship should promote family worship. In 1999 the First Presidency counseled parents and children

to give highest priority to family prayer, family home evening, gospel study and instruction, and wholesome family activities. However worthy and appropriate other demands or activities may be, they must not be permitted to displace the divinely appointed duties that only parents and families can adequately perform. [First Presidency letter, 11 February 1999; cited in "Letter Regarding Parents Teaching Children," *Church News*, 27 February 1999, 3]

Of course these same principles have been repeatedly taught by numerous Church leaders in countless ways over many years.

We live in a world of busyness. Traveling throughout the Church I sometimes privately inquire of local leaders—and these are good Latter-day Saints—"Are you holding family prayer and family home evening?"

Often I receive an embarrassed look and the explanation "We are so busy. Our children's school and extracurricular activities, music and other lessons, social schedule, and Church functions keep them almost fully occupied. My spouse and I are tied up with work, Church, and other commitments. We are seldom together as a family."

The spirit of the First Presidency's counsel is that if we are so busy doing good things that we do not have time for the essential things, we must find solutions.

When children are raised with reverence—when they see parents whose lives are reverent—they are more likely to follow this divine pattern.

PERSONAL WORSHIP

Ultimately, reverence is a personal matter. Public worship leads us to family worship, which leads us to personal worship. This includes personal prayer, personal gospel study, and personal pondering of one's relationship with Deity. "For how knoweth a man the master . . . who is a stranger unto him, and is far from the thoughts and intents of his heart?" (Mosiah 5:13).

Elder D. Todd Christofferson said:

The importance of having a sense of the sacred is simply this—if one does not appreciate holy things, he will lose them. Absent a feeling of reverence, he will grow increasingly casual in attitude and lax in conduct. He will drift from the moorings that his covenants with God could provide. His feeling of accountability to God will diminish and then be forgotten. Thereafter, he will care only about his own comfort and satisfying his uncontrolled appetites. Finally, he will come to despise sacred things, even

God, and then he will despise himself. ["A Sense of the Sacred," CES fireside address, 7 November 2004, BYU, Provo]

Whether it be in public, family, or personal worship or in the mundane affairs of life, it is imperative that we speak the names of Deity only with reverence. The Psalmist David wrote, "He sent redemption unto his people: he hath commanded his covenant for ever: holy and reverend [meaning reverent] is his name" (Psalms 111:9). President Boyd K. Packer stated, "Irreverence suits the purposes of the adversary by obstructing the delicate channels of revelation in both mind and spirit" ("Reverence Invites Revelation," *Ensign*, November 1991, 22).

In our worship we often use the names of the Father and the Son. Every prayer, every talk, and every lesson ends with "in the name of Jesus Christ, amen." For some the use is perfunctory, given without thought or care. Sometimes we hear the phrase slurred in a mindless way as one hurries to conclude and sit down. I, of course, am not suggesting that this important statement of authority be said in some theatrical show—simply that it is sincerely and clearly expressed with our lips, with our mind, and with our heart. That will bring spiritual power to our supplications and teachings.

One of the most powerful reverence lessons in my life occurred nearly thirty-five years ago. After completing our studies at BYU, Diane and I moved to Honolulu to begin the next season of our lives. It turned out to be a long season—twenty-seven years. Only a call from a prophet caused us to leave Hawaii.

The Hawaii Temple—now known as the Laie Hawaii Temple, as there are two temples in Hawaii—was first dedicated by President Heber J. Grant on (appropriately) Thanksgiving Day, November 27, 1919. It was the first temple built outside of Utah, except for the temples in Kirtland and Nauvoo. For nearly six decades it served the Saints in Hawaii and, for much of that time, those throughout the Pacific and Asia. In the mid-1970s there was need for the temple to be closed, enlarged, and renovated. Consequently the temple had need for rededication, which occurred on June 13, 1978.

Presiding at the rededication was the president of the Church, Spencer W. Kimball. With him were his first and second counselors, N. Eldon Tanner and Marion G. Romney. Also attending were Ezra Taft Benson, the president of the Quorum of the Twelve Apostles, and others of the Twelve and the Seventy. It is not something you would see in the larger Church of today, having that many of the senior Brethren together for an event away from Church headquarters. But that was our blessing in 1978.

I was a young priesthood leader at the time and was asked by the temple rededication coordinating committee to be responsible for local security and transportation arrangements for President Kimball and his party. I do not want to overstate my responsibilities—they were simply supportive and "behind the scenes." However, what my assignment did allow was proximity to President Kimball. For a weeklong period that included three days of temple rededication sessions, a solemn assembly, and a large regional conference, I observed the president of the Church close-up. I watched him teach, testify, and prophesy with authority and with power. I saw his tireless effort to minister to "the one," asking to meet privately with individuals he noticed in meetings or along the way. I witnessed him continually being used as "an instrument in the hands of God" (Alma 17:9). I was profoundly impressed!

At the week's conclusion we were at the airport for the departure of President Kimball and his associates. Again, emphasizing my limited and supportive role, I share the following. President Kimball came to me to thank me for my meager efforts. Physically he was not very tall, and I am a large man. He grabbed me by my jacket lapels and sharply yanked me down to be at his height. Then he kissed me on the cheek and thanked me. After walking away a few steps, President Kimball returned. He grasped me in the same way and pulled me down again. This time he kissed me on the other cheek and told me that he loved me. Then he departed.

The year before, a biography of Spencer W. Kimball had been published, written by his son and his grandson. At that time I had obtained it and read it, and I found it interesting. However, after this very personal experience with Spencer Woolley Kimball, I went home from the airport and pulled that thick volume from our library shelf, feeling an intense desire to read it again. Over the next several days—every waking hour I was not otherwise obligated—I was reading and reflecting. You see, I was now reading about someone whom I deeply loved. I was now reading about someone who I knew loved me. I was now reading about someone for whom I would do anything, because I knew whatever he asked would be for my own best good.

Through the exhilaration of that experience I had another experience. This one is too personal to share, but through it I felt deeply ashamed. I comprehended that I did not have that same love and respect—reverence—for Those who matter the most: the members of the Godhead and, specifically, God's Only Begotten, the Savior and the Redeemer. This motivated me to study His "biography" and, through prayer and fasting and pondering, to know that I was now reading about someone whom I deeply loved. I was now reading about someone who I knew loved me. I was now reading about someone for whom I would do anything, because I knew whatever He asked would be for my own best good.

My dear friends, I testify that this knowledge has made all the difference in my life and in our family. I hasten to add that it has not magically made us without blemish and it has not necessarily made life easy. That would be contrary to God's plan. But what it has provided is hope—"a perfect brightness of hope" (2 Nephi 31:20). There has never been a thought of giving up, quitting, or retreating. I wish the same for you.

Even as magnificent as you are, within a congregation of this size there is much joy and much pain. Individually you may deeply feel the weight of life's heavy burdens. Perhaps matters in your family are not as you would wish. Maybe you are struggling with your faith. Possibly you are dealing with something in your past—either something you have done or something that has unfairly been done to you. Some of you may have physical or mental or emotional challenges that seem too much to endure. Whatever your circumstances, living a reverent life will lessen your load. With the message of the oft-sung hymn "I Am a Child of God" in your heart and soul and not simply on your lips, and with a continual reliance on the atoning sacrifice of the Savior Jesus Christ, there can be peace and comfort even in the most difficult of times.

Today can be a pivotal, even historic day in our lives. It can be the day we make the decision and take the disciplined efforts to become more reverent. For some of us it may be by giving up some addictive habit or repugnant practice that is offending God. For others it may be by reprioritizing our lives and making our love for God supreme. A reverent life is worth any price. Indeed, it is the essence of our life's work. Of this I testify in the name of Jesus Christ, amen.

Recognizing and Responding to the Promptings of the Spirit

Gordon E. Limb

In the social work main office in the Joseph F. Smith Building there is a disability access door that has a self-charging mechanism that opens and closes the door. We've had this mechanism on the door for over two years. My office is located next to that door, so I am very aware of every time the door opens and closes. However, it was only very recently that, as I was sitting at my desk in a quiet, thoughtful moment, I heard the door open, and as it closed I heard a unique melodic sound. I was so taken aback that I got up from my desk, walked out of my office, opened the door, and listened again to the melodic tone as it closed. I asked myself, Why hadn't I heard that melody before? Was this the first time that the melodic sound had occurred? My guess is that the door has been making that sound since it was first installed, yet it took me over two years to recognize and respond to that small, soft, melodic sound. It wasn't until I was in tune with the sound that I actually heard it.

Gordon E. Limb was director of the BYU School of Social Work when this devotional address was given on 5 March 2013. © Brigham Young University.

331

Brothers and sisters, in my work at BYU and in my service within the Church, I have been blessed to spend much of my time working with youth and young adults. As important topics and decisions come up during what Elder Robert D. Hales called the "decade of decision" ("To the Aaronic Priesthood: Preparing for the Decade of Decision," *Ensign*, May 2007, 48), I often hear questions such as How can I recognize and respond to the promptings of the Spirit? and, more specifically, as stated by Elder David A. Bednar, How can I tell the difference between my emotions telling me what I want to hear and the Holy Ghost telling me what I need to hear? In fact, while he was president of BYU–Idaho, Elder Bednar said that this last question was the question most frequently asked by the students with whom he met. He said, "During the entire time we have been holding family home evenings with students, I cannot remember a single time when some version of this question was not asked" ("Receiving, Recognizing, and Responding to the Promptings of the Holy Ghost," Ricks College devotional address, 31 August 1999).

I am guessing many of you, like me, have asked this question. How can we tell if we are receiving inspiration from the Spirit or if we are getting a message from our own emotions or from an evil source or if we are receiving any spiritual prompting at all? While I don't have a complete or easy answer to these questions, I would like to discuss with you some of the things I have learned about recognizing and responding to the promptings of the Spirit. I pray for and invite the Holy Ghost to be with each of us today as we discuss this most important topic. Let's begin by discussing how the Lord communicates with us.

HOW THE LORD COMMUNICATES WITH US

When we communicate with Heavenly Father, we do so through prayer. When He speaks to us, He does so through revelation. This two-way divine communication is critical to our understanding of the process of receiving personal revelation (see L. Lionel Kendrick, "Personal Revelation," BYU devotional address, 20 May 1997).

Let's look at this process in action. In sections 6 and 8 of the Doctrine and Covenants, through revelation given to Oliver Cowdery, we learn some important concepts of this two-way divine communication. In Doctrine and Covenants 6:15 the Lord said, "Thou knowest that thou hast inquired of me and I did enlighten thy mind . . . that thou mayest know that thou hast been enlightened by the Spirit of truth." Then, in verse 23, the Lord said: "Did I not speak peace to your mind concerning the matter? What greater witness can you have than from God?" Here we see that after Oliver inquired of the Lord through prayer, his mind was enlightened by the Spirit and he was given a feeling of calmness or peace. In Doctrine and Covenants 8:2 the Lord states, "Behold, I will tell you in your mind and in your heart, by the Holy Ghost, which shall come upon you and which shall dwell in your heart."

Elder Richard G. Scott noted, "When we receive an impression in our *heart*, we can use our *mind* either to rationalize it away or to accomplish it" ("Learning to Recognize Answers to Prayer," *Ensign*, November 1989, 31; emphasis in original). Together the verses in these two sections teach us that when Heavenly Father speaks to us through the Spirit *in its most familiar form*, it most often comes to us through our thoughts and feelings. As President Boyd K. Packer noted:

> *That sweet, quiet voice of inspiration comes more as a feeling than it does as a sound. . . . The Holy Ghost communicates with our spirits through the mind more than through the physical senses. This guidance comes as thoughts, as feelings through promptings and impressions. We may* **feel** *the words of spiritual communication more than* **hear** *them and* **see** *with spiritual rather than with mortal eyes.* ["Prayer and Promptings," *Ensign*, November 2009, 44; emphasis in original]

Therefore, it shouldn't be difficult for us to understand why we are counseled by our Church leaders to avoid anything that negatively impacts our ability to receive promptings through our thoughts and feelings (see Bednar, "Receiving").

In the field of social work we often work with people who are struggling with addictions, including pornography and other addictive substances and behaviors. These types of addictions negatively impact "our ability to recognize and respond to the promptings of the Holy Ghost" (Bednar, "Receiving"). Brothers and sisters, what are the influences in your life and mine that negatively impact our ability to feel the Spirit? What are ways we can better understand the Lord's pattern of communicating with us?

MAKING FAULTY ASSUMPTIONS

All too often we make faulty assumptions and have erroneous expectations regarding recognizing the Spirit. Let me share with you what Elder Bednar said about this:

> Let me suggest that many of us typically assume we will receive **an** answer or **a** prompting to our earnest prayers and pleadings. And we also frequently expect that such **an** answer or **a** prompting will come immediately and **all at once**. Thus we tend to believe the Lord will give us **a big answer quickly and all at one time**. However, the pattern repeatedly described in the scriptures suggests we receive "line upon line, precept upon precept," or, in other words, **many small answers over a period of time**. Recognizing and understanding this pattern is an important key to obtaining inspiration and help from the Holy Ghost.

Elder Bednar then went on to state:

> Sister Bednar and I frequently visit with students who wonder about career choices and how to properly select a school at which to study and receive additional education. Many times a student is perplexed—having felt as though "the" answer about a career or a school was received at one particular point in time, only to feel that a different and perhaps conflicting answer was received at another point in time. The question then is often asked, "Why did the Lord give me two different answers?" In like manner, a student may sincerely seek to know if the person he or she has been dating is "the one." A feeling of "yes" at one time may appear to be

contradicted by a different feeling of "no" at another time. May I simply suggest that what we initially believe is "the" answer may be but one part of a "line upon line, precept upon precept," ongoing, incremental, and unfolding pattern of small answers. It is clearly the case that the Lord did not change His mind; rather, you and I must learn to better recognize the Lord's pattern as a series of related and expanding answers to our most important questions. ["'Line upon Line, Precept upon Precept' (2 Nephi 28:30)," BYU–Idaho devotional address, 11 September 2001; emphasis in original]

Let me share two personal examples that illustrate Elder Bednar's points.

Back in 2000, when I was getting ready to graduate with my doctorate and interviewing for my first faculty position, I found what I thought was the perfect job: a good school fairly close to home, a creative joint faculty position within the school, and a very prominent company that does great work with American Indian children and families—my specialty. My meeting with the company went great. They were onboard, and I thought this appointment would lead to all kinds of research opportunities and funding. In my mind this job was made for me. I prayed, felt good about it, and was moving forward. Then, during my faculty visit to the school, things went from bad to worse. My presentation didn't go well, the faculty members didn't seem to like me, and there was just something that was not right. Well, I didn't get the offer. So why is it that after praying and feeling good about this job, things didn't work out? That was a question my wife and I were asking ourselves.

When this job didn't work out, the other opportunity I had was to go to Washington University in St. Louis to the top social work program in the country, which obviously is a good thing. Their offer was for me to be the assistant director of the Kathryn M. Buder Center for American Indian Studies and a lecturer in the School of Social Work. Although this was a great opportunity, it was not a tenure-track position—something I definitely wanted. So we prayed again, moved forward, and took the job. What a blessing

that position turned out to be! I got to spend three years working
with Eddie Brown, the director of the Buder Center and former
assistant secretary of the interior in charge of the Bureau of Indian
Affairs—an appointment our own Larry Echo Hawk later filled.
Eddie Brown is probably the most influential American Indian social
worker in the country, and during those three years we were able to
travel throughout the country working with Indian tribes and tribal
organizations. Those three years provided me with the foundation
I needed in order to be where I am today.

As a sidenote, I later found out that, shortly after 9/11, when the
economy took a nosedive, the first position was canceled due to lack
of funding from the company for the joint appointment. While it
would have started out as a great job, it would have been short lived.

Here is the lesson I learned in recognizing and responding to
the promptings of the Spirit: Sometimes what we perceive to be a
positive answer followed by a negative outcome is later followed by
a new, unexpected, better answer (i.e., opportunity) if we will but
trust in the Lord and keep moving forward. The Lord knew what I
did not. That first experience prepared me to listen more closely to
the Spirit the next time, to have an increased level of gratitude for
how the Lord works in our lives, and to remember "that all things
work together for good [in the Lord's time frame] to them that love
God" (Romans 8:28). So, in summary, sometimes the right choices
or blessings come in the Lord's time and through promptings that
are often not recognized until after they are acted upon.

Example two: My wife, Erika, and I dated for nearly a year
before we were married. I don't ever recall receiving a one-time
spiritual confirmation that she was "the one." However, the more
we interacted, the more we talked, and the more we learned about
each other in different situations, I received many small, simple, and
quiet promptings that she was a special, talented, spiritual woman.
Together, all of those simple answers over a period of time helped
me to receive an appropriate spiritual confirmation that I should ask
her to marry me. That confirmation did not come all at once during

a single heartfelt prayer of desperation. Rather, it came more in a line-upon-line and precept-upon-precept manner (see Bednar, "Line upon Line").

Here is another key element regarding finding a spouse. Elder Dallin H. Oaks stated:

> *If a revelation is outside the limits of stewardship, you know it is not from the Lord, and you are not bound by it. I have heard of cases where a young man told a young woman she should marry him because he had received a revelation that she was to be his eternal companion. If this is a true revelation, it will be confirmed directly to the woman if she seeks to know. In the meantime, she is under no obligation to heed it. . . . The man can receive revelation to guide his own actions, but he cannot properly receive revelation to direct hers. She is outside his stewardship.*
> ["Revelation," BYU devotional address, 29 September 1981]

Just because I received a witness to marry my wife, that was not enough. She also had to receive her witness—independently. I think it took her a little longer to know whether or not she wanted to spend the rest of eternity with this guy who was pretty average.

Now, your experiences or others' experiences with important decisions may be different. We all know that big answers do come—and sometimes all at once—but those are more the exception than the rule. For our family, the story of the lost binoculars and how my daughter, McKenna, prayed and knew almost instantly where to find them has become legendary and is used as an example of a big answer to a single prayer. However, "we should not feel spiritually inadequate or unqualified if we do not receive a big and immediate answer to a request or plea for help the first time we ask" (Bednar, "Line upon Line").

As we think about things we can do to increase our capacity to follow the Spirit, let me suggest a few ways I have found to better receive and respond to the promptings of the Spirit.

WAYS TO INCREASE OUR CAPACITY TO RECEIVE AND RESPOND TO THE PROMPTINGS OF THE SPIRIT

First, living worthily invites the constant companionship of the Spirit. If you are not now worthy, repent and become worthy. For those who are endowed, go to the temple—the Lord's classroom— and keep your covenants. I've heard students ask, "How can I tell if this is the Spirit I'm feeling?" If you are living worthily, Paul's letter to the Galatians tells us that the fruits of the Spirit are "love, joy, peace, longsuffering, gentleness, goodness, faith, meekness, temperance" (Galatians 5:22–23). These are all examples of what we feel when the Spirit is present.

In striving to live worthily I am also encouraged by the discussion in section 46 of the Doctrine and Covenants about the gifts of the Spirit. Verse 9 states that "they are given for the benefit of those who love me and keep *all* my commandments" (emphasis added). Well, I love the Lord, but I don't always keep *all* of the commandments. The last part of this verse adds an additional element of hope: "and him that seeketh so to do." I am thankful that as I make mistakes and neglect to heed promptings but "seeketh so to" keep the commandments, a loving Father in Heaven and Savior are always there to help me get back on course if I will but keep repenting and keep trying.

One night recently my seven-year-old son was having a hard time and was misbehaving, so I sent him to bed a little early. My two boys share the same room, and I usually read to them before bed. That night as I went down to read to them, I was in a hurry to finish a talk I had coming up in my Church assignment—as well as being a little frustrated with my son's behavior. So I hurriedly read to them and, before leaving, gave my son one more short lecture on proper behavior. During that time I felt something—a feeling—that I should stop and give him a hug and tell him that I loved him. But in my haste and frustration I ignored the prompting, finished reading, and hurried back upstairs to finish my talk. That was a missed opportunity I regret.

Thankfully for me, Heavenly Father is patient—perfectly patient—and was patient with me on that occasion. The next morning, as I was lying in bed getting ready to get up and start the day, I felt that same prompting: give your son a hug and tell him that you love him. This time I followed the prompting. When my son awoke, I called to him and asked if he could come to my room. When he did, I asked him to sit down on my bed.

He did so and looked at me and asked, "What?" like he was expecting to get another lecture like the night before.

I said, "Hayden, I sure love you and am grateful that you are my son." I then gave him a big hug. He got up and left, and a few minutes later I could hear my son in his happy element, making siren sounds while playing with Legos. The experience was nothing spectacular, but it was a tender mercy, and I am thankful for a second prompting from the Spirit to do what I should have done the night before.

Second, sincere prayer invites the constant companionship of the Spirit. President Gordon B. Hinckley observed:

The trouble with most of our prayers is that we give them as if we were picking up the telephone and ordering groceries—we place our order and hang up. We need to meditate, contemplate, think of what we are praying about and for and then speak to the Lord as one man speaketh to another. [*TGBH*, 469]

Another key element in sincere prayer is gratitude. When was the last time you said a prayer and only expressed gratitude? About learning to recognize answers to prayer, Elder Richard G. Scott said:

I have saved the most important part about prayer until the end. It is gratitude! Our sincere efforts to thank our beloved Father generate wondrous feelings of peace, self-worth, and love. No matter how challenging our circumstances, honest appreciation fills our mind to overflowing with gratitude. ["Learning to Recognize Answers," 32]

Obviously there are times we need to ask for help and guidance, but I know I can spend more time giving thanks in my prayers.

Third, immersing ourselves in the scriptures invites the constant companionship of the Spirit. "Studying the scriptures trains us to hear the Lord's voice" and recognize His Spirit (David M. McConkie, "Gospel Learning and Teaching," *Ensign*, November 2010, 15). Scriptural immersion provides us with a unique insight into how others have received and responded to the promptings of the Spirit. Elder Bednar gave a great CES fireside talk entitled "A Reservoir of Living Water" (4 February 2007)—that I highly encourage you to read or reread—in which he talked about feasting on the word by *searching* the scriptures for connections, patterns, and themes. In our Church callings we have a handbook of instructions that tells us how to fulfill our callings. In living the gospel, our handbooks of instruction are the scriptures and the revealed word of God through His prophets.

Fourth, service invites the constant companionship of the Spirit. Do you realize that as others are seeking the Spirit to receive answers to their prayers, often the Lord uses us to answer those prayers? We had a Relief Society president in my ward who would often pray and ask, "Father, help me to be an answer to someone else's prayer today." Then, as she was going into work or coming home, she would drive around the ward enlisting the Spirit's prompting to determine if there was a sister who needed her help. Numerous times as she was driving by a sister's home or thinking of a particular sister, the Spirit would prompt her to stop by, bring dinner, or ask to watch the sister's children. That Relief Society president knew what it meant to follow the promptings of the Spirit and be an answer to someone else's prayer. That is Christlike service.

Finally, taking time to pause, ponder, and listen invites the constant companionship of the Spirit (see Caryn Esplin, "Recognizing and Increasing Personal Revelation," BYU–Idaho devotional address, 31 July 2012). In our fast-paced, immediate-gratification world we can become so preoccupied with good things that we neglect the most important things. I have found that early in the morning, when things are quiet and my mind is focused, I am most receptive to the promptings of the Spirit.

There is a famous social science experiment (see Daniel J. Simons and Christopher F. Chabris, "Gorillas in Our Midst: Sustained Inattentional Blindness for Dynamic Events," *Perception* 28, no. 9 [1999]: 1059–74) in which participants are asked to watch a video of players in white and black passing a basketball and to count the number of passes the white team makes. However, during the middle of the experiment, as participants are counting the passes, a person in a gorilla suit walks between the players and off the other side of the screen. At the end the narrator asks how many passes the white team made. The narrator then asks, "But did you see the gorilla?"

This experiment has been done on a number of occasions, and typically about half of the participants are so focused on counting the number of passes that they do not see the obvious gorilla walking through the players. I have to admit that the first time I saw the video I did not see the gorilla. Brothers and sisters, are we so focused and so busy that we neglect the promptings of the Spirit— even when those promptings appear right in front of us like the gorilla? Or, when the promptings do come, can we tell the difference between the Spirit's promptings and our emotions?

CONCLUSION

There is a line from the musical *Joseph and the Amazing Technicolor Dreamcoat* after Joseph has been sold into Egypt and put in prison. While Joseph is feeling down and hopeless, the narrator sings:

Hang on now Joseph, you'll make it some day.
Don't give up Joseph, fight till you drop.
We've read the book and you come out on top.
["Go Go Go Joseph" (London: The Really Useful Group, 1991)]

Similarly, our Heavenly Father has a plan for us—a perfect plan of happiness—and I testify that as we learn to better recognize and respond to the promptings of the Spirit, we will find answers to our prayers and have increased capacity to know how and whether those promptings are from the Holy Ghost—especially during this "decade of decision" for many of you. Just like the door leading into the social work office, I further testify that as we learn and understand the Lord's pattern for communicating with us, those small, melodic tones of the Spirit will

[lead] *us back into his sight,*
Where we may stay
To share eternal life.
["Our Savior's Love," *Hymns*, 2002, no. 113]

In the name of Jesus Christ, amen.

The Covenant Path

Rosemary M. Wixom

I am honored by the opportunity to speak to you today. I love to come to the BYU campus. I stand before you as "true blue." As it has already been said, my shade of blue was painted in Cache Valley at Utah State University. My husband's blue has a reddish tint and our children's blues are of various hues. Yet when we see the color blue—any blue—we cheer.

There is something very stimulating about a university campus. Where there is a learning atmosphere there is energy, and increasing your knowledge is progressive. You are advancing on the path of life.

Now you may be puzzled at today's devotional and may be asking, "What does the Primary general president have to say to me?" After all, many of you graduated from Primary years ago and have "put away [those] childish things."[1] Yet the messages and principles of the songs you sang in Primary still apply today and hopefully have remained in your heart.

Rosemary M. Wixom was the Primary general president of The Church of Jesus Christ of Latter-day Saints when this devotional address was given on 11 March 2013. © Intellectual Reserve, Inc.

Today we sang "I Will Follow God's Plan." We sang the words "My life is a gift; my life has a plan. My life has a purpose; in heav'n it began."[2]

As a student on this campus you are progressing with your plan. You have a purpose in mind. Can you see the Lord's hand in your life? Can you see the path you took to get here?

I was born in Ogden, Utah, and grew up in Salt Lake City. At age eighteen, when I was about to leave to go to Utah State, my goals were simple. I really had just two. I'm going to be honest with you and tell you what they were: (1) I wanted to be an elementary school teacher, and (2) I wanted to fall in love. Now that seems simple, but I really did not think beyond those two goals. I hoped that somewhere out there was a handsome young man who also had the goal to stay on the path, get an education, and fall in love so we could marry, have a family, and bring children into this world. But I was anxious and nervous inside. What if my plan did not unfold *how* I wanted it to and *when* I wanted it to?

I was looking at the path through a magnifying glass, and all I could see were my shoelaces. I remembered those lessons in Primary about the plan of salvation. I could see the circles and the arrows on the chart, but I could not yet visualize myself in the plan. I wish I would have had the words to the chorus of this Primary song then. They read:

I will follow God's plan for me,
Holding fast to his word and his love.
I will work, and I will pray;
I will always walk in his way.
Then I will be happy on earth
And in my home above.[3]

That is the key, and it is really quite simple: "I will follow *God's plan* for me." And we do it by holding fast to His word, with His love, and through our prayers to Him while simply living life.

Brigham Young said, "Live so that the spirit of our religion [lives] within us."[4] We are a making-and-keeping-covenants people, and nothing better shapes us than the sacred covenants we make to the Lord. We live these covenants when we follow His plan, and we come to know who we really are.

George Bernard Shaw said: "Life isn't about finding yourself. Life is about creating yourself."[5]

That is true. I think of it this way: There are those who see themselves on this earth as simply growing up—helpless in a way. They eat, they sleep, and they live their lives. They watch themselves get taller and older. They let the world mold them and allow their circumstances to dictate their future. It is as if they are watching the wind swirl around a block of sandstone. The years go by until, finally, one day a shape is created. Or we can decide the kind of person we want to become, grip the chisel, and go to work. The sculpture being created is now of our creation. At times we may even stand back in awe at the form it is taking. The pinnacle of our reality is when we come to know we are not alone in our work. The real Artist is standing at our side, and His vision for this exquisite piece is beyond our comprehension.

Elder Joseph B. Wirthlin said:

We see ourselves in terms of yesterday and today. Our Heavenly Father sees us in terms of forever. Although we might settle for less, Heavenly Father won't, for He sees us as the glorious beings we are capable of becoming.[6]

It is as if the Lord has given us tools with which to create this "being." These tools are the covenants we make and keep, beginning with the baptismal covenant.

A covenant is personal. It is so personal that it is given to us individually, and often our very own name is said in conjunction with the ordinance that accompanies the covenant. By living our covenants with the Lord's help, He sculpts us into a masterpiece.

Think of the baptismal covenant. Lately I have viewed the covenant of baptism through a granddaughter's eyes. Lucy Catherine is three years old. In her world she is a princess. She is beginning this earthly path. I think she takes after her grandmother. Lucy is my buddy. She loves to climb up into my lap, and together we watch the Bible videos on my iPad. She can operate the iPad all by herself. Her favorite Bible video is of Jesus being baptized in the River Jordan.

Lucy is only three years old, but she feels something when she watches Jesus being baptized, and so do I.

Elder Robert D. Hales said: "Many members of the Church do not fully understand what happened when they went into the waters of baptism." He then asked:

Do [we] *understand . . . that when* [we were] *baptized* [we were] *changed forever? . . .*

. . . Our baptism and confirmation is the gateway into His kingdom. When we enter, we covenant to be of His kingdom—forever![7]

We see powerful evidences of the magnitude of the baptismal covenant in the history of the Church. In Liverpool, England, in the 1840s, George Cannon and his wife, Ann Quayle Cannon, were converted to the gospel. George wrote in a letter to his sister:

I was sincerely desirous to lead a new life . . . ; and though slow of belief at first, and not seeing the necessity of baptism, yet God in His infinite mercy opened my eyes.[8]

With the covenant of baptism and the promise of more covenants came the desire to join the Saints in America at all costs. Ann tucked a little money away each month so the family would have the funds necessary for the voyage.

The wish to get to Zion became . . . a consuming desire. . . . She began to count the days that must elapse before the ship's sailing. She was impressed that if this season . . . should pass and find the family still in England, she would not be alive to urge the journey another year. . . . She had a sure premonition that she should not live to reach the shores of America, and told her husband so.[9]

Ann was expecting their seventh child at the time, and George tried to persuade her to wait.

[But] *she refused absolutely—she would rather die in trying to go than live* [by] *remaining. . . .*

. . . Both [George and Ann] *prayed . . . that God's blessing would attend them in doing what they believed to be His will.*[10]

On September 17, 1842, George, Ann, and their six children boarded the ship and set sail for America. George later wrote:

We are now launched on the bosom of the mighty deep, and sea-sickness has made the passengers for the most part very ill. My dear Ann is dreadfully affected with this nauseous sickness. . . . Yet I have never heard one complaint from her on her own account. [She] *regret*[s] *. . . not being able to assist me in the care of the children.*[11]

The days and weeks went by, and Ann only worsened. On October 28 she passed away. George wrote, "O God, how mysterious are Thy ways! Teach me resignation to Thy will!"[12]

Both George and Ann Quayle Cannon understood the promise "The Lord God will proceed to make bare his arm . . . in bringing about his covenants and his gospel unto those who are of the house of Israel."[13] George and Ann Cannon lived their lives keeping their covenant of baptism and looking to the promise of more covenants while carving out a future for their posterity.

What did they clearly understand about the covenant of baptism? What was it that drove George and Ann to come to America at all costs? They were simply doing what they believed to be the Lord's will.

Today we are not asked to move to Salt Lake City after our baptism. But we do enter into sacred covenants with God, and we promise to do three things:

- Take upon ourselves the name of Jesus Christ
- Keep His commandments
- Always remember Him

How can we take upon ourselves the name of Christ today? We do more than represent Him and follow Him: "We . . . see ourselves as His. We . . . put Him [and His work] first in our lives. We [seek] what He wants rather than what we want or what the world teaches us to want."[14]

How can we live that baptismal promise in our daily lives here as students at BYU? It is a process, and oftentimes we wrestle to align our lives with the Father's will. At times we may even question our judgment. We may rationalize our actions and say, "But others are doing it." The choices we make follow us into our classrooms, in our conversations, with our callings, and on our dates. The results may alter how we dress, our appearance, what we text, the movies we see, and our very thoughts. When we seek His will, He will magnify our every effort to stay on the path back to Him. We need not ever feel alone. Be patient with yourself as you learn this process.

Our prayers may become different, and we may find ourselves asking, "What would Thou have me do?" and "Help me know what is Thy will." We find ourselves stepping out of the boat, so to speak, to do His will. We prepare spiritually each day with personal prayers to Him, we read His words in the scriptures, and then we trust that He will guide us. His will then becomes ours.

Elder David A. Bednar said:

> You exercised your moral agency to accept the conditions of the baptismal covenant. . . . And as a representative of Jesus Christ, your life is no longer just about what you want but what God wants for you.[15]

Missionaries all over the world literally take upon themselves the name of Christ when they put on that missionary badge. We witnessed prophetic revelation last October 6 when President Thomas S. Monson announced the missionary age changes.[16] The response has been astounding. We are witnessing a modern-day miracle in these latter days.

Many of you have experienced a mission, and you know what it is like. It is not easy. When I served my first mission with my husband, in my first sentence in my first letter home to both our children and my parents, who had also served, I asked, "Why didn't you tell me a mission was this hard?" When it becomes impossible to carry on, it is that covenant to do the Lord's will that causes a missionary to find a private place and get on his or her knees. His or her prayer may be "I cannot do this alone. Only with Thee can I continue; only with Thee can I learn another language; and only with Thee can I teach those older, wiser, and more articulate than I." A mission changes our life for the better because we take upon us His name.

When we are baptized we covenant to keep His commandments. This commitment to come into God's kingdom separates— but, as Elder Robert D. Hales notes, does not isolate[17]—us from the world as we "stand as witnesses of God at all times and in all things, and in all places."[18] To stand as a witness includes everything we do and say.

In living the baptismal covenant we look for ways to keep the commandments rather than look for ways around them.

While I was visiting Buenos Aires, Argentina, I met Marianela, a frail, beautiful mother with two children, ages nine and twelve. All three had been baptized. Marianela was dealing with severe rheumatoid arthritis. She could only stand or lie down; she could not sit. At home she taught her children with what resources she had. She used both the scriptures and the Relief Society manual. I noticed those two books stacked neatly on her table. She wanted her children to keep the commandments and participate on Sunday and partake of the sacrament, so she accepted the invitation from the bishop's wife to pick them up weekly. Marianela would ride to church lying down in the backseat of the car. It was her way of practicing obedience and aligning her heart with His. In Primary we sing the words "Keep the commandments! In this there is safety; in this there is peace."[19] There was peace in Marianela's home.

I saw another example of keeping the commandments in the Ilagan Stake in the Philippines. Just before a meeting I watched a large truck pull up to the chapel entrance. I could see the arms of the members reaching through the slats on the side of the truck to wave to others in the parking lot. The truck was covered with a canvas top. Out jumped numerous happy Filipinos—the men in their white shirts and ties and the women in their dresses. I learned they had ridden for hours to get there, bouncing on the wooden benches inside the truck. We all hurried into the building and sat down. I thought of their sacrifice to be there—and then the tears streamed down my face as they sang the opening song. With smiles they sang "Because I Have Been Given Much."[20]

Part of keeping the commandments is serving the Lord. President Lugo, the president of the Ilagan Stake, is a tiny little man with great faith. He has the image of the Savior in his countenance. I learned that he had been in a serious cycle accident and had been in the hospital. It was nearing the time in their stake for their yearly trip to the temple to do baptisms for the dead. He was devastated at the thought of not going with the youth, but he could not walk.

His wife said, "You cannot go. If you go, the youth would have to carry you, and that would be asking too much."

President Lugo said, "If they will carry me into the temple, I will walk out."

And that is exactly what he did. How can we possibly draw limits on our service to the Lord?

As we keep our covenant to always remember the Lord, He will help us follow His plan. Let's be honest: While trying to live our covenants, we sometimes get discouraged. We may see nothing but our imperfections. We may think our mistakes are impossible to repair, and we may think we cannot change. We may feel like we are failing.

As we chisel in the sandstone to create this new self, we sometimes chip off huge chunks of stone. Doing this may appear to disfigure our ultimate goal. Like Nephi, we may say, "O wretched man [or woman] that I am!"[21] We may lose hope, and we may fear that there is no way to repair our mistakes. But the real Artist, Jesus Christ, patiently and lovingly stands by our side and waits for us to ask for His help. He is ready to heal us. Then, like Nephi, with a broken heart and a contrite spirit, we may ask:

Wilt thou redeem my soul? . . .
  . . . Wilt thou encircle me . . . in the robe of thy righteousness! . . .
Wilt thou make my path straight before me! . . .
  O Lord, I have trusted in thee, and I will trust in thee forever.[22]

One real blessing is that this Sunday we will again have the opportunity to renew the covenant we made at baptism as we partake of the sacrament with the glorious promise that we may always have His Spirit to be with us.

No wonder that when Romans 6 refers to baptism the scripture reads, "Walk in newness of life."[23] That newness of life is the Atonement working within us, and we can experience it weekly. The Artist, Jesus Christ, is our Savior and Redeemer. "He was foreordained to carry out the Atonement—to come to the earth, suffer the penalty for our sins, die on the cross, and be resurrected."[24] He will not halt the sculpturing process or put down the chisel until we are perfect and living in His presence. The Atonement is the supreme expression of the Savior's love for the Father and for us.[25]

The sculptor Michelangelo, "when asked how he had produced the magnificent statue of an angel, . . . is reported to have simply replied, 'I saw the angel in the marble and carved until I set him free.'"[26]

And so it is with the mutual efforts of a loving Savior and a covenant-keeping disciple on the path. The angel is within each one of us. Let us live the covenant we have made at baptism and seek to do His will. We will watch the plan He has masterfully created for each one of us take shape. Regardless of its form, we will stand in awe as the angel emerges, and we will give credit to our Savior Jesus Christ, for He is the perfect Artist.

In the name of Jesus Christ, amen.

NOTES

1. 1 Corinthians 13:11.

2. "I Will Follow God's Plan," *Songbook*, 164.

3. *Songbook*, 165; emphasis added.

4. *DBY*, 204.

5. George Bernard Shaw, quoted in Joseph B. Wirthlin, "Lessons Learned in the Journey of Life," *Ensign*, December 2000, 12.

6. Joseph B. Wirthlin, "The Great Commandment," *Ensign*, November 2007, 29–30.

7. Robert D. Hales, "The Covenant of Baptism: To Be in the Kingdom and of the Kingdom," *Ensign*, November 2000, 8, 9; emphasis in original.

8. Beatrice Cannon Evans and Janath Russell Cannon, eds., *Cannon Family Historical Treasury* (Salt Lake City: George Cannon Family Association, 1967), 36.

9. Evans and Cannon, *Cannon Family*, 44–45.

10. Evans and Cannon, *Cannon Family*, 45.

11. Evans and Cannon, *Cannon Family*, 47.

12. Evans and Cannon, *Cannon Family*, 50.

13. 1 Nephi 22:11.

14. Henry B. Eyring, "That We May Be One," *Ensign*, May 1998, 67.

15. David A. Bednar, in Heather Whittle Wrigley, "Elder Bednar Instructs Members in Caribbean Area," Church News and Events, 24 February 2012; www.lds.org/church/news/elder-bednar-instructs-members-in-caribbean-area.

16. See Thomas S. Monson, "Welcome to Conference," *Ensign*, November 2012, 4–5.

17. See Hales, "The Covenant of Baptism," 8.

18. Mosiah 18:9.

19. "Keep the Commandments," *Songbook*, 146.

20. *Hymns*, 2002, no. 219.

21. 2 Nephi 4:17.

22. 2 Nephi 4:31, 33–34.

23. Romans 6:4.

24. *True to the Faith: A Gospel Reference* (Salt Lake City: The Church of Jesus Christ of Latter-day Saints, 2004), 15.

25. See *True to the Faith*, 15.

26. David S. Baxter, "Overcoming Feelings of Inadequacy," *Ensign*, August 2007, 14.

The Joy of Education
and Lifelong Learning

James D. Gordon III

I am happy to be here with you today. I remember when I was a university student. Like some of you, I had trouble deciding what my major should be. First I thought about majoring in economics. That way, if I couldn't get a job after I graduated, at least I would understand why.

Then I thought I might major in physical education. I went down to the gym to lift weights, but the laughter made it difficult to concentrate.

I sampled some classes, but I didn't always do very well. For example, I took a photography class. I just about went crazy trying to take a close-up of the horizon. The teacher in that class gave me an F minus. He said that giving me an F would be unfair to the people who failed normally.

I studied chemistry, but I thought that there were only four elements on the periodic table: earth, air, fire, and water. I thought that fire had three electrons in the outer shell.

James D. Gordon III[1] *was assistant to the president for planning and assessment and a professor of law at BYU when this devotional address was given on 26 March 2013.* © *Brigham Young University.*

I thought about studying math. It has been reported that 60 percent of Americans cannot do basic math. Sixty percent! That's nearly half! But we shouldn't laugh—and most of you didn't, and I appreciate that.

SEEK LEARNING

Seriously, I would like to speak about the joy of education and lifelong learning. Life is a test, and life is also a school. The Lord has invited us to seek learning. He said, "Seek ye diligently and teach one another words of wisdom; yea, seek ye out of the best books words of wisdom; seek learning, even by study and also by faith."[2] He commanded early Church leaders to "study and learn, and become acquainted with all good books, and with languages, tongues, and people."[3]

Three reasons why we should learn are to develop personally, to increase our ability to serve others, and to be prepared in all things. Brigham Young said, "Our education should be such as to improve our minds and fit us for increased usefulness; to make us of greater service to the human family."[4]

President Thomas S. Monson taught:

Your talents will expand as you study and learn. You will be able to better assist your families in their learning, and you will have peace of mind in knowing that you have prepared yourself for the eventualities that you may encounter in life.[5]

Learning helps us to be prepared in all things. The Lord said:

Teach ye diligently and my grace shall attend you, that you may be instructed more perfectly in theory, in principle, in doctrine, in the law of the gospel, in all things that pertain unto the kingdom of God, that are expedient for you to understand;

Of things both in heaven and in the earth, and under the earth; things which have been, things which are, things which must shortly come to pass; things which are at home, things which are abroad; the wars and the

perplexities of the nations, and the judgments which are on the land; and a
knowledge also of countries and of kingdoms—
      That ye may be prepared in all things when I shall send you again to
magnify the calling whereunto I have called you, and the mission with
which I have commissioned you.[6]

Being prepared in all things includes being prepared for the
world of work so that you can provide for yourself and your family.

It is a great privilege to study at Brigham Young University. You
have the opportunity to learn in an environment that is consistent
with the principles of the gospel. Being a student here is a position
of trust. As you know, the Church pays for much of your education.
You have the responsibility to study hard, to obey the Honor Code,
and to prepare for future service. Hopefully throughout your life
you will look back on your time here with fondness and cherish the
memories.

ON PURSUING A BYU EDUCATION

I would like to offer some advice as you pursue your education
here. I hope that I don't sound like Polonius giving advice to Laertes
in Shakespeare's play *Hamlet*—especially when I remember what
happened to Polonius. I am not referring to the fact that he was
killed behind the arras, but rather to the fact that over the centuries
he has been portrayed by literally thousands of bad actors.

First, do your best in school. You might recall a story about a
person who was asked to build a house. He decided to cut corners,
use cheap materials, and do a poor job. When he was done, the
owner handed him the key and said, "I'd like to give you this house
as a gift."

Attending the university is like that. You can work hard and do
a good job, or you can cut corners and do a poor job. Be fair with
yourself by giving your best effort. I encourage you to work diligently, to learn a lot, and to prepare well for the future.

Second, do things to enrich your education, such as having a
mentored-learning experience with a faculty member, publishing an

article, doing an internship, working in BYUSA, or participating in a student club. Perhaps you can be a teaching assistant or a research assistant or participate in a performing group. BYU offers so many opportunities to develop and grow. When you look back on your education here, these extra activities will have special meaning.

You might participate in intramural sports. Personally, I'm not very athletic. I tell my students that I played football in high school. They had a play designed especially for me. It was called "Pencilneck Right." You know how BYU uses the run to set up the pass? Well, Pencilneck Right was used to set up the injury time-out.

When I was in high school I was in the chess club. I tell my students that I had a rook on my letterman jacket. Do you know what it says when you walk around campus with a rook on your letterman jacket? "Don't mess with me, pal. Checkmate!"

Third, give service. It is important to fulfill Church callings and to perform other service. Y-Serve, the Center for Service and Learning, located in the Wilkinson Student Center, offers many opportunities to serve in the community. Service is important for its own sake, and it helps you to keep a broader perspective and to stay balanced.

Fourth, make friends. Even though your classmates are not as good-looking—and not as humble—as you are, they are bright, good, and interesting people. The friendships you make here can last throughout your whole life and can be a particularly sweet aspect of your university experience. Take time to make friends.

When I was in high school I didn't have many friends. Once I told my dad that the other kids were giving me a hard time about my religion. My father sat down next to me, and, in his fatherly way, he said, "Son, it doesn't matter what race you are or what religion you are. There will always be people who don't like you—because you're irritating."

Fifth, attend devotional and forum addresses and other events, such as academic presentations, concerts, plays, and art exhibits. These are wonderful opportunities.

Sixth, enjoy your university education. It's exciting, fascinating, challenging, and fun. The secret to happiness is not to look forward to some future time when all your problems will be solved. The secret is to be happy today.

THE JOY AND SWEETNESS OF LIFELONG LEARNING

There is joy in learning. In some Hebrew schools a special ceremony occurs on the first day of class. The teacher places a drop of honey on the cover of a book and gives the book to the student, who licks the honey off. The symbolic message is that learning is sweet.

Learning can also be challenging. Sometimes the learning curve is steep. When we are acquiring new knowledge or skills, we may feel uncertain, and we may make mistakes. However, being stretched means that we are growing. If we ask Heavenly Father in prayer, He will increase our ability to learn and help us to overcome our challenges.

Hopefully your university education will provide a foundation for lifelong learning. As *The Aims of a BYU Education* describes:

> *BYU should inspire students to keep alive their curiosity and prepare them to continue learning throughout their lives. BYU should produce careful readers, prayerful thinkers, and active participants in solving family, professional, religious, and social problems. . . . Thus a BYU diploma is a beginning, not an end, pointing the way to a habit of constant learning. In an era of rapid changes in technology and information, the knowledge and skills learned this year may require renewal the next. Therefore, a BYU degree should educate students in how to learn, teach them that there is much still to learn, and implant in them a love of learning "by study and also by faith."[7]*

The most important area of lifelong learning is spiritual learning. We seek answers through prayer. We read the scriptures regularly so that they become part of our lives. Reading the scriptures reminds us of the Lord's commandments, the covenants that we have made to keep them, and the blessings of the gospel. Studying the scriptures also invites the Holy Ghost, who guides our decisions and helps us to learn. Elder Russell M. Nelson said: "Faith is nurtured through knowledge of God. It comes from prayer and feasting upon the words of Christ through diligent study of the scriptures."[8]

Regardless of one's opportunities for formal education, a person can engage in lifelong learning. My grandfather was Jim Gordon. His parents were Scottish immigrants. He was only able to finish the eighth grade before he went to work. He drove a delivery wagon in San Francisco when he was a young man.

Automobiles replaced horse-drawn wagons. Later my grandfather became a mechanic. He brought books about diesel engines home from work, and he read them. Eventually he became the supervisor over all the diesel equipment for a substantial company. Although his opportunity for formal education was limited, he kept learning on his own. His most important learning experiences occurred when, later in life, he decided to enter the waters of baptism and to receive the blessings of the temple.

When my grandfather was young, he drove a horse-drawn wagon. However, his world changed. During his lifetime he flew in passenger planes, and astronauts landed on the moon. Your world will change too. Many of the changes will be positive and exciting; others may present challenges. Will you be prepared to meet the challenges that will arise during your lifetime?

We need to continue to learn throughout our lives. President Gordon B. Hinckley told graduating BYU students:

We live in a world where knowledge is developing at an ever-accelerating rate. Drink deeply from this ever-springing well of wisdom and human experience. If you should stop now, you will only stunt your intellectual and spiritual growth. Keep everlastingly at it. Read. Read. Read. Read the word of God in sacred books of scripture. Read from the great literature of the ages. Read what is being said in our day and time and what will be said in the future.[9]

Personally, I love to read. I tell my students that my first job was as a proofreader in an M&M factory. You have your own patterns for reading. One thing that helps me is that my wife, Nadine, and I belong to a book group with some friends. During the school year we meet almost monthly. We take turns: a couple chooses a book, hosts the book group in their home, leads the discussion, and serves refreshments afterward. We have read books about a wide variety of subjects. I had never even heard of many of these books before, but I have enjoyed reading them very much.

In addition, I have always enjoyed words. When I was a boy and I would encounter a word I didn't know, sometimes I would ask my father what it meant. He would reply, "Look it up." My father usually knew the answer, but he wanted me to learn how to look words up. So I would open the dictionary that sat on the bookshelf in our living room and look the word up.

Later I wanted to learn more words. One summer my friend John Tanner (who later became a BYU English professor) and I worked as groundskeepers at the Oakland California Temple. On some days we would each write five words and their definitions on an index card and put the card in our shirt pocket. Then we would share the words and use them in sentences during the day. My favorite word from that summer was *halcyon*. It means calm, peaceful, tranquil, or golden. As we pulled weeds and performed other physical labor on the beautiful temple grounds, we would exclaim, "Oh, those halcyon days of youth!" Now, as I look back, I see that they really were halcyon days.

In our busy lives, how can we make time to continue learning? I believe in consistent, incremental progress—small steps over time. For example, one doesn't learn to play the piano in a single day. One must practice daily for several years. After many small increments, one can eventually play hymns, popular songs, or classical music. Lifelong learning is like that. We need to schedule some time each day to study the scriptures. We can also regularly read a little in other books. We learn "line upon line" and "precept upon precept."[10]

Elder Dallin H. Oaks and Sister Kristen M. Oaks wrote:

There are few things more fulfilling and fun than learning something new. Great happiness, satisfaction, and financial rewards come from this. An education is not limited to formal study. Lifelong learning can increase our ability to appreciate and relish the workings and beauty of the world around us. This kind of learning goes well beyond books and a selective use of new technology, such as the Internet. It includes artistic endeavors. It also includes experiences with people and places: conversations with friends, visits to museums and concerts, and opportunities for service. We should expand ourselves and enjoy the journey.[11]

TWO STUMBLING BLOCKS OF LEARNING

There are two issues connected with learning about which we must be careful. First, learning can lead to pride. In 2 Nephi Jacob wrote:

O that cunning plan of the evil one! O the vainness, and the frailties, and the foolishness of men! When they are learned they think they are wise, and they hearken not unto the counsel of God, for they set it aside, supposing they know of themselves, wherefore, their wisdom is foolishness and it profiteth them not. And they shall perish.

But to be learned is good if they hearken unto the counsels of God.[12]

President Ezra Taft Benson taught:

Pride is the universal sin, the great vice. . . .
The antidote for pride is humility—meekness, submissiveness. (See Alma 7:23.) It is the broken heart and contrite spirit.[13]

Humility opens our hearts and minds to learning. By contrast, thinking that we already know everything impedes our learning. King Benjamin taught that a person needs to become "as a child, submissive, meek, humble, patient, full of love, willing to submit to all things which the Lord seeth fit to inflict upon him, even as a child doth submit to his father."[14]

Second, we should expect that at times apparent conflicts may arise between secular learning and gospel principles. "[T]he gospel encompasses all truth."[15] At the groundbreaking of the BYU Eyring Science Center in 1948, President George Albert Smith said:

> *I want to say that The Church of Jesus Christ of Latter-day Saints accepts all that is true in the world from whatever source it may come, with the knowledge that it originated with the greatest of all scientists, our Father in Heaven. . . .*
>
> *And so I congratulate the students of this great institution* [BYU] *to think that you have all the advantages that the people of the world have, plus the advantages of faith in God, a belief in the power of our Heavenly Father, and His inspiration.*[16]

> *The Aims of a BYU Education* states:

> *Students need not ignore difficult and important questions. Rather, they should frame their questions in prayerful, faithful ways, leading them to answers that equip them to give "a reason of the hope that is in" them (1 Peter 3:15) and to articulate honestly and thoughtfully their commitments to Christ and to His Church.*[17]

When human knowledge and the gospel appear to conflict, we should remember that human knowledge is limited. Eternal truth is not limited, but our understanding of it is incomplete. After this life, if we are worthy, we will understand all truth. Meanwhile, we seek answers to faithful questions. We study, ponder, pray, and have patience. We exercise faith in God. He blesses us with greater knowledge, understanding, and peace in our lives.

We should be humble about what we know and what we do not know. An angel appeared to Nephi. Nephi wrote:

And he said unto me: Knowest thou the condescension of God?

And I said unto him: I know that he loveth his children; nevertheless, I do not know the meaning of all things.[18]

We do not know the meaning of all things, but we do know that God loves His children.

God's wisdom supersedes human knowledge. Elder Oaks wrote:

We are commanded to seek learning by study, the way of reason, and by faith, the way that relies on revelation. Both are pleasing to God. He uses both ways to reveal light and knowledge to his children. But when it comes to a knowledge of God and the principles of his gospel, we must give primacy to revelation because that is the Lord's way.[19]

We should also remember to put the gospel, not our academic discipline, first in our lives. Jesus said, "But seek ye first the kingdom of God and his righteousness, and all these things shall be added unto you."[20]

THE STRENGTH IN LEARNING

This is a wonderful time to be on the earth. There are so many opportunities for lifelong learning. If we do our best and seek Heavenly Father's help, He will strengthen us beyond our natural abilities and help us to learn. That learning will enable us to develop personally, will increase our ability to serve others, and will help us to be prepared in all things.

I testify that the gospel is true. Heavenly Father lives and loves us, and Jesus Christ is the Son of God, the Savior of the world. In the name of Jesus Christ, amen.

NOTES

1. Marion B. and Rulon A. Earl Professor of Law, J. Reuben Clark Law School, Brigham Young University. Apologies and thanks to Johnny Carson, Jay Leno, Steven Wright, and others.

2. D&C 88:118.

3. D&C 90:15.

4. *JD* 14:83.

5. Thomas S. Monson, "Three Goals to Guide You," *Ensign*, November 2007, 119.

6. D&C 88:78–80.

7. *The Mission of Brigham Young University* and *The Aims of a BYU Education* (Provo: BYU, 1996), 12.

8. Russell M. Nelson, "With God Nothing Shall Be Impossible," *Ensign*, May 1988, 34.

9. Gordon B. Hinckley, "A Three-Point Challenge," BYU commencement address, 27 April 1995; excerpt in *TGBH*, 171.

10. D&C 98:12; 2 Nephi 28:30.

11. Dallin H. Oaks and Kristen M. Oaks, "Learning and Latter-day Saints," *Ensign*, April 2009, 27.

12. 2 Nephi 9:28–29.

13. Ezra Taft Benson, "Beware of Pride," *Ensign*, May 1989, 6.

14. Mosiah 3:19.

15. Elder Cecil O. Samuelson Jr. on Elder Neal A. Maxwell's views, quoted in Bruce C. Hafen, *A Disciple's Life: The Biography of Neal A. Maxwell* (Salt Lake City: Deseret Book, 2002), 167; see also Henry Eyring, quoted in Henry J. Eyring, *Mormon Scientist: The Life and Faith of Henry Eyring* (Salt Lake City: Deseret Book, 2007), 60.

16. George Albert Smith, "Address at Ground Breaking Ceremonies for the Physical Science Building at Brigham Young University," 11 May 1948, 2, 4; this quotation is posted on the fifth floor of the BYU Harold B. Lee Library.

17. *The Aims*, 4.

18. 1 Nephi 11:16–17.

19. Dallin H. Oaks, *The Lord's Way* (Salt Lake City: Deseret Book, 1991), 72.

20. 3 Nephi 13:33.

"My Life Is a Gift; My Life Has a Plan"

Michelle Marchant

Brothers and sisters, I'm very humbled to be standing before you today. I want you to know I am very honored to be among you. I am especially honored to be among the amazing BYU students who continue to edify me daily in my life.

At a recent stake conference I attended, the visiting General Authority opened the evening session for questions, and a man in the congregation asked, "Could it be that I have the wrong patriarchal blessing?"

At first I was startled by his words. But as I pondered the implications of his heartfelt question, I realized that I also had times when I doubted whether or not portions of my patriarchal blessing would really be fulfilled. Can you identify? Are there times in your life's journey when your faith wavers in respect to God's plan for that journey?

In my experience, following God's plan has been made easier by knowing my relationship to God, experiencing the divine nature of

Michelle Marchant was an associate professor in the BYU Department of Counseling Psychology and Special Education when this devotional address was given on 2 April 2013. © Brigham Young University.

love and service, recognizing the examples of prophets, finding joy
and guidance in the temple, learning from the experiences of others,
and ultimately trusting the wisdom of God's plan for me. During our
time together this morning I would like to consider with you these
milestones in the journey God has ordained for us. I invite the Spirit
to be with us.

KNOWING OUR RELATIONSHIP TO GOD

When my sister Natalie delivered her second child, I was blessed
to visit her family in Wisconsin. One night, while preparing for
bedtime, I was singing "I Am a Child of God"[1] with my then three-
year-old niece, Amanda. She looked up at me from her bed and said,
"Aunt Michelle, Heavenly Father made you and He made me." Tears
welled in my eyes as I considered the pure doctrine this toddler had
expressed. At a very young age Amanda understood one of the most
central truths of God's plan: "All human beings—male and female—
are created in the image of God. Each is a beloved spirit son or
daughter of heavenly parents, and, as such, each has a divine nature
and destiny."[2] This principle is so significant to Heavenly Father's
plan that He emphasizes it in "The Family: A Proclamation to the
World," the Young Women theme, and the Relief Society declaration,[3] as well as in Primary, where young children sing many songs
that highlight this simple truth.

Many modern-day prophets have also underscored the message
of our divine nature. Recently our beloved President Thomas S.
Monson declared:

> *I never cease to be amazed by how the Lord can motivate and direct the
> length and breadth of His kingdom and yet have time to provide inspira-
> tion concerning one individual. . . . The fact that He can, that He does, is
> a testimony to me. . . .*
> *. . . The Lord is in all of our lives.*[4]

Brothers and sisters, for the past few years I have felt impressed to
study the nature of God and His plan of salvation. In doing so, I have

come to understand some beautiful truths. I bear witness that what Amanda taught me when she was three years old is true: Heavenly Father did make you and me. He made us for a divine purpose. I testify that He knows you by name and that He loves you. One of His greatest desires is "to guide [your] future as he has [your] past."[5] I testify that the Lord is eager to be in your life by sharing His love and His plan for each of you. "Have confidence in the Lord."[6]

EXPERIENCING THE DIVINE NATURE OF LOVE AND SERVICE

Elder Quentin L. Cook commented:

Understanding how [Heavenly Father] *feels about us* [and the potential that He recognizes in each of us] *gives us the power to love Him more purely and fully. Personally feeling the reality, love, and power of that relationship is the source of the deepest and sweetest emotions and desires that can come to a man or woman in mortality. These deep emotions of love can motivate us.*[7]

We can show that love in so many simple ways. Recently my sister Natalie posted on Facebook that my sweet Amanda, now twelve years old, had shared her coat with her younger sister Maren on their way to school because Maren had left her coat at home. Amanda's understanding of the profound doctrine of love has motivated her in how she treats other people, particularly her own sister. Her example inspires me.

I'd like to believe that a portion of Amanda's understanding of her divine nature is derived from her heritage. Her great-grandmother Beatrice Marchant was a woman of noble faith and continual service. Grandma Marchant wrote in one of her personal histories:

The first and most important fact [for me to share with my posterity] *is that I was born a "Child of God."* . . . *I can appreciate and understand the world and the people around me if only I make an effort to do so. I even have the ability to help change the world for better or for worse. This has made my life an interesting experience.*[8]

Grandma Marchant was a remarkable woman. She raised fifteen children; cared for her invalid husband for ten years prior to his death while simultaneously providing for her many children; fed every person who walked through the doors of her home, despite her limited resources; worked as one of the first female legislators for the state of Utah; served as Relief Society president at age seventy; and, without fail, acknowledged every birthday and anniversary of each of her enormous posterity, including in-laws. I could go on and on about my grandma's loving, giving heart.

It is an honor to have learned from a woman who recognized her divine nature in such a profound way that many around her, particularly her posterity, have felt her influence. Grandma Marchant was the epitome of these words taught by Moroni: "That which is of God inviteth and enticeth to do good continually; wherefore, every thing which inviteth and enticeth to do good, and to love God, and to serve him, is inspired of God."[9]

I am grateful for the examples of my niece and my grandmother, who have followed God's plan by doing good upon the earth. My desire is that I will also live my life loving and doing good continually so that "the Lord [will] guide [me] continually."[10]

RECOGNIZING THE EXAMPLES OF PROPHETS

I likewise find great strength from the examples of prophets, including the brother of Jared and Joseph Smith, who were eager to seek the Lord's guidance to fulfill His divine plan for them.[11] Both of these prophets were impelled by their great faith to turn to the Lord to receive guidance. The brother of Jared sought the Lord's direction for the welfare of his people, particularly their basic needs, such as language, land, and light. Joseph Smith sought wisdom concerning religious truth. Each secluded himself from other people in order to plead with the Lord—one upon a mountain, the other in a grove. Both acknowledged their weaknesses and expressed the desires of their hearts, including ways that their needs might be met. Both men experienced adversity. The brother of Jared and his people lacked light and ventilation in their sea-tight barges; Joseph was seized by a "thick darkness" that threatened him with "despair and . . . destruction."[12]

What transpired next for both of these chosen servants was miraculous and powerful. The Lord appeared to each of them, and light was a significant aspect of both of these divine visitations. The Lord touched the stones provided by the brother of Jared, making them instruments of light for the barges.[13] "A pillar of light . . . descended [and] rested upon" Joseph Smith,[14] and he was invited to voice his question about religious truth to God the Father and His Son, Jesus Christ, receiving a direct answer "that not only changed his life forever but also changed the history of the world."[15]

Despite the transcendent importance of these events, I find what occurred after them to be even more significant. Neither the brother of Jared nor the Prophet Joseph kept the light revealed by the Lord secret; they shared it freely with all who would benefit from it. The Jaredite stones became the source of light so that "men, women, and children . . . might not cross the great waters in darkness [to] land upon the shore of the promised land."[16] Joseph first shared the light of wisdom and truth of the First Vision with his family, then with his close friends and associates, and, ultimately, with the world. Brothers and sisters, we wouldn't be sitting here today in the Marriott Center if Joseph Smith had not shared the light he received, nor would we know about the brother of Jared. The far-reaching effects of the light Joseph Smith received and shared are almost incalculable.

As recorded in the Pearl of Great Price, the Lord revealed to Abraham the doctrine of the eternal nature of spirits. He specifically taught Abraham that there "were organized before the world . . . many . . . noble and great ones."[17] From modern-day revelation we know that prophets like Abraham, the brother of Jared, and Joseph Smith were among those noble and great ones.[18] You too were among the noble and great ones.[19] I testify that your presence and purpose upon this earth are as important to God as the presence and purpose of any of the noble and great ones who have gone before. God is an attentive Father, and, in His eyes, all His children

possess nobility and greatness. I value the way in which Elder
Neal A. Maxwell captured this doctrine:

> *The same God that placed that star in a precise orbit millennia before
> it appeared over Bethlehem in celebration of the birth of the Babe has given
> at least equal attention to placement of each of us in precise orbits so that
> we may, if we will, illuminate the landscape of our individual lives, so that
> our light may not only lead others but warm them as well.*[20]

The lesson I draw from Elder Maxwell's statement is to do like
the brother of Jared and the Prophet Joseph did: have faith in the
Lord's divine plan for us—both past and future—with the intent to
lead others to partake of His light. In doing so we are able to help
others progress toward their divine potential.

FINDING JOY AND GUIDANCE IN THE TEMPLE

I am grateful for the tender experiences of making covenants and
serving within God's holy temples. Participating in temple work has
been a vital part of discovering my nobility and understanding the
Lord's plan for me. Prior to serving my full-time mission to Haiti,
I was blessed to receive my endowment in the Salt Lake Temple. I
count that experience as one of the most glorious of my life. The love
I felt as I passed through the veil into the celestial room, greeted by
family and friends, was unfathomable. I am the oldest of eight children, and my parents have been less active in the Church since I was
twelve years of age. Trusted friends and relatives were gracious to
offer love and support so that I was not alone as I prepared for and
was blessed by this sacred ordinance. I recall feeling a strong desire
to remain in the celestial room, encircled by these good individuals,
so that I could continue to partake of the love that filled my soul.

I soon realized that the feelings I experienced during my first visit
to the temple could be renewed. I've come to appreciate that regularly
entering the Lord's house allows me to partake of His love and gain
a clearer perspective about my divine potential. It is often within
these hallowed walls that I seek and receive the Lord's guidance for

my future. Sometimes my request is related to an everyday need: for example, "What is the best direction for this talk that I've been asked to give?" or "Who should serve alongside me in a calling I have just received?" Other times I have sought direction regarding decisions that are of more eternal consequence, such as "Is this college major the best choice for fulfilling my potential?" "Is this job opportunity the right match for me?" or "Should I continue to date this man?"

Irrespective of the question, the Lord ultimately provides an answer that leads me toward the destiny He has planned for me. In the temple I have become keenly aware that the Lord knows us by name as I hear the name of the person for whom I am performing ordinances repeated over and over. This has confirmed to me that He is aware of me, as He is of each of His children. The power of His words "I say unto you that mine eyes are upon you. I am in your midst"[21] has become more tangible. He has designed an individual-ized plan to help each person to progress so that each can return to live with Him.

This message is one that I am eager to share with others, espe-cially my own family. I feel great joy watching my family members enter the Lord's house and participate in ordinances that will lead them to know God's plan. Many of my siblings provide opportunities for their teenagers to participate in temple work. It is evident that my nieces' and nephews' experiences in the temple have guided them to make righteous choices for their futures, particularly as they progress into their adult years. As they advance their education, serve missions, date people with high moral standards, and accept opportunities to build God's kingdom, they show that they are committed to fulfilling their divinely appointed plan. I testify that worship and service in His holy house is key to seeking and receiving His direction—to being able to fulfill God's plan and share His love with others.

LEARNING FROM THE EXPERIENCES OF OTHERS

I would like to share the experience of a young woman who is truly one of the noble and great ones. With time, this young woman chose to make changes in her life and to covenant with the Lord.

She is a modern-day individual who allowed her faith in the Lord's plan for her to influence others.

A few years ago a student who was enrolled in one of my classes (I will refer to her as Anna) was essentially failing. When Anna attended class she portrayed a passion about becoming a teacher. One day I felt impressed to invite Anna to visit with me in my office. Through the course of our discussion I learned that her family background was complicated and challenging. Unfortunately, participating in school and living the gospel had not been high priorities for Anna's family and, therefore, had not become high priorities for Anna. In her formative years she had become disillusioned and profoundly disappointed by the inconsistency, addictions, and destructive behaviors she saw swirling around her.

Because of her turbulent family situation, Anna was taken into the home of relatives. Her aunt and uncle encouraged her to attend school and participate in extracurricular activities, particularly dance. Anna was wary about church but acknowledged that the young women in her ward unconditionally reached out to her despite her values and minimal church activity. Over time, participation in school and in dance, as well as the love of her relatives, helped Anna develop self-confidence. Ultimately, Anna's relatives encouraged her to apply to BYU. To their delight she was accepted.

Being accepted at BYU wasn't necessarily the golden ticket for Anna. Her family continued to be unstable, she avoided religious activity, old habits began to resurface, and old wounds refused to heal. At this time in her college experience Anna was enrolled in my class. I felt prompted that I needed to provide Anna another opportunity to demonstrate her commitment to becoming a teacher. Together we created a plan that would help her acquire the knowledge and skills necessary to pass my class and be on the road to becoming a professional educator. To my delight, Anna embraced the plan and passed my class. To my disappointment, I didn't hear from her once the semester ended.

More than two years later I was working in my office when a young woman appeared at my door—it was Anna. She radiated peace and joy. Something had changed since I had last seen her. When I probed, Anna told me that she had just returned from serving a full-time mission. I was overcome by the complete transformation I saw and felt in her.

Anna recently disclosed to me that during much of her youth and early young adult years she had felt trapped and angry. Many "things" influenced Anna's journey of change—friends, relatives, roommates, the testimonies of others, the Book of Mormon, the temple, and so forth. The turning point for Anna was when she realized a need to anchor herself in Christ. She began to feel the light and power of Christ's atoning love, especially when she read the Book of Mormon. Eventually she could not contain the light and love she felt, and she knew that she needed to share them, so she worked with her bishop to prepare to serve a mission. As a missionary Anna found that the more she served, the more she wanted to serve.

Anna's story doesn't end there. Last December I was jogging along Ninth East near the MTC entrance. As I crossed the street I was pleasantly surprised to see Anna approaching me. This young woman who had struggled with the Church during her youth and had nearly failed my class is now sharing her light and love with the missionaries as an MTC teacher. My heart was full.

When I asked Anna's permission to share her experiences, she readily agreed and quickly told me that the essence of her story is the transforming influence of the Lord's love and light in her life. While acknowledging that her journey has not been easy, she is quick to add, "The Lord has guided me. He has taken me by the hand and guided my life. Now I can be His instrument. All of the things I have are because of God's hand in my life."

TRUSTING GOD'S PLAN FOR YOU

Anna's experience reminds me of these tender words:

May today there be peace within. May you trust that you are exactly where you are meant to be. May you not forget the infinite possibilities that are born of faith in yourself and others. May you use the gifts that you have received, and pass on the love that has been given to you. . . . Allow your soul the freedom to sing, dance, and love.[22]

I am honored to know Anna and others like her at BYU. Your commitment to rise above the temporal and partake of the divine is inspiring. Clearly you chose to seek your divine nature in your first estate, and, as a result, you were granted the privilege to live in this second estate.[23] So the question before you is, "How will you embrace your *second* estate?"

The examples of my niece Amanda, my Grandma Marchant, modern and ancient prophets, and BYU students like Anna have inspired me to embrace my second estate with hope.

A few years ago a friend gave me a framed quote from an alternate translation of Jeremiah 29:11, which reads, "For I know the plans I have for you. . . . They are plans for good . . . to give you a future and a hope."[24] I have positioned this framed quote in my bedroom so that I see it every morning and night as a reminder that "the promises of the Lord, if perhaps not always swift, are always certain."[25]

As one who has yet to experience the blessings of marriage, I have shared with you today truths I have wrestled to understand and accept. My tears have wet my pillow many a night over the timing of marriage. I do not know the reason why Heavenly Father's plan for me is a bit different than His plan for my sisters, various friends, and even many of my BYU students and former Young Women. But this I do know: I am a child of God, just as each of you is a noble child of God. He loves us, and He has sent each of us here for an individual and distinct purpose. I am learning that "[His] words are sure and shall not fail, . . . but all things must come to pass in their time."[26]

I rejoice in His plan for me. I know that His promises are sure for each child of God in this room and beyond, even when you cannot fully see or understand His complete design for you individually. Because I have fervently supplicated the Lord and experienced His tender mercies, I can now bear witness that the Lord will reveal His plan to you if you "cheerfully do all things that lie in [your] power; and then . . . stand still."[27]

So rather than question the promises in my patriarchal blessing, I have chosen to show faith, believing the truth found in a Primary song: "My life is a gift; my life has a plan."[28] I promise that your patriarchal blessing is for you to keep! What I have learned in my life's journey is that the Lord will not tell me the end from the beginning, but He is eager "to guide [my] future as he has [my] past."[29]

We read these powerful words in the Bible Dictionary: "Faith . . . must be cultured. . . . The effects of true faith . . . include . . . an actual knowledge that the course of life one is pursuing is acceptable to the Lord."[30] I bear witness that the Lord knows you by name, just as He knows the brother of Jared and the Prophet Joseph. He is so eager to share His infinite love with you. He wants you to feel His love so that you will embrace your life's plan and cherish the gift that it is. Moreover, He wants you to share His love and light with others. Will you accept the invitation to be still, to come to know Him, and to trust His plan for you so that you can in turn share His light and love with others?

I testify that "He is the light, the life, and the hope of the world."[31] I know this to be true because I have felt His light and love, which have guided me to know His plan for me. It is the greatest desire of my heart to go forth and share His light, His life, and His hope with all who are within my circle of influence. In His sacred name, even Jesus Christ, the Resurrected Lord, amen.

NOTES

1. *Hymns*, 2002, no. 301; *Songbook*, 2–3.

2. "The Family: A Proclamation to the World," *Ensign*, November 1995, 102.

3. See "The Family," 102; *Young Women Personal Progress: Standing as a Witness of God* (Salt Lake City: The Church of Jesus Christ of Latter-day Saints, 2009), 3; and the Relief Society declaration, in Mary Ellen Smoot, "Rejoice, Daughters of Zion," *Ensign*, November 1999, 92.

4. Thomas S. Monson, "Consider the Blessings," *Ensign*, November 2012, 89.

5. "Be Still, My Soul," *Hymns*, 2002, no. 124.

6. 2 Thessalonians 3:4.

7. Quentin L. Cook, "The Doctrine of the Father," *Ensign*, February 2012, 34.

8. Beatrice A. Peterson Marchant, *My Heritage*, personal history and letter to her grandchildren, 8 June 1980, 1.

9. Moroni 7:13.

10. Isaiah 58:11.

11. See Ether 1–3 and 6; JS—H 1.

12. JS—H 1:15–16.

13. See Ether 3:4, 6.

14. JS—H 1:16–17.

15. Cecil O. Samuelson Jr., "Stand by My Servant Joseph," *Ensign*, February 2013, 34.

16. Ether 6:3, 12.

17. Abraham 3:22.

18. See Bruce R. McConkie, "Joseph Smith: A Revealer of Christ," BYU devotional address, 3 September 1978.

19. See "Carry On," *Hymns*, 2002, no. 255.

20. Neal A. Maxwell, *That My Family Should Partake* (Salt Lake City: Deseret Book, 1974), 86.

21. D&C 38:7.

22. Author unknown, but this prayer is often attributed to Saint Thérèse of Lisieux or Saint Teresa of Avila.

23. See Abraham 3:26.

24. The New Living Translation (NLT) of the Bible (1996).

25. Dieter F. Uchtdorf, "Continue in Patience," *Ensign*, May 2010, 58.

26. D&C 64:31–32.

27. D&C 123:17.

28. "I Will Follow God's Plan," *Songbook*, 164.

29. "Be Still, My Soul."

30. Bible Dictionary, s.v. "faith," 670.

31. The First Presidency and the Quorum of the Twelve Apostles, "The Living Christ: The Testimony of the Apostles," 1 January 2000.